UNDER PRESSURE

COOKING SOUS VIDE

THOMAS KELLER

JONATHAN BENNO, COREY LEE, AND SEBASTIEN ROUXEL

WITH SUSIE HELLER, MICHAEL RUHLMAN, AND AMY VOGLER

PHOTOGRAPHY BY DEBORAH JONES

INTRODUCTION BY HAROLD McGEE

ARTISAN

Published by Artisan

A Division of Workman Publishing Company, Inc.

225 Varick Street

New York, NY 10014-4381

www.artisanbooks.com

Library of Congress Cataloging-in-Publication Data

Under pressure : cooking sous vide /

Thomas Keller . . . [et al.] ; photography by Deborah Jones ; foreword by Harold McGee.

p. cm.

ISBN 978-1-57965-351-4

1. Sous vide (Cookery) 2. Food—Effect of heat on. I. Keller, Thomas.

TX690.7.U47 2008

641.5´87—dc22   2007049387

Design by Level, Calistoga, California

Printed in Singapore

First printing, September 2008

1 3 5 7 9 10 8 6 4 2

To all the chefs who have inspired and mentored me throughout my career—those who, like
Roland Henin, helped guide me and remind me why we cook: to nurture others.
And foremost, to all those who have worked tirelessly at The French Laundry, per se, Bouchon,
Bouchon Bakeries, and Ad Hoc, both past and present, for their contributions to the evolution
of our restaurants. Only through such a collaborative effort is this book possible.

—THOMAS KELLER

To my mother, Margery; my father, Howard; and my wife, Elizabeth
—for supporting me in life, education, and cuisine.

—JONATHAN BENNO

To the cooks at The French Laundry, past and present,
with whom these recipes were developed.

—COREY LEE

To my wife, Andrea, and daughters, Ava and Grace, for their
constant support. To my grandmother, Marie, and my aunt, Jeannette,
whose passions for cuisine inspire my own. And to my staff.

—SEBASTIEN ROUXEL

CONTENTS

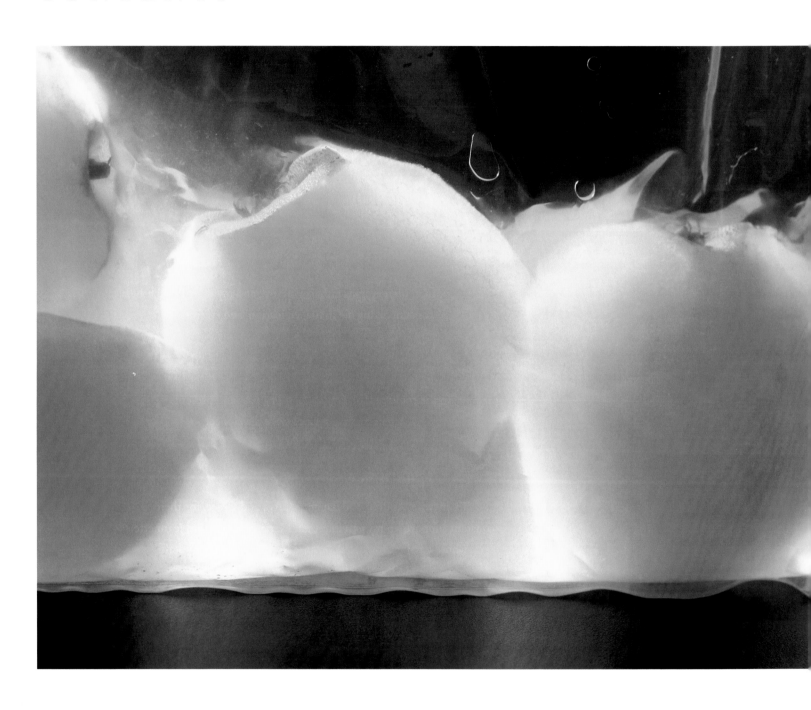

Though I am a scientist and not a cook, I love the art of cooking, the techniques, the equipment, the organization, and the proud and intrepid men who continually go back and back to improve on their work. In cooking, success is not extemporized. It is built on precision, the quest for truth, and the purity of flavors and textures.

My life with sous vide over the years had been aligned to its use in industry, but nearly thirty years ago I had the good fortune to work with Joël Robuchon, when I was able to display the many benefits chefs might enjoy when they understood the power of precise temperatures in cooking.

Thanks to my friend Stanislas Vilgrain, I was given the opportunity to come live in the United States, where I discovered another world of cooking, another perception of culinary science, and, in this, Thomas was an inestimable mentor. I met Thomas and his kitchen staff when several of his recipes were being adjusted and reworked to fit within the framework of sous vide cooking for Cuisine Solutions. I trained his staff in both of his restaurants, where I found the same exactness I had experienced with the Michelin-starred chefs of France.

Here at last is an excellent book about the technique of cooking sous vide. It's both thoughtful and well documented, and it has been written by a chef of immense talent and modesty. Every page is a tribute to his open-mindedness and to his preciseness, and to the talents of those he works with—including Harold McGee, who has made the science so easy to understand.

Due to its exactness, sous vide cooking ushers us into the realm of temperature control so far unprecedented. And it is likely to continue to amaze us in the future as its usage evolves, and as more chefs embrace sous vide for their own imaginative ends. It is already playing an important part in a restaurant kitchen's everyday repertoire. It is clearly going to become the pillar of food safety. A packaged product wherein all vegetative types of pathogenic bacteria have been destroyed and for which the risk of recontamination has been all but eradicated is a safer product.

Bruno Goussault
Chief Scientist

UNDER PRESSURE

A POWERFUL NEW COOKING TOOL HAROLD MCGEE

THIS BOOK INTRODUCES AMERICAN COOKS TO ONE OF THE MOST IMPORTANT

culinary innovations of modern times. And what is this great advance? A way of heating foods precisely. At last! Heat is the most important ingredient in cooking, the one that can transform all the others into something delicious— or into something dry and dull. It's also the ingredient that has been the hardest to measure or control. But in this book, Thomas Keller and his chefs illustrate the powers of precision heating with dozens of dishes that wouldn't be as fine, or even conceivable, without it.

This new heating method is the twenty-first-century version of the *bain-marie,* or water bath, which goes back to medieval times. It goes by the name *sous vide,* meaning "under vacuum," and it involves two new appliances and two basic steps. First you use a vacuum-packing machine to seal food tightly in a plastic bag. Then you immerse the bag in a water bath heated exactly to the optimal cooking temperature. The vacuum-packed bag hugs the food, protecting it from contact with the water while transferring the heat directly from the hot water. The bath is regulated by a device called an immersion circulator, a combination of thermometer, heater, and pump that monitors the temperature, heats the water just enough to

maintain the temperature you set it to, and moves the water around so the temperature is even throughout the bath.

"Sous vide" isn't really the best name for this method, because the vacuum-packing the term actually refers to is less important than temperature control. "Precision cooking" would be a better term. But for now, sous vide is it.

The heart of sous vide cooking is the controlled application of relatively low heat—just hot enough to cook the food properly, no more. A pot of boiling water or a hot oven cooks food at a higher temperature, so that by the time the center of the food reaches the proper temperature, the outside is at least partly overcooked. If you don't get the timing just right, meats end up dry and vegetables mushy. But if you heat food in water maintained at exactly the temperature you want the food itself to reach, it will end up cooked properly throughout.

As discussed on page 13, the sous vide method was developed in France in the early 1970s. Cooks in the United States first heard about it a decade later, but the Food and Drug Administration raised safety concerns, and the equipment was unfamiliar and expensive. Sous vide cooking more or less faded from the scene until 2000, when Gérard Bertholon, a French chef turned food-company executive, demonstrated its virtues to Daniel Boulud, Thomas Keller, and other leading American chefs and showed them how to use it safely. The chefs then discovered what remarkable things they could do with it, and the word spread.

It's fitting that the first book to present the sous vide method to English-speaking cooks comes from Thomas Keller, one of the most creative and admired chefs of his generation, whose cooking is deeply rooted in the French tradition. No one is in a better position to show that, far from being some passing high-tech fad, sous vide is a lasting contribution to fine cooking, a technique that makes it possible to cook foods more consistently and delicately than ever before.

The most important and obvious benefit of temperature control is that it ensures against under- or overcooking food. But as they've experimented with degree-by-degree precision cooking, chefs have made some unanticipated discoveries. In the past, we've defined the doneness of meats and fish and eggs in terms of three or four broad categories spanning a total temperature range of 10 degrees C (18 degrees F) or more. Yet it turns out that just 1 degree C

(2 or 3 degrees F) can make a difference! Cooking salmon gently keeps it moist, but salmon cooked to 48.9°C (120°F) is moist and slightly tacky, while salmon cooked to 50.6°C (123°F) is slightly firmer and no longer tacky. An egg soft-cooked at 60°C (140°F) is barely jelled throughout; at 62.8°C (145°F), the yolk is actually firmer than the surrounding white. Sous vide cooking has opened up new realms of texture and flavor that weren't discernible before and that still aren't fully understood.

Sous vide has also opened up a new frontier in cooking times. Traditionally, tough cuts of meat were cooked for several hours at 82.2° to 93.3°C (180° to 200°F) to dissolve their connective tissues into soft gelatin. But those high temperatures also squeeze moisture from the meat fibers and dry them out. Today cooks using sous vide can serve short ribs and brisket at an untraditional medium-rare, tender yet moist, by cooking them at 57.2°C (135°F) for 48 hours. Here again cooks are coaxing new textures and flavors from familiar ingredients and raising new questions for food science.

Kitchen ingenuity has even turned the vacuum-packing machine itself into a tool for refining traditional dishes and inventing new ones. The original industrial purpose of

vacuum-packing was to make foods easier to handle, limit their exposure to the air, and give them a longer shelf life. Restaurant chefs derive these same benefits from it, but they have also discovered that vacuum-packing can make food look and taste better. It maintains the shape of fish and meats during cooking, for example, and compresses fruit slices so that they become translucent, intense, almost meaty.

Do the advantages of the sous vide method portend the mechanization of professional cooking, the triumph of technology over craft? I don't think so. Precision heating offers unprecedented control over texture and flavor, and consequently more textures and flavors to choose among—just as cooks can now choose from an unprecedented range of ingredients and techniques from all over the world. Cooking is certainly becoming less simply traditional, but at the same time it's becoming more personal, more expressive of each cook's individual imagination and taste.

In this book, four gifted chefs explain the principles of sous vide cooking and share what they've created with its help. They'll give you an extensive view of this new territory and its possibilities. And then it's your turn to explore.

PRECISION OF EXECUTION

THE FUNDAMENTAL ADVANTAGE OF SOUS VIDE IS PRECISION. BEFORE SOUS VIDE,

every time we applied heat to food, we relied on our senses and our experience to know when the food had reached the right temperature—that is, to know when to *stop* the cooking, because you almost always cook food at a higher temperature than you want the food to reach. When we roast a saddle of lamb, for example, the cooking temperature is hundreds of degrees higher than the 54.4°C (130°F) we want the finished lamb to be. With sous vide, we can cook it at 54.4°C for as long as it takes.

The degree of precision sous vide allows is extraordinary, but you still have to know how to cook. Sous vide enables you to be precise in determining cooking temperatures, but you're still cutting that lamb saddle, tying it, engaged in the repetition of techniques that results in a perfect lamb saddle day after day. The precision sous vide allows is a reminder of how precision underlies everything we do at our restaurants. Precision of craft, precision of execution is a daily, hourly, minute-by-minute striving.

From a practical standpoint, precision's goal is consistency, and consistency may be the single most important factor in any restaurant's success, whether that restaurant is a casual or a fine-dining destination. Consistency not the progressiveness or refinement of the cuisine, the depth of the wine list, the design of the room, the quality of the product—is ultimately what the best restaurants are judged on.

Any restaurant raises certain expectations in the mind of the customer, and the restaurant succeeds only by matching or exceeding those expectations. For those restaurants that promise dining of the highest quality, expectations are very high. Precision of execution, from the cooking of the lamb to the way the server puts his or her thumb on the rim of the plate, rather than on top of it, and everything before, after, and in between, is what we are judged on. It is critical at every level, from the moment the first commis arrives in the morning to the moment when the counters are wiped down before the kitchens empty for the night. It's not enough to succeed at our goal 90 percent of the time. We fail if we are not consistent.

When I noticed one evening at per se that the painter's tape that holds down the night's menus at the pass had been cut at right angles with a knife, I was surprised, then gratified. That one of the servers, Zion Curiel, had decided to take this small, arguably irrelevant detail, something the customer never sees, and bring some precision to it, exemplifies the overriding ethos of the restaurant.

Precision is also about setting examples. Examples are important to us culturally; without them, we don't lay a foundation for the next generation. In the restaurants, the precision with which we accomplish the same tasks over and over reinforces the importance of that precision for our younger staff—whether

it's cutting the painter's tape, or the way we put things away, or buying the lamb, acknowledging the quality of that lamb, having the same suppliers, and so on. Precision goes beyond the restaurant.

Cutting brunoise, the very fine vegetable dice, is another example of precision. You cannot have precision without repetition. You perform a technique over and over and over and over again until it becomes part of you, in your movements, in your muscles, in the way you feel. Consistency is taking precision of action and making it routine.

Part of what so appeals to me about repetition is ritual. Precision is not just a matter of doing the same thing over and over—it's about really loving repetition, the chance to do something again and again, ideally at the same point in the day. The repetition of doing it over and over every day results in being able to have a cut that leaves little flesh on the bone, giving you the best yield from the best possible fish. You get really good at it. You get closer and closer to the perfect cut.

And sous vide allows us, after we've done all that work, to apply heat in the most exacting way, to cook the food with the precision that we began with when we got to work. If you don't cook it right, all your work is lost. So precision in this sense is simply a respect for life, not wasting anything.

In the same way that sous vide is one component in a broad spectrum of cooking techniques, it is also one component in our quest for precision at every level. In other words, sous vide is this: another step in our culinary evolution.

WHY SOUS VIDE?

WHY USE SOUS VIDE? YOU CAN, AND SHOULD, ASK THE SAME ABOUT ANY

technique. Why sauté, why roast, why grill? Yet we don't think to question these techniques, because they have been around for so long. Sous vide techniques are new, and so we're naturally a little quizzical, even skeptical. The answer is: we use sous vide because it allows us to achieve specific results that can be achieved only this way.

Sous vide is not complicated or mysterious, but rather straightforward and exact. Like all cooking techniques, it is defined by a temperature-time equation: a given temperature is applied to food for a given time.

The two basic facts that distinguish sous vide from the other cooking techniques are these: we vacuum-pack the food in plastic (using a vacuum packer), and we cook it in water that rarely exceeds 85°C (185°F), well below simmering, and usually a good deal lower. We program and maintain temperature with an immersion circulator.

Sous vide is no more complicated than that. And it gives us the extraordinary ability to cook food at the same temperature we want it to reach. When we use most other cooking techniques, we subject the food to temperatures far hotter than we want that food to be. When we roast a beef tenderloin, we may only want it to reach 51.7°C (125°F) at its center, and yet we put it in an oven that's 107.2°C

(225°F) higher than that. To cook that same beef tenderloin sous vide, we would vacuum-pack it and put it into 51.7°C (125°F) water. The advantage here over roasting is that when you use the oven, you have to determine, either by intuition and experience or by using a thermometer, when it reaches 51.7°C (125°F) because the internal temperature is racing upward toward the oven temperature; when you use sous vide, that tenderloin *can't* go higher than 51.7°C (125°F). It hits the optimum temperature and it stays there until you're ready to serve it.

Moreover, when you use a high-heat method such as roasting, the exterior of the meat gets very hot, past well-done, and inside you get what we call the bull's-eye effect—successive rings of well-done, medium-well, medium, and rare. With sous vide, our entire tenderloin, not just the center, is the temperature we want it to be.

Indeed, sous vide is considerably easier than the other techniques because it takes all the guesswork out of cooking. If we want to sauté, say, a lamb loin to an internal temperature of 54.4°C (130°F), so that it will rise to 60°C (140°F) by the time we slice and serve it, we have to be vigilant. But with an immersion circulator, we can program a temperature of exactly 60°C (140°F) into our cooking vessel.

We can't heat our sauté pan to exact temperatures; we can only judge when it's the right temperature by observing the ripple in the oil or the smoke beginning to rise from the pan.

If you were to prepare this lamb loin for a party using sous vide, you could do the initial preparation ahead and then, when the guests arrived, you could drop the vacuum-packed lamb loin into the water you'd heated to 60°C (140°F). Within a half hour or so, the lamb would be a perfect medium-rare, and it would stay that way until you were ready for it.

Again, sous vide is very forgiving—your window for taking it out of the heat is larger than with the more familiar techniques because the food is cooked at the same temperature at which we want it to finish. But we couldn't leave that lamb in the water for a day. Even though it would never go above 60°C (140°F) and it would still look perfectly cooked, it would feel overcooked and taste unpleasant—you can overcook food sous vide even if it never looks overcooked.

Because we still like that seared exterior we get from high heat, we sear the lamb after it comes out of the bag (see Medallions of Elysian Fields Farm Lamb Saddle, page 160, for one such example). Indeed, how we prepare the meat before it goes into the bag and

what we do when it's out are part of the craft of cooking sous vide.

Another example of the benefits of cooking sous vide that simply aren't possible using any other technique: When you braise meats, you usually simmer them in liquid at temperatures ranging from 82.2° to 98.9°C (180° to 210°F). But at about 68.3°C (155°F) the meat releases most of its juices to the cooking liquid—that's why most of the flavor ends up in the sauce. With sous vide, you can cook short ribs below 65.6°C (150.1°F) for 48 hours, long enough to render the meat tender but without heating the meat past the point where it loses all its juices. The tender meat still has an explosive flavor of its own but none of the drab gray color that comes from long braising.

Cooked sous vide, nongreen vegetables, such as carrots and turnips, emerge with no loss of flavor to the cooking medium, nor do they fall apart. Fruits such as watermelon and pineapple acquire an unusual, wonderfully dense texture when compressed by vacuum-packing. Pale fruits such as apples and pears don't oxidize and their color stays vivid, and fruits such as cherries take on a gorgeous translucent appearance.

These are a few of the many wonders of sous vide. Because sous vide simplifies so many aspects of cooking, I believe it will one day be as familiar to home cooks as roasting or frying is now. Microwaving food was once unfamiliar, after all, and sous vide, in my estimation, has many more applications than does the microwave oven.

SOUS VIDE EQUIPMENT

The two pieces of equipment required to cook sous vide are a chamber vacuum-packing machine and an immersion circulator. Vacuum packers remove air from a plastic bag and seal it. Removing the air ensures efficient heat transfer between the water and the food and, because oxygen encourages spoilage and freezer burn, it improves the shelf life of the food in the bag.

There are many different sizes of chamber packers, from big box-shaped countertop appliances 1 foot tall, 1½ feet wide, and 1 foot deep with a clear dome-like lid to stand-alone models on rollers. The bagged food is laid inside the chamber, the air is sucked out of the bag, and the bag is sealed.

Chamber vacuum packers can exert a lot of pressure or a little pressure on the food in the bag. An important consideration in cooking sous vide is just how much pressure to use. If you're cooking a delicate fish, you don't want to crush it. If you're cooking a hard root vegetable, you want it vacuum-packed as tightly as possible in order to ensure the most efficient heating possible.

Perhaps one of the most important abilities chamber vacuum packers have is that they can seal bags containing liquid ingredients, such as a custard base or a marinade, or any number of items that we want to cook with a fat (such as olive oil) or with stock. Packers intended for home use (and a home budget) can't really compress food, and if you have liquids in the bag, those tend to be sucked out along with the air, making a good seal difficult. If you are unable to seal liquids in plastic, your ability to cook sous vide is restricted.

Bag choice is a consideration as well, since there are many manufacturers and bags are made in varying thicknesses. We use an all-purpose .003-inch-thick bag, sturdy enough that it won't puncture when a lot of pressure is used but also cost-efficient. Whatever material you choose, it should be rated for use with food products and for use at boiling temperatures, 100°C (212°F).

Immersion circulators have three key features: a heating element that heats the water, a temperature control that maintains precise temperatures, and a pump that circulates the water. The immersion circulator is attached to whatever sort of container or tank you're cooking the food in, plugged in, and turned on, and the temperature is then set to whatever degree is called for. It couldn't be simpler or more convenient.

FINDING THE BALANCE

It is important to keep in mind that sous vide does not replace other cooking methods. It is an additional technique, with a range of advantages. For instance, at The French Laundry, we do a lamb's neck dish in which the neck is first oven-roasted low and slow until the meat is meltingly tender. Then we remove the meat from the neck, season it, shape it into a roulade, and chill it until we are ready to portion and cook it. We could cook the neck sous vide rather than roast it, but the finished dish acquires a certain quality that we like when the meat is slow-roasted for eight hours. The meat browns and takes on a special texture, and the juices that caramelize in the pan can be deglazed with reduced stock and added to the meat. We want all of those flavors in the finished dish.

On the other hand, for cuts that require long, slow cooking, we use only sous vide because the advantages of making the cut tender without bringing it above 65.5°C (149.9°F) exceed the advantages of braising it in the oven. This point is important: The technique does not define the dish—we define our goals for the dish and choose the technique that will help us to achieve those goals.

Although the meats we would traditionally braise are better on so many levels when cooked sous vide, even here we don't go over completely to sous vide. We still flour, sear, and braise beef cheeks and oxtail in the traditional fashion, because it's essential that we don't lose the experience of cooking these specific dishes: when you sauté floured meat in hot fat, the aromas and sounds are important. Some dishes are wrapped up in the emotions of cooking itself and help us to appreciate what we're cooking, and I don't want to lose that.

Other cooking techniques require a level of craftsmanship that's worth maintaining. Glazing carrots is a good example, and, in fact, it represents my biggest conflict about sous vide. Glazing vegetables is an elemental technique, but it is difficult to do perfectly. Most cooks don't glaze vegetables properly, because they don't pay attention to the process. It requires thought and the experience of having done it over and over to develop an innate sense of how much water, butter, salt, and sugar to use; how to know when the carrots are done; how to achieve that beautiful lacquered glaze just at the moment the carrots are cooked through but not overcooked.

But with sous vide you have perfectly glazed carrots every time. Yet there's some danger in cooking techniques that don't require much attention. Eliminate the need to pay attention and you eliminate the craft. And when you eliminate craft, you eliminate some of the spiritual rewards and soulfulness of cooking.

This became clear to me at per se when the New York City Health Department, unfamiliar with sous vide techniques, asked us to stop cooking shellfish sous vide. We'd been cooking lobster tail sous vide for several years there and at The French Laundry, sealing an uncooked shelled lobster tail with butter in plastic and dropping it into a water bath kept at 59.5°C (139.1°F). The lobster was perfectly cooked in fifteen minutes, and it would stay perfectly cooked for another ten minutes if we wanted to hold it. Previously we'd poached the lobster tails in butter (also in a warm, airless environment, just like sous vide). But in a busy restaurant, when you're serving sixty of these, among many other items, the lobster can overcook. Sous vide produced a more economical (because it required much less butter) and error-free lobster, consistent every time.

But for a while, because of the health department's concerns, we had to return to the original butter-poaching method. And all my

chefs thought, "Oh, how exciting—this is great!" We'd returned lobster cooking to a craft by introducing the capacity for error. It had become challenging—and therefore satisfying when done well. There's no craft to putting a plastic bag in water for twenty minutes. In the ongoing evolution of dishes and techniques, we now heat the butter using the immersion circulator and cook the lobster in the butter (see page 82), true butter poaching but with the control of sous vide.

On the one hand, sous vide is liberating. You don't have to continually monitor the artichokes or carrots or any of those vegetables that have traditionally taken so much time and attention. There are also a number of purely practical advantages, especially for a restaurant. Sous vide is very clean. If you're marinating chicken, you don't have a big container filled with a lot of marinade that can splash or spill; instead, you have chicken neatly sealed in a bag with a small amount of marinade. Because we cook so many things sous vide, the stovetops and ovens are freed up for other preparations. And storing food sous vide is neat and efficient.

On the other hand, I value the craft of cooking probably more than anything. So for

me, the question becomes how to bridge the two realms, the ease and consistency of sous vide and the risk-filled craft of cooking. How do we both respect tradition and embrace progress? These are challenging questions, because there is a wonderment in the ease and precision of cooking sous vide, in the ability to cook a piece of meat uniformly, so that it's medium-rare at both the edges and in the center. In the end, we all still want to advance the craft of cooking and the techniques that have been handed down to us over the years, but that doesn't mean ignoring the new tools that become available to us.

I hope this book is used in two ways. First, of course, as a learning tool, a way of exploring these valuable new techniques, deepening our appreciation of familiar ones, and understanding the recipes and dishes executed by chefs at The French Laundry and per se. Just as important, I hope that you will be inspired by the techniques and recipes and that you will want to head into your own kitchen and compose new dishes, take the applications you learn here, and move them in all new directions. Inspiration, to me, is the most important and most exciting part of cooking.

MY PATH TO SOUS VIDE

and its exciting uses in haute cuisine. I'd been using a machine to vacuum-pack foie gras as far back as 1986, when I was chef and co-owner of Rakel in lower Manhattan. Foie gras is an expensive item that tends to oxidize. When we removed oxygen from its environment, it stayed fresher longer, and we could also portion it in advance. Occasionally we'd cook carrots and a few other vegetables in a vacuum-packed bag in a pot of simmering water on the stove because it was easier to cook and to pick them up for service that way, but even though it was being used by some of Europe's great chefs, we didn't really think much about sous vide. When I left Rakel in 1990, I left the vacuum-packing machine behind as well. I didn't have an inkling that it represented the beginnings of a revolution in cooking.

I opened The French Laundry in 1994. By 1995, we'd done well enough to invest in a bigger and better kitchen, one with room for a vacuum-packing machine, which again we were using to store foie gras and cook some vegetables. Meanwhile, we'd also begun cooking duck breasts wrapped in plastic. We wanted to serve the duck wrapped in a bright green leaf—blanched Napa cabbage or chard. We couldn't roast or sauté it, so we decided to do it in water. We'd blanch a leaf of Napa cabbage, wrap it around a seasoned duck breast, roll it up in plastic to create a small roulade, and tie it off, then poach it for six minutes. This is a technique one uses to cook extra pâté *farce,* so it wasn't much of a leap of the imagination to shape and cook other foods this way. The duck came out a beautiful, uniform medium-rare with a vivid green wrapper and a perfect shape.

In 2000, Gérard Bertholon at Cuisine Solutions approached me, along with Daniel Boulud, Charlie Trotter, and a few other chefs, to create specific dishes that the company intended to market under the label Five Leaf—restaurant-style meals that would be cooked sous vide and sold frozen. Whatever meals we designed had to be sous-vide friendly, so I couldn't design a dish that relied on a crunchy texture and, of course, I had to choose foods that would hold up well in the bag. This was really my first encounter with applying formal sous vide techniques to a range of foods, and I did my "Mac 'n' Cheese" lobster tail and a monkfish stew. The starch, the protein, and the sauce are all packed separately. After each is brought to temperature, the dish gets assembled. We leaped at the chance to work with Cuisine Solutions because it gave us access to technology that we knew would be beneficial to our repertoire.

That summer, Bertholon came to The French Laundry. He brought with him his main tool: an immersion circulator. I'd never seen one before, and when we tasted numerous proteins prepared with the circulator at low heat, the effects of slow cooking in water were remarkable. I think all chefs are fascinated by unfamiliar tools and want to see what can be done with them. Now we had the ability to regulate and maintain precise temperatures, and we experimented with just about everything.

I wrapped sole around brioche and raisins, sealed it in plastic, and poached it for a version of sole Véronique. The gentle, uniform temperature of the water was perfect for the delicate fish. This low-temperature, moist cooking environment, which defines sous vide cooking, even worked without plastic. For a milk-fed chicken breast, we'd bring a pot of milk to a boil, then take it off the stove, drop the chicken into the milk, cover it, and put it in the plate warmer. We never had to monitor the temperature, and it always came out perfectly done.

So although we'd been using related techniques for a couple of years, it was only after Cuisine Solutions introduced us to the immersion circulator that I started to understand the science of slow cooking in plastic in water and its ramifications. It was immediately apparent to all the chefs how exciting and varied the applications of "boil in a bag" were. The sous vide techniques quickly lent themselves to numerous uses, and we have worked with these for countless dishes at The French Laundry, per se, both Bouchons, and Ad Hoc.

A BRIEF HISTORY

Sous vide cooking has long been part of commercial food production for its economy, safety, and efficiency, but only recently has it reached the kitchens of fine-dining restaurants, where its most exciting applications are being explored every day.

The modern era of sous vide began in the early 1970s, when a French biochemist and microbiologist in love with food, Bruno Goussault, realized that you could make an inexpensive, tough cut of beef tender by cooking it at a very low temperature.

Vacuum-packing food had already been around for several decades, a process first credited to the Hills Bros. coffee company early in the twentieth century. In the 1940s, a company called Cryovac used plastic to shrink-wrap turkey for freezing. (The increased shelf life helped turn what had been a seasonal food into a year-round supermarket and deli meat staple.) In the 1960s, hams and sausages were being vacuum-packed for preservation in Europe, and a little later they were also cooked in that hermetic environment, in effect being pasteurized. In other words, when these items were cooked in plastic, the bacteria that caused their spoilage were eliminated, and thus our food sources became much safer.

In 1972, Goussault, employed by a company called Sepial, was asked by Jacques Borel, who ran Wimpy's, a European fast-food chain, to figure out a way to make inexpensive cuts of beef—meat that normally dried out during the long cooking time required—tender and juicy. Goussault found that by cooking the meat vacuum-packed in a water bath in an oven that could maintain very low temperatures (in this case 60°C [140°F]), he was able to create a tender, juicy product.

Goussault also traveled to a hospital in Sweden that was sealing food in plastic and cooking it at 85°C (185°F) for the purposes of pasteurization. He compared cooking food in plastic in water at low temperatures with high-pasteurization temperatures and found that the lower temperatures resulted in better food. At a conference of the Institut International du Froid in Strasbourg in 1974, he delivered a paper that he'd written with a colleague describing these favorable results of low-temperature cooking.

That same year, in Roanne, France, Jean Troisgros, the Michelin three-star chef, was trying to improve his costs on a very expensive item—foie gras, the fattened liver of geese or ducks. When Troisgros cooked it using traditional methods, he was frustrated by the quantity of fat that melted out. He wondered if there was a way to cook foie gras that resulted in less fat loss, and he asked a local charcutier named Georges Pralus for help. Pralus was revered for a green peppercorn ham he made, and Troisgros knew him to be clever with food. He jumped at the foie gras challenge.

Pralus found that if he wrapped the liver in several layers of plastic wrap and cooked it in hot, but not boiling, water, the foie gras retained considerably more fat than when cooked conventionally. His discovery marked the arrival of the sous vide technique in the high-end restaurant kitchen.

Both Pralus and Goussault continued to explore the applications of this low-heat form of cooking, Pralus in the chef's kitchen, Goussault in the industrial kitchen. In 1979, Pralus founded a cooking school to teach chefs about sous vide technique. In 1981, the Cryovac company hired Goussault to work with Pralus in his kitchen to systematize what was still a craft guided primarily by intuition. Here Goussault began to measure the behavior of meat at various temperatures.

In 1982, Henri Gault, an original author of the restaurant guide *Gault Millau,* asked Goussault to help him with a project. France's national train system, SNCF, hoped to lure people back onto long-distance trains via upscale dining. The two men then approached Joël Robuchon, the Parisian chef considered second to none in the world. Could he bring his three-star cuisine to a speeding long-distance train?

Yes, Robuchon replied, but only if they could ensure the quality and consistency that he demanded of his brigade at his restaurant, Jamin. And so Goussault set about registering and recording the internal temperature of every food that was to be cooked, at every step of the way, from before it was heated through carryover. Only in this way would he be able to produce the results Robuchon wanted. The two men worked for more than two years to develop a menu for the Paris-to-Strasbourg line. The train was launched in 1985.

Both Goussault and Pralus continued to pursue sous vide expertise and to teach it. Goussault, with Robuchon and Gault, eventually opened a school to instruct chefs in this new kind of cooking. One of the men who took this class in 1987 was Stanislas Vilgrain, whose family had been in the commercial food business for seven generations. Vilgrain immediately sensed that sous vide techniques could be used with many of the foods his company prepared, and he enlisted Goussault's help when his firm expanded into a new company called Cuisine Solutions, which would be based in Alexandria, Virginia. In 1989, Goussault began working in Washington on a consultant basis (he later became the company's chief scientist).

That same year, a French chef in Rye, New York, took a salary cut to work for the budding company. Gérard Bertholon had trained under several Michelin-starred chefs in Europe and learned enough about sous vide there to sense how important it might be. While in the United States, he had continued to hear about European chefs expounding on the remarkable qualities of sous vide cooking. When he learned that the company in Alexandria was hiring a research-and-development chef, he seized the opportunity.

Cuisine Solutions would grow into a business with $90 million in annual sales wholly reliant on sous vide applications. It prepares 100,000 to 130,000 fully cooked, pasteurized, and then frozen meals a day for clients as diverse as the U.S. Armed Forces, Costco, and TGI Friday's in Japan, as well as creating lines of retail gourmet foods (in this case, cooked but not frozen) for such French luminaries as Alain Senderens. But in America in the early 1990s, sous vide still implied factory food. Bertholon and Vilgrain knew they needed top American chefs to validate the technique, so Bertholon approached chef-restaurateur Daniel Boulud to discuss creating a line of restaurant-style meals that would be cooked sous vide. By 2000, Bertholon's line had expanded to include meals created by a number of chefs.

Numerous other chefs who have worked in French kitchens have also embraced sous vide. And many of their innovations take advantage of precision of temperature to advance gastronomy in new directions.

THE CHEFS

As the chef-owner of The French Laundry and per se, I get most of the attention. I'd like to focus attention here on the three chefs who lead these two restaurants in their daily work.

Jonathan Benno, a 1993 graduate of the Culinary Institute of America, arrived at The French Laundry in 1995 as we were making some definitive changes with the new kitchen. His ideas were instrumental in how we decided the kitchen would run. Jonathan then left to work at Restaurant Daniel and, under my old friend Tom Colicchio, at Gramercy Tavern, before returning in 2002.

Corey Lee, foregoing culinary school for *stages* in Michelin-starred kitchens in Europe, arrived at The French Laundry at about the same time as Jonathan returned. He and Jonathan traveled to New York in 2004 to open per se. Corey returned to California in 2005 to lead The French Laundry kitchen, while Jonathan remained as chef de cuisine of per se.

Sebastien Rouxel, the pastry chef at per se, was one of the youngest ever to earn a *brevet technique de métiers*, a master's in pastry making, in France. A friend lured him to Los Angeles in 1996, but he quickly found his way to New York and a job under Eberhard Müller at Lutéce. In 1999 he became the pastry chef at The French Laundry. He'd hoped all along to return to New York, and when we opened per se, that's what he did.

This broad description of these three instrumental people, of course, does none of them justice. If you and I were at a table sharing a meal and you asked me who they were, I would say this: that while they are the chefs of two of the most respected restaurants in the country, they are also businessmen, teachers, dishwashers, mentors, partners, colleagues, travel agents, farmers, chemists, artisans, public speakers, and friends.

Here they are in their own words on the subject of sous vide.

JONATHAN BENNO Not long ago, I demonstrated a per se recipe at the Culinary Institute of America. A lamb dish, it included wedges of fennel, artichoke hearts, lamb cheeks, and lamb leg, each of which had been cooked sous vide. Afterward, there were a lot of questions about so-called molecular gastronomy, a catch-all phrase for unconventional cooking, including sous vide techniques. I often get asked about molecular gastronomy by young cooks. I tell them, "When you know everything there is to know about the chemical NaCl, come back and talk to me about 'molecular gastronomy.'" Meaning this: Before you can move into experimental territory as a cook and a chef, you have to understand the fundamentals of cooking, which begin with how to use salt (NaCl), how to make a stock, and how to cook a green vegetable.

The same applies to sous vide. It's not a replacement for our fundamental skill set, and you can't forget or disregard where we came from and what we've learned throughout the history of cooking. We still need to know and learn to perfect basic cooking techniques. If you don't have those, you can't use sous vide properly. A chef needs to know how to season and sear a piece of meat he intends to braise, to know how to cook it until it's done, to know that it should cool slowly in the cooking liquid. All this knowledge is an essential foundation that allows you to move on and apply sous vide techniques properly.

But many foods are extraordinary cooked sous vide. Just the other day, I had a revelation when cooking Swiss chard ribs. I had put four ribs in a bag with olive oil, garlic, thyme, and bay and cooked them as we cook most vegetables sous vide. We all tasted them, and Thomas said, "There is too much thyme." He was right, yet I'd used just a small sprig. If I'd cooked the chard conventionally, I would have had to put a big bundle of thyme in the cooking liquid to get that same impact. It showed me how powerful sous vide is, the force of keeping all the flavors in the bag.

Artichokes are especially great prepared sous vide. They cook through without oxidizing and retain all their flavor. To do a great *barigoule,* artichoke hearts cooked in stock and olive oil with aromatic vegetables, you've got to be a really good cook—working quickly so

they don't oxidize, knowing exactly when they're done, stopping the cooking before they begin to fall apart.

My father is a carpenter. He's been pounding nails for forty years, and sometimes he still hits his thumb. As experienced chefs, we still hit our thumbs too. All of us are striving to get better, always learning, always paying attention. A carpenter's joins can always be tighter. A barigoule can always be better. So my ultimate interest in sous vide is to find ways to make food better.

Thirty years ago, my mom used to make a big pot of beef stew. She'd let the stew cool and then package portions of it with her Seal-a-Meal device. On a busy day, she'd take a bag out of the freezer in the morning to thaw, and when she got home, she'd pop it into boiling water while she cooked the egg noodles. Even when she had been on the run all day, we still got a hot meal of beef stew and noodles. My mom was on the cutting edge of sous vide cooking!

That use of sous vide was about convenience. The way we prepare our food at per se has little to do with convenience. It is about precision, about learning and moving forward. As cooks, we're always trying to improve our food, to look at it in new ways, and sous vide helps us do that. That's part of the excitement of sous vide. Of course, as a chef in charge of forty people in a sprawling kitchen, I like the fact that the artichokes are always cooked consistently, no matter who's cooking them. I can't tell you how important that is to me in my work. For me, as a chef, sous vide is important for precision, for consistency, and for safety.

COREY LEE

I was uncomfortable with sous vide at first, though I didn't quite realize why. It was an interesting addition to our cooking repertoire, but I didn't have the knowledge to evaluate it completely. Sous vide is different from roasting, braising, sautéing, poaching, and other types of cooking: it doesn't require you to use your senses the way traditional cooking techniques do. When you seal something in a bag and put it in water, you're not smelling it as it cooks, or tasting it, or listening to the sizzle as it roasts or sautés. Cooking is one of the few things in life that requires the use of all your

senses. It should please all your senses as well. A technique that took most of those things away was strange for me, and this is one of the main criticisms I hear about sous vide. But as I worked with it, I began to realize I wasn't really giving up the use of my senses as a cook.

To understand sous vide, you must take a broader view of it, one in which sous vide is a single element of a much larger process—because the results are so great. While it's true that you don't get to smell the beef if it's braising in a bag rather than in the oven, you're still butchering it and seasoning it; you may be searing it and you are adding other flavors before it goes into the bag; and, after it comes out of the bag, you're often roasting or searing it or glazing it for the finished plate. So you're still engaging all your senses. I don't think sous vide will prove to be a passing trend—nor will it replace anything that's already here.

Sous vide produces different results from traditional methods, so it's important to know when to use sous vide and when to rely on a traditional method. Essentially, you decide which kind of heat to use according to what you want the final result to be. If you have a cut that requires braising, you have to think about how you want the final braise to be. Do you want to use both wet and dry heat to produce something that's really broken down so that it's almost meltingly tender? Then you braise traditionally. Or do you want the meat to retain more texture and structure, to keep the flavor in the bag—and in the cooking liquid? Sous vide will give you that. If you're cooking fish, do you want it to have a very delicate texture and a pure flavor? Cook it sous vide. Or do you want to give it complex roasted flavors and a crispy skin? Use direct high heat. While all cuts and especially certain fish behave differently cooked sous vide, generally sous vide offers huge advantages in retaining moisture and structure, giving these proteins the desired tenderness without overcooking them.

Say you want to use beef tendons as a garnish for a dish. You'll want to dice them, so they need to retain their shape after cooking. Sous vide will do this, and give a better yield, than conventional cooking. But if you want to use them in a sauce, so they should be virtually melted, cook them traditionally.

With vegetables, "big-pot blanching" is undeniably a great method. If you want to serve, for example, baby turnips with their tops, you can't cook them sous vide, because the tops will turn brown. Big-pot-blanch them and you retain the vivid green tops. But if you want to enrich the turnips and introduce additional flavors—say foie gras fat and mint—sous vide is the best way to accomplish this goal. It all depends on what you're looking for.

At home, sous vide is about convenience and ease—and, perhaps, allowing a less experienced cook to achieve really great results in terms of temperature, flavor, and overall quality of a finished dish. In a restaurant serving fine food, sous vide is used to achieve specific results—despite the fact that the process may add more steps to the cooking and requires more time, more equipment, and more expense.

While cooking sous vide gives you extraordinary results, the excitement for me is in everything that happens before and after the food is out of the bag, when you use all your senses. I might cook a pork belly sous vide, at a much lower temperature than conventionally, so that it becomes tender, but not falling-apart tender, so it retains its structure and is sliceable. Then what garnish should I prepare for it? Should I cut a piece of the fat off and fry that as part of the garnish? Should I glaze the meat? Sauté the skin until crispy? Cut it long like an *aiguillette,* like a slice of bacon, and serve it with a poached egg? That's where the excitement is for me.

My favorite thing to cook is risotto. Working with the rice is a real pleasure. And yet I sometimes bring in sous vide even here, to create a great garnish for the rice that I enjoy so much. For an oxtail garnish, I could cook the meat traditionally and get a meltingly tender finished result that I'd fold into the rice. If I cook the oxtail sous vide, though, the meat retains its structure and I can dice it, glaze it, and sprinkle it on top of the rice. It's visually distinct and results in a different finished dish.

So, yes, there is a gap in the pleasures of cooking when you use sous vide, but it's bridged by the fact that the results are so fine—and, ultimately, you don't give up any of the soulful delights that make cooking truly satisfying.

SEBASTIEN ROUXEL

We began using sous vide techniques in the pastry kitchen when we opened per se in 2004. This has dramatically changed the way we prepare and serve desserts, from making custards to cooking fruit, and from compressing melon to how we portion and store our food.

People often think that sous vide cooking is used only for mass-produced food or airline food, but that's no longer accurate. Remember, the freezer was once a modern tool, and in France, it was first looked upon with skepti-

cism in the pâtisserie. Sous vide also is a modern tool, one we use for many different reasons. For many basic preparations, it has replaced the traditional methods.

For example, we rarely make custards on the stovetop anymore. We have figured out how to make custards sous vide exactly the way we like them; because sous vide allows us to control most variables, the custards are of the ideal consistency every time. Moreover, they keep for a week when properly stored because we have effectively pasteurized the custard and heated it to a point where the bacteria that cause spoilage have been substantially reduced. In addition, because the custard remains in a sealed bag, no additional bacteria have a chance to get into it.

Using sous vide doesn't eliminate the need to understand the fundamentals of custard making. Cooks still must know how the various ingredients work together, what temperatures affect the custard, how varying quantities of yolk or fat give you differing results, and so on. Without a solid grasp of the fundamentals of the pastry kitchen, you won't be able to take full advantage of sous vide techniques.

Nor does knowing the fundamentals of pâtisserie allow you to replace everything with sous vide. You can't make a cake sous vide, for instance, and many preparations in the sweet kitchen still require high heat. But for those dessert preparations that benefit from the low-temperature, anaerobic environment that defines sous vide, we never hesitate to use it.

In fact, one of the great, underappreciated benefits of sous vide is that anaerobic environment. We use many fruits and vegetables in our desserts. However, fruits and vegetables begin to oxidize or discolor as soon as you cut them. When we remove oxygen from the environment, we substantially slow these undesirable effects. Bananas, which discolor rapidly upon being cut, are a great example. We use two modern inventions to ensure that the banana stays very white after it's cut in the preparation of our banana sherbet (page 223). First we freeze them—bananas freeze very well. Once they are frozen and we've cut them up and put them into the sous vide bag with

the other sherbet ingredients, they do not begin to oxidize noticeably. Then we seal the bag, which removes the oxygen, and cook the fruit in a custard; it remains very bright. This is all but impossible to achieve on the stovetop.

Fruits and vegetables are superb cooked sous vide, becoming tender without losing their vibrant color and flavor. Cherries become vivid and dramatically translucent when cooked sous vide. As for vegetables, one that I like to use in desserts is cucumber—it's refreshing and provides a good transition from the savory part of the meal to the sweeter desserts. Cucumber compressed sous vide is tender, bright, and has a very pure flavor.

Many of the effects of sous vide can be achieved through traditional methods, but these require more attention and time tending them, and there are many variables in a busy kitchen with chefs of differing experience working the stoves. Sous vide eliminates many of these variables and results in a consistent finished product, which is what a restaurant kitchen strives for.

Finally, there are practical matters unique to restaurant cooking to which we apply sous vide—namely, in making and storing various preparations in specific portion sizes that allow for more efficient service and reduce waste. But what I like to say most to cooks who want to use sous vide techniques—and these are ideas that we all stress repeatedly—is that you must have a solid grasp of the fundamentals of pâtisserie before you can take advantage of sous vide, and that sous vide is not a replacement for anything but, rather, a modern tool that we are very lucky to be able to use.

THE FUNDAMENTALS

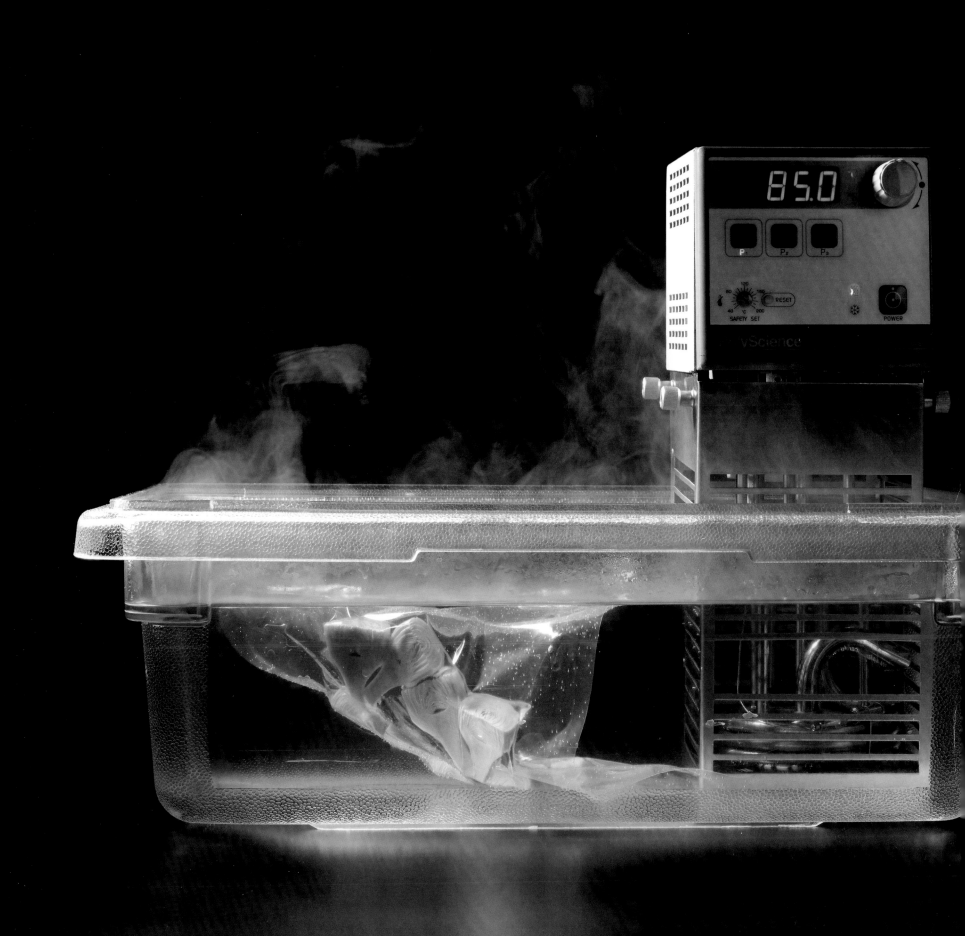

WHAT SOUS VIDE CAN ACHIEVE, AT A GLANCE

In many of the recipes, we explain specifically why sous vide applications are valuable. Most foods can be cooked sous vide with great success, but some foods should not be cooked sous vide. The color of green vegetables—broccoli, asparagus, peas, etc.—is harmed by sous vide. Grains and cereals (rice and pasta, for example) do not benefit in any appreciable way from sous vide. But sous vide can be applied to the majority of food. Here's a rundown of some of sous vide's most important assets.

FOR TENDER CUTS OF MEAT

- Sous vide allows us to achieve the exact internal temperature—for example, the perfect medium in a lamb loin, or the perfect medium-rare in a squab breast—every time.
- With sous vide, we can get the same temperature throughout the entire cut, not just at the center.

FOR TOUGH CUTS OF MEAT

- Half the meats we cook are tough—from variety meats, such as heart, gizzard, and tongue, to shank and shoulder cuts. All of these, without exception, benefit from sous vide techniques.
- We can cook tough cuts of meat at temperatures that are low enough that they don't dry out the meat (as braising does) but that are still hot enough to dissolve, over time, the connective tissue that makes the meat tough.
- We can cook medium-rare short ribs. We can cook a pot roast to medium-rare, yet cook it long enough so that it's meltingly tender and pink.
- Often we confit the tough cuts—for instance, duck legs, pork bellies, and gizzards. In a traditional confit, the meat is submerged in a large quantity of rendered fat and cooked gently for hours, then cooled in that fat. With sous vide, you can achieve exactly the same results with considerably less fat; moreover, you're not using valuable oven space that, when you're confiting traditionally, must be kept at a very low temperature for a long time.

Overleaf, from left: Fennel and radishes; artichoke hearts

- Tough cuts can be brought to different consistencies as desired. For example, a pork belly might be cooked until it is falling-apart tender or just until it is tender but not falling apart, still firm enough to be sliced.

FOR FISH

- Fish, perhaps more than any protein, has such a small window of doneness that it requires the most finesse on the part of the cook. Sous vide makes cooking fish easier and more consistent, especially in a busy kitchen.
- Because no high-heat flavors (the complex flavors from roasting or sautéing) will develop, fish cooked sous vide has a very pure flavor.
- Some fish, such as salmon, cooked sous vide at a very low temperature develop a voluptuous texture that is impossible to achieve any other way.
- Fish we once poached in a court bouillon can now be cooked in a small amount of liquid with a small amount of aromatic vegetables, for a bigger and better flavor.

FOR SEAFOOD

- Seafood such as lobster, octopus, and squid can easily become tough when using high heat. The low heat of sous vide allows us to cook them through and keep them extraordinarily tender.

FOR HARD ROOT VEGETABLES

- All root vegetables can be cooked sous vide with excellent results in terms of texture, flavor, and color. For example, potatoes cook through without their exterior overcooking, turnips cook through elegantly enhanced with a flavorful fat, and carrots remain vivid orange.

FOR OTHER VEGETABLES

- Some softer vegetables are excellent cooked sous vide—onion and fennel, for instance, become tender without overcooking or falling apart. All nongreen vegetables, from corn and radishes to endive, can be efficiently and elegantly flavored in the sous vide bag.

FOR FRUITS

- Fruits are perfectly and consistently cooked in the same way tender vegetables are. In addition, fruits, which are especially susceptible to rapid oxidation and discoloration, remain bright when cooked sous vide rather than becoming dull and brown.

NONCOOKING TECHNIQUES

- Marinating meats sous vide is neat and efficient.
- Compressing food sous vide can result in dramatic textures and brighter colors.
- Gently compressing food can maintain a desired shape, such as a roulade.

GENERAL KITCHEN ISSUES

- Sous vide allows us to cook food before service and chill it or hold it so that it can be finished *à la minute,* at the last minute, with no compromise whatsoever of quality.
- Stove and oven space, valuable assets in busy, crowded kitchens, are freed up when one or more circulators are being used.
- Sous vide requires less "people power"—the cooks' time is not spent tending the pot, so they are free to concentrate on other work.
- Consistency: everything can be cooked to its optimal temperature and texture every time.
- Circulators are portable, allowing us to cook anywhere.
- Cooler space is efficiently used with food stored sous vide. When we seal food sous vide, we are in effect creating the perfect-size container, rather than storing, for example, 750 milliliters of custard base in a 1-liter container.
- Sealing food sous vide prevents damage from oxidation.
- Food sealed and cooked sous vide, then cooled and stored, has a dramatically increased shelf life. This is especially so with custard bases, which are in effect pasteurized by the cooking process and so keep for more than a week if well chilled.
- Sous vide allows us to pick up, or serve, the food efficiently.

THREE BASIC PRINCIPLES

3

Three basic principles govern sous vide cooking: pressure, temperature, and time.

PRESSURE

Pressure is determined by the power of the vacuum packer. The vacuum packer extracts air from the sous vide bag, squeezing the bag tightly against the food, sometimes even compressing the food. The questions to ask in order to determine the desired pressure are these: Do you want the item sealed very, very tightly or even compressed? Or is the item so delicate that it will be crushed by too much pressure? Is there a bone that might puncture the bag if too much pressure is used?

Chamber vacuum packers typically have one gauge for the amount of pressure and a second gauge for the duration of packing. Because vacuum-packing machines vary, general settings for packing are recommended (low, medium, and high) in the recipes here. Many factors determine the appropriate pressure; sealing time is determined by the thickness of the bag. The gauge on the packing bar records how hot it gets. Thicker bags need more heat to fuse completely.

For hard items, such as carrots, we want high pressure so that oxygen is removed and the plastic is as tight against the vegetable as possible, resulting in the maximum surface area coming into contact with the water's heat. The need for maximum surface area is true for meat as well, but sealing pressure may vary depending on how delicate the cut is. For items we want to compress, such as porous fruits and vegetables, we also use high pressure. We compress melon to transform its texture and intensify its color. For some dishes, we compress two different proteins

together (ham and mackerel, for instance; or chicken thigh and a *farce,* or stuffing; or layers of rabbit and bacon), not to change their shape and texture but to ensure that they bond as tightly as possible. For items such as a delicate piece of fish, we use less pressure so that we don't bruise them; if you're cooking a medallion of cod, you don't want to flatten it out.

It's also essential to keep in mind that the food must be cold when it's packed and sealed. This is far more important than most people realize. In fact, Bruno Goussault says that when he trains chefs in sous vide technique, the number one error they make is not chilling the food properly before it's sealed. The problem is related to the fact that in very low pressure situations, water vaporizes at a lower temperature. To demonstrate, Goussault will put one pan of cold water and another one of warm water in a vacuum chamber. When the chamber is locked and the vacuum turned on, the warm water will begin to boil vigorously almost immediately, as the water vaporizes. When warm food is put in a vacuum, the same vaporization will happen, drying it out and affecting its texture.

This is why, in addition to safety issues, when one of these recipes calls for a piece of meat to be seared before it is cooked sous vide, *it must be thoroughly chilled for several hours, or overnight, before sealing it.* If you don't have the refrigerator space to allow the meat to cool uncovered, put the meat in a Zip-loc bag and submerge it in an ice bath until it's thoroughly chilled before packing—below 6°C (42.8°F).

The temperatures used in sous vide cooking are always below that of simmering water, which is about 87° to 93°C (190° to 200°F). The highest temperature we use, almost without exception, is 85°C (185°F), and this is exclusively for vegetables. Plant cell walls are weakened at this temperature, and so the vegetable becomes tender.

Meat and fish cooking temperatures are more varied. Fish proteins generally are delicate, and they denature and coagulate—that is, cook—at about 6.6°C (11.9°F) lower than meat proteins do. For meat, the cells begin to contract and thus squeeze out water and become tough at about 60°C (140°F). At about 70°C (160°F), the meat will have squeezed out much of its moisture, but the cells are easier to pull apart and the collagen will have begun to melt into gelatin (resulting in the very tender meat we expect from a braise).

Cooking a braise cut sous vide at 65.5°C (150°F) for a longer time, however, serves to break down the collagen without squeezing out all the juices, resulting in meat that is as tender as that from a traditional braise but more flavorful.

For tender breasts of poularde, we use 62°C (143.6°F), but we cook the thighs at 64°C (147.2°F). We cook delicate fish, such as St. Peter's (John Dory), at 60°C (140°F).

These temperatures are basic guidelines, not hard-and-fast rules. They may vary slightly depending on how the food is to be treated before and after it goes into the bag. A chicken breast that will be seared after it's removed from the bag may be cooked at a lower temperature than a breast that will simply be cooked sous vide, then sliced and served.

In conventional cooking, timing can be thought of in terms not of how long to cook something, but of how long before you must *stop* its cooking. And this is tricky in conventional cooking, because you're usually using temperatures far higher than the one you want the food to reach. If you're sautéing a medallion of beef, for example, you may want the internal temperature to reach only 54.4°C (130°F), but you're cooking it at about 200°C (400°F). That means that once the beef is at just the right temperature, the window of time you have to get it out of the heat is very small. Further complicating matters is the fact that the temperature of the food will rise at least a few degrees after it's out of the heat, an effect called carryover cooking.

In sous vide cooking, however, once the food reaches the desired internal temperature, it stays there, even when left in the water. And there is no carryover cooking when the food is removed from the water.

This does not mean, however, that the window of time for perfectly cooked food is unlimited. If the meat spends too long in the heat, the color won't change, but the texture and feel will—so it may look beautifully rare but the taste and texture will not be what you expect. It is meat that is rare yet overcooked.

FOUR BASIC TECHNIQUES

We use four specific sous vide techniques: storage, compression, marination, and cooking.

STORAGE

Food vacuum-packed for storage will last considerably longer in the refrigerator than food that's simply wrapped in plastic. It will also hold up better in the freezer. The main reason is the removal of oxygen from the food's environment. Lack of oxygen greatly reduces the activity of many bacteria that cause spoilage. In the freezer, the vacuum-sealing keeps the food from losing moisture to the air, preventing freezer burn. And in some cases, perhaps most notably with foie gras, artichokes, and fruit like apples and pears, vacuum-sealing can prevent discoloration from oxidation. Cooking and then storing food sous vide has the additional benefit that there's no chance for recontamination from airborne bacteria, a cutting board, or a cook's hands, and that will further delay spoilage. Storing food this way is also neater and cleaner, and it helps to maintain the shape of the food.

COMPRESSION

Compression is our newest sous vide technique, discovered (if you will) by Mark Hopper, chef de cuisine at Bouchon in Las Vegas. We use it almost exclusively to change the texture of a food, specifically porous fruits such as pineapple and melon. Compression, which requires a great deal of pressure, can transform a crisp, light bite of fruit into a dense, almost meaty one. We also compress cucumbers, celery, and tomatoes.

A secondary effect of compression is what might be called "setting"—in other words, using the pressure to bring a food to a specific shape and maintain it, so that when it's briefly cooked, the food sets in that shape but remains raw inside. It can then be finished using another cooking method without losing its shape. We set the shapes of different fish and meat this way—a loin of rabbit wrapped in bacon, a piece of delicate St. Peter's fish (John Dory), a stuffed squab breast.

MARINATION

We marinate food sous vide because it is neat, convenient, and efficient. Vacuum-sealing itself doesn't speed up marinating, but when the bag is opened, releasing the vacuum, some marinade can penetrate the food, enhancing its effects. From a restaurant standpoint, the economy of space afforded by marinating food in sealed plastic bags, rather than in plastic containers, is especially useful. The sealed package prevents the possibility of the marinade accidentally spilling, and it also makes it easy to redistribute the marinade ingredients around the food.

COOKING

The most valuable and versatile sous vide technique is, of course, cooking. The three main types of sous vide cooking are short-time cooking (*à la minute*), long-time cooking (up to several days), and fruit and vegetable cooking.

Food that's naturally tender—most fish, for example—requires a relatively short time in the water bath, as little as 10 minutes or so, and is typically served immediately. Meats that are tough require a long time to break down the connective tissues and become tender. Some meats that are braised may fall between short- and long-time cooking, in that they are cooked through but do not become meltingly tender (the chicken thighs in Chestnut-Stuffed Four Story Hills Farm Chicken with Celery and Honey-Poached Cranberries, page 114, for example). Vegetables generally require between 30 and 90 minutes. They are almost always cooked at 85°C (185°F).

These are the general rules, but there are countless variations and points of finesse, as the recipes that follow will demonstrate.

SAFETY ISSUES REGARDING THE THREE BASIC SOUS VIDE STEPS

Certain basic safety rules apply to each step of sous vide.

SEALING

1. Chill the food, or sear the food if that is called for and then chill it immediately and thoroughly.
2. Seal the chilled food and either cook it immediately or store it at 3.3°C (38°F) or below.

COOKING

1. Cook the food, remove it from the bag, and serve it.
2. Cook the food, leave it in the bag, and chill it in an ice bath to 1°C (34°F), then refrigerate or freeze.

STORING

1. Store the food (chilled first if it has been cooked) in the refrigerator at or below about 3.3°C (38°F) or freeze it.
2. Defrost food in the refrigerator before using.

SAFETY

The safety issues of concern in cooking sous vide are different from those cooks are used to addressing in more conventional forms of cooking. They're not complicated, but they're very important to understand and respect; if we ignore them, the potential pathogens can be considerably more dangerous than in other situations because of their opportunity to multiply to dangerous levels.

The bacteria we're mainly concerned with in sous vide cooking are *Salmonella, Clostridium botulinum, E. coli* O157:H7, and *Listeria*. All of these bacteria can live in the anaerobic environment of a vacuum-packed bag, and if they do exist in the bag and it is put in warm water, they can multiply to dangerous levels. The longer bacteria are in what is referred to as the "danger zone"—temperatures between 4.4° and 60°C (40° and 140°F)—the faster they multiply and the more dangerous they become. Bacteria grow with exceptional speed at temperatures between about 40° and 50°C (100° and 120°F), doubling in number every 20 to 30 minutes.

In order to prevent our bagged food from turning into bacteria bombs, we need to understand how bacteria work and how to treat the food in ways that limit their growth. As a general rule, *treat everything you seal in a bag as though it carries harmful bacteria.*

Most bacteria are found on the exterior of food. Some notable exceptions include ground meats (such as hamburger, in which surface bacteria is spread throughout the meat) and eggs (*Salmonella* from the infected ovaries of chickens can contaminate the interior of eggs). Also, if contaminated food is cut into, bacteria can be brought inside the food. Generally, we restrict bacterial growth by keeping the food either cold or hot and by limiting the time it spends in the warm-temperature danger zone. Because most bacteria exist only on the exterior of the food, only the exterior, not the center of the food, must reach temperatures at which the bacteria are killed. But keep in mind that if food that has only a harmless number of bacteria on it is left out at room temperature, those bacteria can multiply rapidly to harmful levels.

Moreover, cooking food to 60° to 82.2°C (140° to 180°F) doesn't mean you've killed all the bacteria. Thousands to millions of bacteria can exist on any given piece of food, and generally accepted cooking times and temperatures kill most but not necessarily all bacteria—until you get up to sterilization temperatures and times. So all safety measures are based on statistics and odds and cannot be ironclad guarantees.

A special note about meats: Always buy the freshest meat possible, and cook it as soon after buying it as you can. All meat is, by definition, contaminated, and the longer it sits before being sealed in a sous vide bag and cooked, the more bacteria can grow—and the more bacteria you'll end up with if you cook and hold it at danger-zone temperatures.

Salmonella bacteria, of which there are more than 2,000 kinds, cause more illnesses than any other food-borne pathogen. *Salmonella* poisoning sickens 1.4 million people each year, according to the Centers for Disease Control, and kills 600 of those who are particularly vulnerable to illness (the very old, the very young, and those with compromised immune systems). Fortunately, most people recover without treatment. *Salmonella* bacteria live in the intestines of animals and humans and can contaminate any raw food. They are a serious problem in the chicken industry, and raw chicken and eggs are among the foods most commonly carrying the bacteria. *Salmonella* are the most heat-resistant bacteria, so measures to protect food from them will likely take care of most other pathogens as well.

Clostridium botulinum is different from the other pathogens we worry about and potentially the most dangerous. The bacterium produces spores that can lie dormant in soil, where *Clostridium* is commonly found. The spores, which are extremely heat-resistant, grow in anaerobic or low-oxygen environments (such as a can or a jar, a dry-cured sausage, even a baked potato wrapped in foil and allowed to cool—or a vacuum-packed bag). The bacteria produce a neurotoxin that is extremely dangerous but that is killed at high temperatures (80°C [176°F]). About 100 people a year in this country are made sick by botulism, mostly from home-canned foods. The main reason the dangers posed by botulism are different from those of other bacteria, besides the potency of the botulism toxin, is the fact that, with the exception of canning, most cooking doesn't include anaerobic environments. *But because sous vide techniques are defined by an anaerobic environment, botulism is of particular concern when using sous vide.*

E. coli O157:H7 is a serious bacterium that can be found on meats and vegetables and is responsible for about sixty deaths a year. Like *Salmonella,* it lives in the intestines of animals and people. It is most prevalent in ground meat and green leafy vegetables.

Listeria, a bacterium present in soil and water, is particularly harmful to pregnant women. Known to grow rapidly in floor drains, it is a special concern at food processing plants, and so products such as hot dogs and other processed meats are often the cause of listeriosis. Unlike the other bacteria discussed here, *Listeria* can grow at near-freezing temperatures.

But by keeping food cold and chilling cooked food as quickly as possible, you can drastically reduce its rate of growth. This is why, when cooking sous vide, cooked food that will be refrigerated in the bag for later use must be chilled thoroughly and completely in an ice bath.

The maximum time food sealed sous vide can safely remain in the bag in danger-zone temperatures (this includes cooking time if cooking below 60°C [140°F]) is 4 hours. But the sooner cooked food is out of the danger zone (meaning the faster it's chilled), the better, from both a safety and a spoilage standpoint. This safety window does give you plenty of leeway. You can safely cook at danger-zone temperatures, and you can leave food out to rest for a half hour or so after cooking so that it can reabsorb the cooking juices—as long as you then chill it completely as quickly as possible in an ice bath. If any vacuum-packed protein, either cooked or raw, has been in the danger zone for 4 hours or longer, we recommend that it be discarded.

To reiterate: *Food to be cooked sous vide must be cold when it's sealed and then either cooked immediately or stored in the refrigerator until ready to cook. After food is cooked sous vide, it must either be served immediately or quickly and thoroughly chilled in an ice bath within 4 hours of entering danger-zone temperatures, then held very cold.*

At per se, sous-chef Rory Herrmann developed a protocol for all of our restaurants, called a HAACP plan, that was accepted by the New York City Health Department for ensuring the safety of food cooked and stored sous vide. While this protocol addresses virtually every ingredient and method the restaurants use, identifying risks and ways to control the risk, the common denominators are the ones just mentioned. Again, all food must be kept refrigerated at 3°C (38°F) or below until it's sealed. Then it should be cooked and served or chilled to a temperature of 1°C (34°F) or below in an ice bath and refrigerated.

What constitutes an ice bath? A minimum of 50 percent ice, but more ice than that is better. An ice bath is not a big pot of water with some ice floating in it—an ice bath should appear to be mostly ice. If there's any doubt, take the temperature of the ice bath to make sure it's at 1°C (34°F). And it's a good idea to agitate the bag every so often to prevent a "dead zone" of warm water from surrounding it. Add more ice as soon as the heat of the bag has melted some of the ice. Adding salt to the ice will further reduce the temperature.

After food has been cooked sous vide and chilled, how long will it keep? Even when the food is chilled and in the cooler, some bacteria, such as *Listeria*, can continue to grow.

Clostridium spores can germinate at 5°C (41°F). Complicating the situation is the fact that coolers vary widely in the temperature they can hold, and within any cooler, there are cold spots and warm spots. We recommend that you check your cooler frequently to make sure at least part of it maintains a temperature of 3.3°C (38°F) or lower, and always keep food that has been sealed sous vide in the coldest part of the cooler. If you're concerned about your cooler's temperatures, you may want to store sealed food packed in ice.

As a general rule, if you're not going to use the food within 3 days, freeze it (still in the plastic).

There may be times when you have reason to be concerned about food you've sealed sous vide—say you've accidentally left a package out, or your power went off, so the food has been in the bag at room temperature for several hours. In these cases, we recommend that you discard the food.

Safety considerations are built into all the recipes here, so be sure to follow the recipes closely with regard to heating and chilling food that is sealed sous vide. Generally, though, food pathogens are something to be aware of and to understand, not to fear. Know where they may be present, know the conditions in which they flourish, and prevent those conditions.

IN OUR KITCHENS

Sous vide use at our restaurants is so pervasive as to be completely integrated into the system. From the built-in circulator tank at per se's fish station to the 80-gallon tank that resides in the storeroom of the Bouchon kitchen in Las Vegas—used for cooking large quantities of braised short ribs and other such cuts—chamber sealers, immersion heaters, water-filled tanks, and plastic bags are all part of our kitchens.

The French Laundry, per se, Bouchon, and Ad Hoc kitchens all have numerous immersion circulators. Because most are portable, they can move from station to station or on busy weekends out of the kitchen altogether—anywhere the water tank, often a tall Lexan container, will fit. We usually have at least one designated immersion circulator on the line during service and one in the prep area.

Each chef using the circulator is responsible for the item he or she puts into it. If that item requires brief cooking, the chef sets a timer. If the item requires many hours or a couple of days, the time of removal is posted on the tank. Because vegetables are usually cooked at the same temperature, often many bags of different vegetables will be in the same tank.

The circulators can be used in virtually any container they'll fit into. Some containers are large enough that they require two circulators to ensure even heating of the water. Use your common sense here. Tanks that will be kept running for a long time can be covered to make the heating more efficient and to limit evaporation.

Finally, there's an appliance that stands in for a circulator when all the rest are being used, or for large quantities. It's generically referred to as a "combi"—a combination oven—and it uses dry heat or steam heat or a combination of both. This oven can be set to precise temperatures, and the steam heat can act just as efficiently as water heated with an immersion circulator.

IN THE HOME KITCHEN

The recipes that follow are the exact ones used by the kitchens at The French Laundry and at per se. They've been written for the professional kitchen, from one chef to another. No modifications have been made to accommodate cooks preparing them at home, even though some of them certainly can be done at home with the right equipment. The recipes have been developed through trial and error and, of course, countless repetitions. They've been tested using chamber vacuum packers and immersion circulators. They include the full range of techniques we use in the restaurants, not just sous vide, but the sous vide applications are the newest and most exciting of these techniques.

The recipes here are for the finished dishes as served at per se and The French Laundry. Each dish comprises several components; some of these components are quick and simple, others require long cooking times or involved preparation. We've organized the recipes component by component rather than in the sequential or chronological order more familiar to the home cook, because restaurant kitchens will have different chefs preparing various components of a single dish. This is why, also, the yield of a compo-

nent may be more than you will need for that specific dish.

That said, once you get used to this format, we hope you'll find it useful. Many of the components of a dish can be prepared ahead of time, or, if you're cooking with other people, the various components can easily be divvied up. This is how restaurant kitchens operate, and it can be an excellent strategy at home—cooking together is something we encourage! And it will make these dishes far more satisfying and manageable for home cooks.

Another way this book differs from other American cookbooks is that the quantities for most ingredients in these recipes are given in metric weights. A digital scale that goes to the tenth of a gram is an important kitchen tool generally, and it is a must for this book. We weigh most ingredients to ensure accuracy. Even liquids are generally measured by weight, not volume—a recipe might call for 100 grams of water, for instance (however, in the basic recipes starting on page 255, some large quantities of liquids are listed in liters). We hope you'll find that learning to use metric measurements, a vastly more logical and consistent system than American or imperial weights and measures, actually makes cooking easier.

A FEW ADDITIONAL TIPS TO KEEP IN MIND AS YOU COOK FROM THIS BOOK

1. Read the preceding pages (26–38) closely, taking particular note of the section on safety. Safety issues involved with sous vide cooking are different from those for traditional forms of cooking. They are not difficult to understand or follow, and they are very important. Please adhere to safety recommendations scrupulously.

2. Read the recipe through before you begin. Again, each dish has been broken down into its components, and each component has its own recipe. Use this format to create your own game plan when preparing a complete dish. Note that more than one ingredient can go into the water bath at the same time if they require the same temperature.

3. Ingredients must be thoroughly chilled, and cold throughout before they are vacuum-packed (see page 35).

4. Herbs should not come in direct contact with food that is vacuum-packed. Doing so will cause some areas of the food to take on more flavor than others. For this reason, we roll herbs and aromatics in food-safe plastic wrap (we call it a sachet) before putting them in the main bag (see page 269).

5. Always bag food in a single layer to ensure even cooking.

6. Many, if not most, of these recipes call for including some sort of liquid in the bag—fat, stock, or a dairy product. All these recipes have been tested using a chamber vacuum packer. We don't recommend you attempt recipes that include liquids in the bag unless you have a chamber packer.

7. Timing in these recipes is based on the cold vacuum-packed food being submerged in water that is at the proper temperature. The heating element and the quantity of water being heated will determine the length of preheating time, but in a test of one of our circulators, it took 1 hour for 11.4 liters (3 gallons) of water to go from 10°C (50°F) to 60°C (140°F) and 1¼ hours to reach 85°C (185°F). Of course, you can start with hot tap water, or heat water on the stove, to reduce the time.

8. Our stocks do not have added salt. If you are using stock that has been salted, take that into consideration as you season.

9. Certain components of dishes are prepared in larger proportions than are needed in the individual recipe. There are a myriad of uses for any of these.

10. When recipes call for the use of a chinois, use a fine-mesh chinois (*chinois fine* in French), not a perforated one.

11. Few plating instructions are given in these recipes, because plating in restaurants is often up to the chef preparing the dish and will be defined as much by his or her personality as by the food. The size and shape of the plate used also determines how a dish will be plated.

VEGETABLES AND FRUITS

SOUS VIDE HAS DRAMATICALLY CHANGED THE WAY WE COOK VEGETABLES.

It hasn't replaced other techniques, but from the standpoint of flavor, preventing oxidation, and convenience, it is dramatically effective.

First and foremost, always, is flavor; A carrot cooked sous vide has a very pure flavor; it has not lost flavor to a liquid cooking environment, and the flavor is not complicated by high temperatures that cause browning. That in itself is remarkable. But put a single bay leaf in a big bag of carrots, and the flavor of bay is both more pronounced and more nuanced than it would be if the carrots were cooked conventionally; the carrots are permeated with the aromatic but have lost none of their own flavor to the cooking medium. (The effect of aromatics in the bag, in fact, is so powerful that we first wrap them in food-safe plastic wrap. You've got to be careful with any herbs you include with vegetables.) The carrots come out of the bag at the perfect point of doneness, so that

if you want to finish them in some way with a higher-heat technique, by bringing roasted flavors to them or by glazing them, it's very quick—an especially valuable quality in restaurant cooking.

The way sous vide enables you to retain texture and shape is unmatched. You can cook vegetables so that they become tender, without the possibility that they will overcook or begin to fragment or fall apart. This is especially useful when the vegetables must be sliced before being reheated; a bulb of fennel cooked sous vide, for example, slices cleanly. (The gentleness of the heat is particularly advantageous with vegetables, which become increasingly delicate as they cook.)

Oxidation, a part of nature, can affect fruits and vegetables in ways we struggle to prevent. Artichokes, for instance, will begin to darken as soon as you cut them unless you immediately put them into acidic water or into heat that will

neutralize the enzymes responsible. Sealing vegetables sous vide also reduces the effects of oxidation. This can be invaluable when you don't want to put the vegetable into a high-heat or acidic environment. But if you do want flavors from high-heat techniques, they're easy to introduce after the vegetable comes out of the bag.

Last, sous vide techniques offer convenience: the ability to cook a large amount of vegetables so that they are ready to go at a moment's notice. They're easily cooked, cooled, and stored without compromising flavor or texture.

The only vegetables we don't cook sous vide are green vegetables—they lose their vivid color when locked in a sous vide bag. They're best cooked in a big pot of vigorously boiling heavily salted water (see Big-Pot Blanching, page 268). But for all the others, sous vide is a great technique.

MARINATED TOY BOX TOMATOES
WITH COMPRESSED CUCUMBER–RED ONION RELISH, TOASTED BRIOCHE, AND DIANE ST. CLAIRE BUTTER

RED ONION RELISH

100 grams small dice red onion

23 grams granulated sugar

125 grams water

12 grams red wine vinegar

1 English cucumber

TOMATOES

35 grams roughly chopped basil

140 grams water

140 grams granulated sugar

290 grams sweet Toy Box tomatoes, peeled

Extra virgin olive oil

Small basil leaves

High-quality unsalted butter, such as Diane St. Claire, at room temperature

Four ½-inch-thick slices Brioche (page 262), crusts removed and toasted

Maldon salt

The inspiration for this dish was the technique of compressing tomatoes in syrup. We thought of it when the first tomatoes began to arrive one year and, while they were good, they weren't height-of-season tomatoes—they lacked the sugar content that builds as you move into summer. Many of our vegetable purveyors now use refractometers to measure the Brix, the sugar content, of their vegetables. And we thought we might be able to counter the tomatoes' lack of sugar by infusing them with sweetness. We vacuum-packed them in a simple syrup infused with basil, and the results were extraordinary. Not only did the sweetness penetrate the tomatoes, but so did the basil flavor. You can't achieve the same effect by simply marinating the tomatoes in the syrup—those taste like tomatoes lacquered with syrup. We first tried compressing tomato fillets, but the flavor scarcely changed and so we thought of using peeled whole small tomatoes instead. You can use the technique with many flavors—other fresh herbs, such as thyme or tarragon, or aromatic vegetables or spices—depending on the dish. And you can adjust the sweetness as well. This is a savory course, but we could increase the sweetness of the tomatoes, say, to make a sorbet, or serve the candied tomatoes with an olive oil ice cream as a sweet course.

With the cucumber-onion relish—the compressed cucumbers become beautiful, vibrant, and almost translucent—this is a great dish. All the fruit, sweetness, and acidity here needs the balance of some fat, and we finish this with some brioche toast and the extraordinary hand-kneaded butter made by Diane St. Clair at her Animal Farm in Orwell, Vermont. Unfortunately, Diane can make only a small amount of butter each year, but you can use any high-quality butter.

FOR THE ONION RELISH: Combine the onion, sugar, and water in a saucepan, bring to a simmer, and cook for about 15 minutes. The onions should be tender. Add the vinegar and cook for another 20 minutes, or until there is only a very small amount of liquid left. Cool, then transfer to the refrigerator to chill.

Cut the cucumber into 3-inch lengths. Trim the sides away to square off the edges, then cut 8 even rectangles about 1 inch wide by ⅛ inch thick from each piece (2 per side); cut only until you reach the seeds, and discard the seedy centers. Lay the cucumber slices side by side in one layer in a bag. Vacuum-pack on high, then refrigerate for at least 1 hour, or overnight.

Cut the cucumber into small dice, about ⅛ inch. You should have about 85 grams of cucumber.

FOR THE TOMATOES: Combine the chopped basil, water, and sugar in a saucepan and bring to a simmer, stirring to dissolve the sugar. Chill this simple syrup over an ice bath, whisking until cold.

Place the tomatoes in a large bag and strain in enough simple syrup to cover them (see photograph, page 46); you may not use all of it. Vacuum-pack on high, then refrigerate for at least 1 hour, or overnight.

AT SERVICE: Toss the cucumber and onion together. Drain the tomatoes and toss with a little olive oil and small basil leaves. Whip the butter until smooth. Serve with the brioche toast and Maldon salt.

MAKES 4 SERVINGS

"STEAK TARTARE"
COMPRESSED WATERMELON AND HAYDEN MANGO "YOLK"

WATERMELON

¼ ripe seedless watermelon, rind removed

Kosher salt

Extra virgin olive oil

MANGO "YOLK"

125 grams mango juice

0.8 gram Kelcogel F (see Sources, page 282)

0.2 gram sodium hydroxymetaphosphate
   (see Sources, page 282)

30 grams calcium gluconate
   (see Sources, page 282)

0.4 gram ascorbic acid

75 grams granulated sugar

½ lime

Freshly ground black pepper

Ferran Adrià, chef-owner of the renowned El Bulli outside Barcelona, brought the technique of spherification, using alginate and calcium gluconate to gel the exterior of a liquid, to fine dining. Ferran''s technique piqued our interest in spherification and its applications. The great team at CP Kelco in San Diego helped us to develop this one, using different hydrocolloids—natural substances that affect the properties of liquids—to achieve similar effects.

When we were looking for a canapé we could offer to vegetarians and vegans, we came up with this play on beef tartare, using the technique of spherification. The compressed watermelon mimics the beef and a ball of encapsulated mango juice replaces the traditional egg yolk. Mango juice actually tends to set up a little on its own, taking on a viscosity that's very similar to that of egg yolk. The dish is finished with a squeeze of lime.

PHOTOGRAPH ON PAGE 47

FOR THE WATERMELON: Place the piece of watermelon in a bag and vacuum-pack at the highest setting. Refrigerate for at least 3 hours.

To complete: Cut the watermelon into a fine dice and then finely mince to resemble tartare. Drain in a chinois or fine-mesh conical strainer. Toss the watermelon with a pinch of salt and a drizzle of olive oil.

FOR THE MANGO "YOLK": Put the mango juice in a Vita-Prep. Place the Kelcogel F and sodium hydroxymetaphosphate on a saucer.

Hold it above the Vita-Prep and, with the machine running on low speed, slowly tap in the powders in steady small amounts until they are all incorporated. Turn to high speed for 2 to 3 seconds, then strain the mixture through a chinois or fine-mesh conical strainer.

To complete: Pour 500 grams of cold water into a deep bowl. Whisk in the calcium gluconate, ascorbic acid, and sugar to dissolve. Put another deep bowl of cold water next to it. Drop a teaspoonful of the mango mixture (keeping it as close to a ball as possible) into the calcium gluconate mixture and let sit for 1 minute. Remove with a slotted spoon and place into the bowl of cold water. Repeat with the remaining mango mixture. Use the best yolks.   **MAKES 10 "YOLKS"**

AT SERVICE: Spread one-quarter of the watermelon in a ring mold on each plate. Lift off the mold and top with a mango "yolk." Finish with a squeeze of lime juice and a grind of black pepper.

MAKES 4 SERVINGS

NOTE

One-quarter of a small seedless watermelon will yield about 120 grams of tartare, serving 4. You'll get approximately 20 "yolks" from 125 grams of mango juice. It is best not to work with less mango juice. Any unused mango should be discarded. Additional servings can be made from the remaining watermelon.

Opposite: marinated Toy Box tomatoes (see page 44); above: "Steak
Tartare": Compressed Watermelon and Hayden Mango "Yolk" (page 45)

SWEET CORN SOUP
WITH SUMMER SUCCOTASH AND PORK BELLY DUMPLINGS

DUMPLINGS

150 grams cooked pork belly (see page 148)

Canola oil

35 grams minced Spanish onion

50 grams red wine vinegar

50 grams granulated sugar

80 grams Quick Pork Sauce (page 260)

Kosher salt and freshly ground black pepper

¼ recipe Pasta Dough for Rolling (page 262)

Durum semolina flour

CORN SOUP

3 to 4 large ears corn

400 grams Chicken Stock
    (page 257)

400 grams heavy cream

20 grams granulated sugar

Kosher salt

1 tarragon sprig

SUCCOTASH

1 red bell pepper

1 yellow bell pepper

10 haricots verts

Extra virgin olive oil

Tarragon leaves

Pork belly is one of the most gratifying cuts for a chef to cook, and at The French Laundry we serve it in many forms. We cut it to precise shapes for various dishes, which results in a lot of leftover trim, oddly shaped pieces of exquisite, perfectly cooked pork belly. One way to make use of these delicious trimmings is to dice them and use them as a stuffing, or *farce*, gently sautéed to crisp them but leaving them very succulent (most braised meats can be transformed into a delicious *farce*).

Because of the pork, we thought of dumplings. But not the dim sum kind of dumplings—our pasta is egg-based, and the dumplings are shaped like tortellini. We had a soup in mind and knew the tortellini would work well. (It could have been any kind of wrapper, though, depending what we wanted to do—ravioli, pierogi, or even a vol-au-vent.) Corn and pork is always a good combination. Like the pork belly, the corn is cooked sous vide, and it is extraordinary. All its aromatic qualities seem to be preserved when corn is cooked sous vide, and so the flavor is intense. The corn made us think of succotash, so we make a summer version, with fresh green beans instead of fresh limes and bell peppers, for garnish.

FOR THE DUMPLING FILLING: Cut the pork belly into ⅛-inch dice. Heat a film of canola oil in a sauté pan over high heat. Add the pork belly and sauté for 3 to 5 minutes to render some of the fat and lightly brown the meat; it should not crisp. Drain in a fine-mesh basket strainer and discard the fat.

Heat a film of oil in a pot over medium heat. Add the onion and sweat until softened. Add the red wine vinegar and sugar. Bring to a simmer and reduce the liquid by half, to make a gastrique.

Add the pork and pork sauce and reduce the liquid over low heat until it becomes a heavy glaze, coating the pork. There should be enough liquid to come just to the top of the pork. Season to taste with salt and pepper, remove from the heat, and let cool in the pan.

Line a small baking pan with parchment and spread the filling in the pan. Refrigerate until cold. The glaze will become thicker, but it will melt when the pasta cooks.

FOR THE DUMPLINGS: Divide the pasta dough into 2 pieces. Set the rollers of a pasta machine at the widest setting. Run one piece of the dough (keep the other piece wrapped in plastic) through the machine. As you roll it out, dust the dough with flour as necessary to keep it from sticking to the machine. Fold the dough in half, end to end, turn it a quarter turn, and run it through the same setting again. Repeat this procedure 5 more times, or until the pasta is extremely smooth and silky, then fold the pasta lengthwise in half to give you a narrow sheet of pasta and run it through the machine.

Set the openings of the rollers down one notch and run the pasta through (do not fold it). Reduce the opening another notch and run the dough through again. Continue the process until the sheet is about $\frac{1}{32}$ inch thick. Run it through the machine twice on the final setting. Cover the sheet of pasta with plastic wrap or a towel to keep it from drying out and repeat with the second piece of dough.

Spread a $\frac{1}{4}$-inch layer of flour on a sheet pan to hold the shaped dumplings. Lay one sheet of pasta on a lightly floured work surface with a long side facing you. Trim the edges so they are straight. Starting about $1\frac{1}{2}$ inches from one end, spoon about 10-gram mounds of filling 3 inches apart down the center of the strip of dough. Fold the top edge of the dough over to meet the other edge and use your fingers and the dull side of a $2\frac{1}{2}$-inch round cutter to shape the filling and eliminate any air bubbles trapped in the pasta. With the sharp side of the cutter, cut out half-moon dumplings. Lift up each dumpling, making sure that the edges are sealed, and bring up the two points to meet over the center, overlapping them slightly; press the dough together to seal. Place the shaped dumplings on the sheet pan. Repeat with the remaining dough and filling. If you will not be cooking the dumplings shortly, freeze them on the baking sheet, then store in freezer bags for up to 10 days. Cook while still frozen.

FOR THE SOUP—85°C (185°F); 30 MINUTES

Cut the kernels from the ears of corn; reserve 3 of the cobs. You need 400 grams of corn kernels.

Put the 3 corn cobs in a pot with the chicken stock, cream, sugar, and salt to taste. Bring to a simmer and simmer for 20 minutes, to reduce the liquid by about half. Strain the liquid into a bowl (discard the cobs), and cool over an ice bath, stirring occasionally.

Make an herb sachet (see page 269) with the tarragon.

Combine the liquid, corn kernels, and the sachet in a large plastic bag and vacuum-pack on high.

Cook at 85°C (185°F) for 30 minutes.

Pour the soup into a Vita-Prep and puree until completely smooth. Strain through a chinois or fine-mesh conical strainer and season with additional salt to taste. Refrigerate until ready to serve.

MAKES 575 GRAMS

FOR THE SUCCOTASH: Char the peppers on all sides over a flame or with a blowtorch. Put in a plastic bag to steam and loosen the skins, and let cool. Peel the peppers and, working around each pepper, cut the flesh away from the core into sheets. Discard the seeds and trim away the ribs to make even sheets of pepper. Cut into $\frac{1}{8}$-inch dice. You will need 20 grams of each color of diced peppers; reserve any extra peppers for another use.

Trim the ends of the haricot verts on a bias, then cut them in half on a severe bias. Blanch the haricot verts (see Big-Pot Blanching, page 268), chill in an ice bath, and dry on C-fold towels.

AT SERVICE: Cook the dumplings in simmering water for 3 to 4 minutes (5 to 6 minutes if frozen). Reheat the soup. Warm the peppers and haricots verts in oil in a sauté pan.

Drain the dumplings and add to the sauté pan, then arrange the dumplings and vegetables in soup bowls. Garnish with tarragon and add the soup.

MAKES 4 SERVINGS

PUREE OF SUNCHOKE SOUP
WITH ARUGULA PUDDING AND PICKLED RADISHES

RADISHES

150 grams water

75 grams champagne vinegar

75 grams granulated sugar

4 large red French breakfast radishes

4 Flambeau radishes

4 icicle (white) radishes

SUNCHOKE SOUP

50 grams unsalted butter

50 grams thinly sliced Spanish onion

400 grams thinly sliced peeled sunchokes

4 grams granulated sugar

12 grams kosher salt

1 kilogram Chicken Stock (page 257)

100 grams heavy cream

ARUGULA PUDDING

300 grams arugula leaves

Canola oil

70 grams sliced shallots

1 bay leaf

2 thyme sprigs

100 grams Vegetable Stock

   (page 260)

100 grams heavy cream

5 grams kosher salt

10 grams Beurre Manié (page 261)

10 grams beaten egg yolk (about ½ large)

CROUTONS

100 grams Clarified Butter (page 261)

100 grams Brioche (page 262),

   frozen and cut into ⅛-inch dice

Kosher salt

Radish sprouts

Sunchokes are very sweet and rich, so we pair them with the sharp, peppery flavors of arugula and three types of radishes, which are gently pickled and cooked sous vide. The arugula is blanched and pureed, then combined with a basic creamy vegetable stock that is thickened with beurre manié and egg yolk to make a savory pudding. My favorite element in this dish is the radishes. The sous vide technique really sets their vivid color and cooks them in a way that leaves them powerfully flavored.

FOR THE RADISHES—85°C (185°F); 25 MINUTES

Bring the water and vinegar to a boil. Add the sugar and stir to dissolve. Remove from the heat and chill over an ice bath until cold.

Meanwhile, rub the radishes in a damp towel to clean. Trim the ends from the radishes. With a #12 parisienne baller, cut balls of red radish. Cut the Flambeau radishes into small disks. Cut the icicle radishes into oblique (roll-cut) shapes.

Place the 3 types of radish in separate bags. Pour in enough of the liquid to just cover the radishes and vacuum-pack on medium.

Cook at 85°C (185°F) for about 25 minutes; the radishes should still have some crunch. Cool in an ice bath.

To complete: Drain the radishes and let dry on C-fold towels.

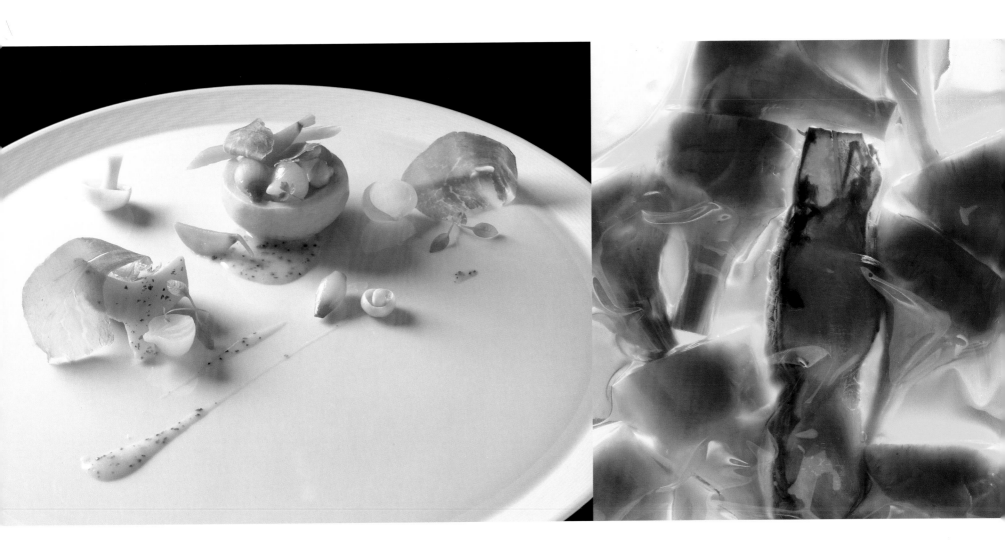

Left: Globe Artichokes *à la Barigoule,* Spring Garlic, Flat-leaf Parsley, and Shaved Serrano Ham (page 52); right: globe artichoke hearts with herb sachet; opposite (left): violet artichokes; opposite (right): *Artichauts en Vierge* (page 56)

GLOBE ARTICHOKES À LA BARIGOULE, SPRING GARLIC, FLAT-LEAF PARSLEY, AND SHAVED SERRANO HAM

1 stalk spring garlic

CUISSON

30 grams extra virgin olive oil

40 grams thinly sliced carrot

35 grams thinly sliced shallot

30 grams thinly sliced onion

Kosher salt

30 grams serrano ham, cut into ¼-inch dice

5 grams minced garlic

2 globe artichoke hearts (see page 269),
    cut into ¾-inch pieces

70 grams dry white wine,
    such as Sauvignon Blanc

150 grams Chicken Stock (page 257)

150 grams White Veal Stock (page 255)

VEGETABLES

8 Thumbelina carrots

4 cipollini, peeled

8 red pearl onions, peeled

8 white pearl onions, peeled

Extra virgin olive oil

Kosher salt

Granulated sugar

Champagne vinegar

Red wine vinegar

ARTICHOKES

8 medium (36 count) globe artichokes

Kosher salt

8 grams balsamic vinegar

25 grams extra virgin olive oil

Minced flat-leaf parsley

MUSHROOMS

Canola oil

12 honshiminji (beech) mushrooms,
    with some stem still attached

Kosher salt

Shavings of serrano ham

Parsley shoots

Artichokes *à la barigoule* is a type of stew, and stewing is almost always suited to sous vide. A perfect barigoule can be a little tricky, requiring some experience to get the cooking of the artichoke hearts just right, but sous vide makes it easier. The *cuisson*, or cooking liquid, which will become part of the final sauce, is prepared like a quick vegetable stock: aromatic vegetables are sweated in oil, then diced artichokes and ham are added along with stock and cooked. The cuisson is strained and cooled, and the artichoke hearts are cooked sous vide in it. The artichokes absorb the flavors of the cuisson, and then the cuisson, enhanced by the flavor of the artichokes, is blended with pureed cooked artichokes and olive oil to make the sauce for the hearty vegetable dish.

When it's available, we use spring garlic, or green garlic, young garlic pulled from the ground just when the bulb has formed, or even before it forms. It's very sweet, without the bite of more mature garlic. And it is as tender as garlic that has been confited. **PHOTOGRAPH ON PAGE 54**

FOR THE GARLIC: Blanch the garlic (see Big-Pot Blanching, page 268). Chill in an ice bath, then drain and dry. Trim and cut on the diagonal into ¼-inch slices. Set aside.

FOR THE CUISSON: Gently heat the olive oil in a wide saucepan. Add the carrot and sweat for 2½ minutes. Add the shallot, onion, and a pinch of salt and cook for 1½ minutes. Stir in the ham and cook for about 30 seconds, then add the garlic and cook for 30 seconds. Add the artichokes and cook for another 2 minutes. Add the white wine and turn the artichokes in the wine for about 30 seconds (the wine will help keep the artichokes from oxidizing). Add the chicken and veal stock, bring to a simmer, and cook for 10 minutes to infuse the broth with flavor. Check the cuisson by tasting; the artichokes should be fully cooked.

Strain the cuisson through a chinois or fine-mesh conical strainer; discard the solids. Chill until cold.

Peel the carrots. Cut them lengthwise in half and use a paring knife to round the cut edges.

Place the carrots and the three types of onion into four separate bags, adding a drizzle of olive oil and a pinch each of salt and sugar to each one. Vacuum-pack on high.

Cook at 85°C (185°F) for 35 to 40 minutes, or until tender. Chill the bags in an ice bath.

Trim the artichokes (see page 269): Cut the stems flush with the bottoms of 4 of the artichokes. Trim the bottoms of the stems of 2 of the remaining artichokes, leaving about 1 inch attached. Trim the stems of the 2 remaining artichokes.

Place the 4 whole hearts in a bag with about 90 grams of the cuisson and a pinch of salt. Cut the 2 hearts with the 1-inch stems in half and place in another bag with about 45 grams of the cuisson and a pinch of salt. Place the remaining 2 hearts in a bag with the remaining cuisson and a pinch of salt. Vacuum-pack all of the artichokes on high.

Cook all of the artichokes at 85°C (185°F). Cook the bag of 4 artichokes and the bag of 4 halves for 45 minutes to 1¼ hours, or until tender. Cook the 2 whole hearts, which will be used for the puree, for 1½ hours, or until completely soft. When they are tender, place the bags of the 4 artichokes and the 4 halves in an ice bath to chill.

When they are completely soft, transfer the 2 artichokes for the puree to a Vita-Prep; reserve the cuisson in the bag. Pulse to puree the artichokes, adding just enough of the cuisson to achieve a puree. Then slowly add additional cuisson as necessary to loosen the puree to the consistency of a thick sauce. Add the balsamic vinegar and olive oil.

To complete: Just before serving, stir in the parsley.

FOR THE MUSHROOMS: Heat a film of oil in a sauté pan. Add the mushrooms, sprinkle with salt, and cook until tender, adjusting the heat so that they do not brown. Remove the mushrooms from the pan and drain on a C-fold towel.

AT SERVICE: Drain all the artichokes. Spoon the artichoke puree into four bowls and top with the whole artichoke hearts. Toss the artichoke heart halves with a little parsley and add one to each bowl. Squeeze the cipollini to remove the centers and separate the outer layers into rings. Toss the cipollini rings, the white pearl onions, the carrots, and spring garlic with a drizzle of olive oil and champagne vinegar. Toss the red pearl onions with olive oil and red wine vinegar. Sprinkle all the vegetables with salt. Arrange the vegetables in the bowls and garnish with shavings of ham and parsley shoots.   MAKES 4 SERVINGS

FOR THE SOUP: Melt the butter in a saucepan. Add the onion and sweat until completely soft. Add the sunchokes, stir in the sugar and salt, and add the chicken stock. Bring to a simmer and cook until the sunchokes are completely soft and the stock is reduced by about half. Add the cream and bring to a simmer.

Puree the soup in a Vita-Prep, then pass through a chinois or fine-mesh conical strainer. Refrigerate if not serving right away.

MAKES ABOUT 1 KILOGRAM

FOR THE ARUGULA PUDDING: Blanch the arugula leaves (see Big-Pot Blanching, page 268). Cool in an ice bath. Drain, wrap in a towel, and wring out as much water as possible.

Put the arugula in the Vita-Prep with 4 ice cubes (the ice will help the arugula maintain its color). Puree, then pass through a chinois or fine-mesh conical strainer. Set aside.

Heat a film of canola oil in a saucepan. Add the shallots and sweat until softened, about 3 minutes; they should not develop any color. Add the bay leaf and thyme and cook gently for another 3 to 4 minutes. Add the vegetable stock and cook for about 3 minutes, until the shallots are very soft. Add the cream and salt. Reduce by half, then strain through a chinois or fine-mesh conical strainer into a small saucepan.

To complete: Bring the cream mixture to a simmer and whisk in the beurre manié. Keeping it at a low simmer, cook for 15 minutes to remove any taste of raw flour. Whisk in the egg yolk. Remove from the heat.

Using two parts arugula puree to one part cream base, stir the puree into the cream and heat over low heat.

MAKES ABOUT 250 GRAMS

FOR THE CROUTONS: Heat the clarified butter in a sauté pan. Add the brioche and stir to color evenly to a golden brown. Season with salt, and drain on C-fold towels.

AT SERVICE: Reheat the soup if necessary. Place a spoonful of the pudding, some radishes, and the radish sprouts in the bottom of each bowl. At the table, pour the soup around the garnishes. Sprinkle the croutons on top.

MAKES 10 SERVINGS

Preparing the parsley chips (see page 57)

FOR THE SUNCHOKES—85°C (185°F); 40 TO 60 MINUTES

Peel 2 of the sunchokes. Slice them paper-thin on a Japanese mandoline; you need 12 rounds of equal diameter. As they are sliced, lay them out on a C-fold towel—these will become your 12 sunchoke chips. Deep-fry the chips in 138°C (about 280°F) oil until very lightly colored, about 2 minutes, moving them around so they cook evenly, then drain on C-fold towels.

Cut off both ends of the remaining 2 sunchokes. Using a vegetable peeler, peel the sunchokes and put them in cold water to chill.

Make an herb sachet (see page 269) with the bay leaf and thyme. Drain and dry the sunchokes, then place in a bag with the oil, juice, and sachet. Vacuum-pack on medium.

Cook at 85°C (185°F) for 40 to 60 minutes, or until tender.

FOR THE CROSNES—85°C (185°F); 30 MINUTES

Scrub the crosnes and cut both ends off each. Place in a single layer in a bag.

Make an herb sachet (see page 269) with the bay leaf and thyme. Add to the bag, along with the oil and juice. Vacuum-pack on medium.

Cook at 85°C (185°F) for about 30 minutes, until tender. Remove from the bag and trim if needed.

FOR THE PARSLEY CHIPS: Wrap a small plate or a plastic lid tightly in food-safe plastic wrap. Brush the plastic wrap lightly with oil and lay the parsley leaves on the plastic. Lightly brush the leaves with oil. Wrap in a second piece of plastic wrap (see photograph, page 58).

Microwave for 1½ to 2 minutes, until the leaves are crisp. Unwrap and sprinkle with salt.

The parsley chips should be made only a few hours before service to ensure that they stay crisp.

FOR THE OLIVES: Cut off both ends of each olive. Punch out the centers (including the pits) of the olives with a ½-inch cutter; discard. Cut the olives into rings about ⅛ inch thick.

AT SERVICE: Drain the artichokes. Cut the globe artichoke hearts into wedges or other shapes. Cut each violet artichoke lengthwise in half. Drain the sunchokes.

For each serving, gently toss together one-quarter of the artichokes, crosnes, and sunchokes in a bowl with some lemon suprêmes, juice, and Trappitu olive oil. Season to taste with fleur de sel and pepper. Arrange on serving plates, spooning the oil and juice over the salad. Top with the olive slices, parsley shoots, parsley chips, and sunchoke chips.

MAKES 4 SERVINGS

GLOBE ARTICHOKES, SUNCHOKES, CROSNES, MEYER LEMON SUPRÊMES, CASTELVETRANO OLIVES, AND TRAPPITU EXTRA VIRGIN OLIVE OIL

ARTICHOKES

2 globe artichoke hearts (see page 269)

8 violet artichokes, trimmed (see page 269)

2 small rosemary sprigs

2 small thyme sprigs

2 small garlic cloves, crushed, skin left on

2 small bay leaves

8 black peppercorns

210 grams extra virgin olive oil

70 grams champagne vinegar

4 grams kosher salt

SUNCHOKES

4 golf-ball-sized sunchokes

(about 150 grams total)

Canola oil for deep-frying

1 bay leaf

1 thyme sprig

10 grams extra virgin olive oil

2 grams Meyer lemon juice

CROSNES

12 crosnes

1 bay leaf

1 thyme sprig

10 grams extra virgin olive oil

2 grams Meyer lemon juice

PARSLEY CHIPS

Canola oil

12 flat-leaf parsley leaves

Kosher salt

Sicilian green olives, preferably Castelvetrano

(see Sources, page 282)

8 to 12 Meyer lemon suprêmes

Meyer lemon juice

Trappitu extra virgin olive oil

(see Sources, page 282)

Fleur de sel

Freshly ground black pepper

Parsley shoots

A rtichokes are stellar when cooked sous vide for several reasons: They're less likely to oxidize; they cook through at a low temperature but don't get soft; and they're consistent every time. Further, we're very easily able to infuse them with all the aromatics of a traditional barigoule. (The same, generally speaking, goes for the sunchokes here.) Moreover, the oil that the artichokes cook in becomes very flavorful, and we can use it in the vinaigrette.

Crosnes, also known as Chinese artichokes, are small, ribbed tubers with a sweet, nutty flavor. Castelvetrano olives from Sicily are big, bright, firm fruit that's not heavily cured. We also use olive oil made from those same olives. Artichokes, sunchokes, citrus fruits, and olives are abundant and beautiful at the same time and they combine for a great salad. We use the word *vierge* to denote a warm vinaigrette.

When selecting the sunchokes for this dish, look for those that are as round as possible. **PHOTOGRAPH ON PAGE 55**

FOR THE ARTICHOKES—85°C (185°F); 40 TO 75 MINUTES

Place the globe artichokes side by side in one bag and the violet artichokes in one layer in another. Make 2 herb sachets (see page 269) with the rosemary, thyme, garlic cloves, bay leaves, and peppercorns. Put 1 sachet in each bag.

Whisk the olive oil, vinegar, and salt together. Pour half into each bag. Vacuum-pack on medium.

Cook at 85°C (185°F) until completely tender, approximately 40 minutes for the smaller artichokes and up to to 1¼ hours for the larger ones. Feel both the stems and hearts to check for tenderness. Once they are tender, put the bags in an ice bath to chill completely.

SALAD OF NEW-CROP ONIONS, PICKLED RAMPS, AND SAUCE SOUBISE

SOUBISE SAUCE

300 grams white onion, sliced ⅛ inch thick

100 grams Vegetable Stock (page 260), cold

50 grams heavy cream, cold

50 grams canola oil

25 grams champagne vinegar

SWEET ONION

4 slices sweet onion, about 2 inches wide and
⅜ inch thick

Extra virgin olive oil

Kosher salt and freshly ground white pepper

25 grams Vegetable Stock (page 260), cold

10 grams champagne vinegar

PICKLED RAMPS

50 grams water

50 grams granulated sugar

50 grams champagne vinegar

8 ramps, trimmed and blanched (see Big-Pot
Blanching, page 268)

CIPOLLINI AND PEARL ONIONS

8 cipollini, peeled

8 red pearl onions, peeled

12 white pearl onions, peeled

6 grams granulated sugar

6 grams kosher salt

75 grams water, cold

15 grams canola oil

30 grams unsalted butter, cold

15 grams champagne vinegar

15 grams red wine vinegar

Onion sprouts

Mizuna leaves

Chives

Fleur de sel

We developed this for our vegetable tasting menu in the spring when we had all sorts of beautiful onions available and could use up to seven varieties on one plate. Onions are excellent prepared sous vide because they cook through consistently but still maintain their shape, as well as absorb the aromatic flavors in the cooking liquid. But in this dish the biggest advantage of sous vide is for the sauce, a soubise. For a soubise, which is simply onions, milk, and/or cream (and we also add some stock), it's important that the onions be thoroughly cooked without taking on any color. Cooking them conventionally can be time-consuming, since you have to pay close attention to them so they don't brown. But cooking the sliced onions in milk and cream sous vide and pureeing them results in a sauce that is a very pure white. The process is easy, and all the flavors stay in the bag.

We also pickle the ramps sous vide, but this is more a matter of convenience. We cook the red onions with some vinegar, which helps maintain their vivid color. You can use any onions that are available to you in the spring, making sure you have a good variety of shapes and colors and textures.

FOR THE SAUCE—85°C (185°F); 6 HOURS

Combine the onion and all the remaining ingredients in a bag and vacuum-pack on medium-high.

Cook at 85°C (185°F) for 6 hours. The onion should be extremely soft.

Transfer the onion to a Vita-Prep and puree, adding enough of the liquid from the bag to make a smooth puree. (Do not strain.)

MAKES ABOUT 450 GRAMS

FOR THE SWEET ONION—85°C (185°F); 25 MINUTES

Heat a grill pan until hot. Rub the onion rounds with oil and sprinkle lightly and evenly with salt and pepper. Lay the onions on the grill pan and cook to mark them. Rotate the onions to mark in a crosshatch pattern. (They need to be marked on only one side.) Refrigerate the onions until cold.

Place the onion slices in a bag with the stock and vinegar. Vacuum-pack on medium.

Cook at 85°C (185°F) for 25 minutes. Chill the bag in an ice bath.

FOR THE PICKLED RAMPS: Combine the water, sugar, and vinegar in a small saucepan and bring to a simmer, stirring to dissolve the sugar. Remove from the heat and pour over the ramps. Chill over an ice bath until cold.

Place the ramps in a bag with enough of the pickling liquid to cover them. Vacuum-pack on medium. Refrigerate until ready to use.

FOR THE CIPOLLINI AND PEARL ONIONS—85°C (185°F); 35 MINUTES

Trim the roots off the onions, leaving enough to keep the onions together. Cut off the top of the cipollini to expose the rings.

Place the cipollini, red pearl onions, and white pearl onions in separate bags. Divide the sugar, salt, and water among the bags. Add the oil to the bag with the cipollini, and add half the butter to each bag of pearl onions. Vacuum-pack on medium.

Cook at 85°C (185°F) for about 35 minutes, or until tender. Chill in an ice bath.

To complete: Drain the cipollini and pat dry with C-fold towels. Put the white and red onions and their liquid in separate small saucepans. Simmer to reduce the liquid by about two-thirds, then add the champagne vinegar to the white pearl onions and the red wine vinegar to the red pearl onions. Continue to reduce the liquid to a glaze, rolling the vegetables around to coat them.

AT SERVICE: Drain the ramps. Spoon some of the soubise vinaigrette onto each plate. Arrange the onion slices, ramps, cipollini, and red and white pearl onions on the plates. Garnish with onion sprouts, mizuna, and chives. Sprinkle with fleur de sel.   **MAKES 4 SERVINGS**

MUSQUÉE DE PROVENCE, ROASTED BRUSSELS SPROUTS, KING TRUMPET MUSHROOMS, AND BLACK TRUFFLE SYRUP

TRUFFLE SYRUP

100 grams granulated sugar

200 grams truffle juice

75 grams champagne vinegar

140 grams liquid glucose

PUMPKIN

1 small Musquée de Provence pumpkin

2 bay leaves

2 sage sprigs

30 grams extra virgin olive oil

Kosher salt and freshly ground black pepper

Vegetable Stock (page 260)

BRUSSELS SPROUTS

12 Brussels sprouts

Canola oil

Kosher salt and freshly ground black pepper

MUSHROOMS

6 king trumpet mushrooms

Canola oil

50 grams unsalted butter

1 garlic clove, minced

1 thyme sprig

Kosher salt and freshly ground black pepper

TRUFFLE

1 black truffle

Truffle oil

Fleur de sel

Musquée de Provence is a thick, meaty pumpkin that we cut into any number of interesting shapes. We cook the pieces sous vide so that they maintain their shape, without becoming too soft, and they absorb the flavors of the aromatic herbs we include in the bag—predominantly sage and bay, since this is a fall dish. Once the pumpkin has been cooked and chilled, it's sautéed to give it an appealing caramelized surface. We pair it with another hearty fall vegetable, Brussels sprouts, as well as big king trumpet mushrooms, which are seasoned and scored so that the seasoning penetrates deeply, then slow-roasted with garlic, butter, and thyme. The dish is finished with what is in effect an *aigre-doux,* made with truffle juice, champagne vinegar, and chopped truffle.

FOR THE TRUFFLE SYRUP: Combine all the ingredients in a medium saucepan and bring to a boil over medium-high heat, stirring to dissolve the sugar. Lower the heat to reduce the liquid to a low boil, and keep at about 105°C (about 220°F) until reduced by half.

The syrup can be stored, covered, in the refrigerator. Bring to room temperature before serving.   **MAKES ABOUT 250 GRAMS**

FOR THE PUMPKIN—85°C (185°F); 20 MINUTES

Peel the pumpkin, halve it, and remove the seeds and membranes. Make two herb sachets (see page 269), dividing the bay leaves and sage between them. Cut eight 2- to 2½-inch batons of pumpkin about ⅝ inch thick. Toss with 20 grams of the olive oil, sprinkle with salt and pepper, and place in a bag with one of the herb sachets.

With a #22 melon baller, cut 12 balls of pumpkin. Toss with the remaining 10 grams olive oil, sprinkle with salt and pepper, and place in a bag with the remaining herb sachet. Discard the remaining pumpkin, or reserve for another use.

Vacuum-pack on medium.

Cook at 85°C (185°F) for 20 minutes. Remove the pumpkin from the bags. Cut 4 of the batons into 3 pieces each.

To complete: Heat the pumpkin in a bit of vegetable stock in a small pan.

FOR THE BRUSSELS SPROUTS: Remove the outer leaves from the Brussels sprouts. Trim the stems flush and cut each Brussels sprout lengthwise in half. Blanch (see Big-Pot Blanching, page 268) until tender. Chill in an ice bath. Drain on C-fold towels.

To complete: Heat a film of canola oil in a sauté pan and brown the Brussels sprouts. Season with salt and pepper.

FOR THE TRUMPET MUSHROOMS: Clean the mushrooms if necessary. Slice vertically in half. Score the sliced sides in a crosshatch pattern.

To complete: Heat a film of canola oil in a sauté pan. Brown the mushrooms cut side down, then turn to brown the second side and add the butter, garlic, and thyme; baste the mushrooms as they continue to brown. Season with salt and pepper. Drain on a C-fold towel.

FOR THE TRUFFLES: Using a Japanese mandoline or a truffle slicer, cut the truffle into thin rounds. Use as large a cutter as possible to punch out disks of truffle, then cut the truffle disks into shapes: *For crescents,* move the cutter down from the edge of one side of each disk and, using the edge of the cutter, cut the inside arc of a crescent. Do the same on the opposite side to get 2 crescents per disk. *For rings,* use a smaller cutter to punch a hole from the center of each disk, leaving a ring. You will need about 32 truffle pieces. (Mince the trimmings and add to the truffle syrup.) Brush the top of each slice with a drop of truffle oil.

AT SERVICE: Spoon a little truffle syrup into each bowl. Divide the pumpkin, mushrooms, Brussels sprouts, and black truffle shapes among the bowls, and sprinkle with fleur de sel. **MAKES 4 SERVINGS**

CARAMELIZED FENNEL, MARCONA ALMONDS, NAVEL ORANGE CONFIT, CARAWAY SEEDS, AND FENNEL PUREE

FENNEL

2 medium fennel bulbs

8 baby fennel bulbs or very small fennel bulbs

50 grams Pernod

100 grams extra virgin olive oil, plus additional for sautéing

Pinch of kosher salt

2 tarragon sprigs

2 thyme sprigs

2 bay leaves

2 star anise

3 grams caraway seeds

FENNEL PUREE

230 grams fennel trimmings or fennel bulb

Extra virgin olive oil

Kosher salt

Granulated sugar

ALMOND PUREE

200 grams raw Marcona almonds

1 kilogram milk

Kosher salt

ORANGE CONFIT

125 grams water

125 grams granulated sugar

8 naval orange suprêmes

Finely chopped caraway seeds

Sel gris

Toasted Marcona almonds, split lengthwise

Baby watercress leaves

Fennel cooked sous vide epitomizes the advantages of using this technique for vegetables. Placed in the bag with some tarragon and Pernod, it absorbs flavor without giving up any of its own to the cooking medium—as would happen if it were braised. Its shape means that the broad base and thick stalks may not be fully cooked by the time its more slender ends are—i.e., it's easy to overcook and undercook. But with sous vide, once the thinner parts of the vegetable hit perfect doneness, they stay there, without overcooking while the thicker parts cook through. And the fennel comes out of the bag pristine, it hasn't gotten beaten up by agitation of the water as can happen when cooked conventionally, and it slices beautifully. But be aware that the aromatics in the bag have a powerful effect and if you're not careful, the vegetable can taste only of Pernod.

For this dish, the cooked fennel is sautéed briefly before being served with a Marcona almond puree, fennel puree, and orange confit.

FOR THE FENNEL—85°C (185°F); 40 MINUTES

Trim the root ends of all the fennel. Remove the outer layers from the 2 medium fennel bulbs and set them aside for the puree. Cut off the tops and reserve the fronds. Cut the fennel into ½-inch wedges. You will need 12 wedges; reserve any remaining fennel for the puree.

Cut off any dark tips from the baby or very small fennel on the diagonal. Make a slit in the bottom of each fennel bulb for even cooking.

Put the fennel wedges and baby fennel in separate bowls. Divide the Pernod, oil, and salt between the bowls and toss well.

Make two herb sachets (see page 269), dividing the tarragon, thyme, bay leaf, star anise, and caraway seeds between them. Place each type of fennel, with its liquid, in a separate bag, add an herb sachet to each one, and vacuum-pack on medium.

Cook at 85°C (185°F) for 40 minutes, or until tender. Chill the bags in an ice bath.

To complete: Heat a film of oil in a sauté pan. Add the fennel wedges and sauté for about 3 minutes to caramelize. Transfer to a C-fold towel to drain. Mince the reserved fennel fronds for garnish.

If using a fennel bulb, cut into 1-inch pieces. Toss the fennel or trimmings with a drizzle of olive oil and a light sprinkling of salt and sugar. Place into a bag and vacuum-pack on medium-high.

Cook at 85°C (185°F) for 45 minutes to 1 hour, or until the fennel is extremely soft. Puree in a Vita-Prep.   MAKES ABOUT 200 GRAMS

FOR THE ALMOND PUREE: Roast the raw almonds in a 350°F oven until they are a rich golden brown, about 35 minutes.

Transfer to a saucepan and cover with the milk. Bring to a simmer and simmer gently for about 1½ hours, until the nuts are soft enough to puree. If the liquid reduces below the level of the nuts, add water to just cover the nuts.

Drain the almonds, reserving the liquid. Put the nuts into a Vita-Prep and, with the machine running, begin adding enough liquid to allow the nuts to spin. Continue to add liquid as necessary and blend on high speed for several minutes, stopping to add salt to taste and to stir the puree from time to time, until you have a silky-smooth puree.

Pass through a chinois or fine-mesh conical strainer. Refrigerate until serving.   MAKES ABOUT 200 GRAMS

FOR THE ORANGE CONFIT: Combine the water and sugar in a small saucepan and bring to a boil, stirring to dissolve the sugar. Put the orange suprêmes in a container and pour the hot syrup over them. Let cool to room temperature.

AT SERVICE: Spoon some fennel puree and almond puree onto each serving plate. Arrange the caramelized fennel, baby fennel, and orange suprêmes on the plates. Sprinkle the almond puree with a dusting of caraway seeds. Sprinkle the baby fennel with the minced fennel fronds and sel gris. Garnish with the toasted almonds and watercress leaves.

MAKES 4 SERVINGS

WHITE ASPARAGUS
WITH FIELD RHUBARB AND BLACK TRUFFLE COULIS

ASPARAGUS

8 jumbo spears white asparagus

Granulated sugar

Kosher salt

55 grams milk, cold

RHUBARB

210 grams rhubarb (about 4 stalks)

30 grams orange juice, cold

30 grams red wine vinegar

2 strips orange zest

30 grams granulated sugar

BLACK TRUFFLE COULIS

100 grams peeled, cleaned,
  and chopped black truffle

100 grams black truffle juice

20 grams peeled and sliced Yukon Gold potatoes

20 grams sliced button mushrooms

About 200 grams Mushroom Stock
  (page 259)

0.5 gram white truffle oil, or to taste

1.5 grams truffle vinegar, or to taste

12 thin slices peeled black truffle

16 sprigs mâche

Extra virgin olive oil

Champagne vinegar

Fleur de sel

This dish may not seem immediately conventional but, in fact, it's a different version of a common side, asparagus paired with a luxurious butter sauce and seasoned with tart lemon. Here the sauce is an aromatic truffle coulis (extra coulis can be frozen), and rhubarb provides the acidity. This very tart rhubarb is cooked sous vide with a sweet-sour combination of orange juice, vinegar, and sugar. The sauce is simply truffles, potatoes, mushrooms, and truffle juice cooked and pureed. The cooked vegetables are lightly dressed and served with the coulis.

We use very big white asparagus for this dish, about 1 inch thick, from the Netherlands or Belgium, the first of the season and very tender. Because white asparagus can be bitter, you have to balance it with other sweeter components or remove the bitterness during cooking. In order to do that, we usually cook white asparagus in milk or in milk and cream, with a little sugar. If you don't want the flavor of the cream, the subtle sour notes it can contribute, use only milk. In that case, the milk will curdle and the asparagus will need to be cleaned of the curds before being served. If the flavor of the cream is desired or if you're cooking the asparagus *à la minute* and don't have time to clean the curds, then we recommend adding about half as much cream, which prevents the milk from curdling.

Choose the darkest-red rhubarb available. Not peeling the rhubarb keeps the color bright.

FOR THE ASPARAGUS—85°C (185°F); 30 MINUTES

Bend the spears to break off the tough ends. Peel the spears and trim the ends to make the spears the same size.

Line up the asparagus in a single layer in a bag, tips facing up. Add a pinch each of sugar and salt and the milk. Vacuum-pack on medium-high.

Cook at 85°C (185°F) for 30 minutes. Submerge the bag in an ice bath to chill.

To complete: Drain the asparagus and rinse well with cold water. Cut away the ends on a diagonal, then cut each spear on the diagonal into 3 pieces.

Wipe the rhubarb with a damp cloth and trim so the stalks are equal in length. Place in a bag with the remaining ingredients and vacuum-pack on medium-high.

Cook at 61°C (141.8°F) for 15 minutes, or until the rhubarb is tender when squeezed through the bag. Remove from the water and let cool to room temperature, then submerge in an ice bath to chill.

To complete: Drain the rhubarb and pat dry. Cut on a severe diagonal into slices about ¼ inch thick and 1½ inches long.

FOR THE COULIS: Combine the truffle, truffle juice, potatoes, and mushrooms in a small saucepan and add enough mushroom stock to cover them. Bring to a simmer and cook until the potatoes and mushrooms are softened and the liquid is reduced by at least half, about 20 minutes.

While the mixture is hot, blend in a Vita-Prep until completely smooth, about 5 minutes. Pass through a chinois or fine-mesh conical strainer. Add the truffle oil and vinegar. MAKES ABOUT 135 GRAMS

AT SERVICE: Using a cutter, cut the slices of truffle into equal rounds. Dress the mâche, asparagus, rhubarb, and truffle slices with a small amount of olive oil, vinegar, and fleur de sel.

Spread a swath of truffle coulis on each serving plate. Arrange the asparagus, rhubarb, mâche, and black truffle on the plates. Sprinkle with fleur de sel. MAKES 4 SERVINGS

GRATIN OF SALSIFY, BLACK TRUMPET DUXELLES, AND PRESERVED MEYER LEMON *GLAÇAGE*

SALSIFY	MUSHROOMS	GLAÇAGE
400 grams Vegetable Stock (page 260), cold, plus a little extra	75 grams heavy cream	275 grams heavy cream
20 grams lemon juice	1 garlic clove, crushed and peeled	10 grams minced Preserved Lemons (page 264; use Meyer lemons)
2 grams granulated sugar	1 small thyme sprig	
Kosher salt	1 small rosemary sprig	
About 500 grams salsify	½ bay leaf	
1 bay leaf	Canola oil	
1 thyme sprig	25 grams minced shallot	
1 small rosemary sprig	225 grams black trumpet mushrooms, cleaned and diced	
1 garlic clove	45 grams dry Madeira	
5 black peppercorns	45 grams Veal Stock (page 255)	

Salsify is a tricky vegetable because the roots all seem to cook differently. When cooking it traditionally, you almost have to stand over the pot testing each one for doneness and pulling them out individually as they are done. With sous vide, we're able to group them according to size and bag them that way so that they cook in about the same time. We serve them in ovenproof serving dishes that have a shallow well, the salsify sitting atop a duxelles of black trumpet mushrooms and finished with a citrusy *glaçage*, which is spooned over the salsify and quickly run under the salamander to color it lightly.

FOR THE SALSIFY—85°C (185°F); 1 HOUR

Whisk together the stock, lemon juice, sugar, and a sprinkling of salt in a bowl. Peel the salsify, adding it to the liquid as you peel it. Chill.

Make an herb sachet (see page 269) with the bay leaf, thyme, rosemary, garlic, and peppercorns. Transfer the salsify and all of the liquid to a bag and add the sachet. Vacuum-pack on medium.

Cook at 85°C (185°F) for 1 hour. Chill the bag in an ice bath.

To complete: Drain the salsify and cut into equal lengths to fit into the wells of the serving dishes (see headnote) or rimmed ovenproof serving plates. Combine the salsify, a sprinkling of salt, and a small amount of vegetable stock in a medium saucepan and heat just to warm, without coloring.

FOR THE MUSHROOMS: Combine the cream, garlic, thyme, rosemary, and bay in a small saucepan, bring to a simmer, and simmer until very thick, 15 to 20 minutes. Set aside.

Heat a film of oil in a sauté pan. Add the shallots and sweat to soften. Add the mushrooms and cook until they have softened and any liquid has evaporated. Add the Madeira and veal stock and cook until most of the liquid has evaporated.

To complete: Strain the cream mixture over the mushrooms and cook until the cream has reduced and coats the mushrooms. Keep warm.

FOR THE GLAÇAGE: Measure 25 grams of the cream and keep cold. Bring the remaining 250 grams cream to a simmer in a large wide saucepan over medium-high heat. Stir constantly, scraping the bottom, corners, and sides of the pan, to prevent scorching. After about 7 to 10 minutes, the cream will be thickened and coat the bottom of the pan if the pan is tilted. Pour the cream into a small bowl, stir in the preserved lemon, and let cool to room temperature.

To complete: Just before using, whip the reserved heavy cream. Fold the two cream mixtures together.

AT SERVICE: Spread a layer of duxelles on each plate. Top the duxelles with the salsify. Spoon the *glaçage* over the salsify, and run under the salamander to lightly brown the top. **MAKES 4 SERVINGS**

GRATIN OF SALSIFY, BLACK TRUMPET DUXELLES, AND PRESERVED MEYER LEMON *GLAÇAGE*

SALSIFY

400 grams Vegetable Stock (page 260), cold,
　　plus a little extra

20 grams lemon juice

2 grams granulated sugar

Kosher salt

About 500 grams salsify

1 bay leaf

1 thyme sprig

1 small rosemary sprig

1 garlic clove

5 black peppercorns

MUSHROOMS

75 grams heavy cream

1 garlic clove, crushed and peeled

1 small thyme sprig

1 small rosemary sprig

½ bay leaf

Canola oil

25 grams minced shallot

225 grams black trumpet mushrooms, cleaned
　　and diced

45 grams dry Madeira

45 grams Veal Stock (page 255)

GLAÇAGE

275 grams heavy cream

10 grams minced Preserved Lemons
　　(page 264; use Meyer lemons)

Salsify is a tricky vegetable because the roots all seem to cook differently. When cooking it traditionally, you almost have to stand over the pot testing each one for doneness and pulling them out individually as they are done. With sous vide, we're able to group them according to size and bag them that way so that they cook in about the same time. We serve them in ovenproof serving dishes that have a shallow well, the salsify sitting atop a duxelles of black trumpet mushrooms and finished with a citrusy *glaçage*, which is spooned over the salsify and quickly run under the salamander to color it lightly.

FOR THE SALSIFY—85°C (185°F); 1 HOUR

Whisk together the stock, lemon juice, sugar, and a sprinkling of salt in a bowl. Peel the salsify, adding it to the liquid as you peel it. Chill.

Make an herb sachet (see page 269) with the bay leaf, thyme, rosemary, garlic, and peppercorns. Transfer the salsify and all of the liquid to a bag and add the sachet. Vacuum-pack on medium.

Cook at 85°C (185°F) for 1 hour. Chill the bag in an ice bath.

To complete: Drain the salsify and cut into equal lengths to fit into the wells of the serving dishes (see headnote) or rimmed ovenproof serving plates. Combine the salsify, a sprinkling of salt, and a small amount of vegetable stock in a medium saucepan and heat just to warm, without coloring.

FOR THE MUSHROOMS: Combine the cream, garlic, thyme, rosemary, and bay in a small saucepan, bring to a simmer, and simmer until very thick, 15 to 20 minutes. Set aside.

Heat a film of oil in a sauté pan. Add the shallots and sweat to soften. Add the mushrooms and cook until they have softened and any liquid has evaporated. Add the Madeira and veal stock and cook until most of the liquid has evaporated.

To complete: Strain the cream mixture over the mushrooms and cook until the cream has reduced and coats the mushrooms. Keep warm.

FOR THE GLAÇAGE: Measure 25 grams of the cream and keep cold. Bring the remaining 250 grams cream to a simmer in a large wide saucepan over medium-high heat. Stir constantly, scraping the bottom, corners, and sides of the pan, to prevent scorching. After about 7 to 10 minutes, the cream will be thickened and coat the bottom of the pan if the pan is tilted. Pour the cream into a small bowl, stir in the preserved lemon, and let cool to room temperature.

To complete: Just before using, whip the reserved heavy cream. Fold the two cream mixtures together.

AT SERVICE: Spread a layer of duxelles on each plate. Top the duxelles with the salsify. Spoon the *glaçage* over the salsify, and run under the salamander to lightly brown the top. **MAKES 4 SERVINGS**

FOR THE RHUBARB—61°C (141.8°F); 15 MINUTES

Wipe the rhubarb with a damp cloth and trim so the stalks are equal in length. Place in a bag with the remaining ingredients and vacuum-pack on medium-high.

Cook at 61°C (141.8°F) for 15 minutes, or until the rhubarb is tender when squeezed through the bag. Remove from the water and let cool to room temperature, then submerge in an ice bath to chill.

To complete: Drain the rhubarb and pat dry. Cut on a severe diagonal into slices about ¼ inch thick and 1½ inches long.

FOR THE COULIS: Combine the truffle, truffle juice, potatoes, and mushrooms in a small saucepan and add enough mushroom stock to cover them. Bring to a simmer and cook until the potatoes and mushrooms are softened and the liquid is reduced by at least half, about 20 minutes.

While the mixture is hot, blend in a Vita-Prep until completely smooth, about 5 minutes. Pass through a chinois or fine-mesh conical strainer. Add the truffle oil and vinegar.   MAKES ABOUT 135 GRAMS

AT SERVICE: Using a cutter, cut the slices of truffle into equal rounds. Dress the mâche, asparagus, rhubarb, and truffle slices with a small amount of olive oil, vinegar, and fleur de sel.

Spread a swath of truffle coulis on each serving plate. Arrange the asparagus, rhubarb, mâche, and black truffle on the plates. Sprinkle with fleur de sel.   MAKES 4 SERVINGS

SOFT-BOILED HEN EGG WITH GREEN ASPARAGUS, CRÈME FRAÎCHE AUX FINES HERBES, AND BUTTER-FRIED CROUTONS

SAUCE

135 grams crème fraîche

3 grams minced chives

3 grams minced chervil

3 grams minced flat-leaf parsley

1 gram minced tarragon

5 grams water

Kosher salt and freshly ground black pepper

4 large eggs, cold

28 spears medium asparagus (about 565 grams)

CROUTONS

15 to 20 grams unsalted butter

30 grams ⅛-inch cubes crustless Brioche
(page 262)

Kosher salt

Herb leaves

Fleur de sel

Freshly ground black pepper

This dish takes advantage of two common but exquisite pairings—eggs and fines herbes, eggs and asparagus—so simple and so delicious. A soft-boiled egg on a bed of asparagus, sauced with a loose crème fraîche seasoned with tarragon, chervil, chives, and parsley and garnished with sautéed croutons, is a light, elegant preparation that's appropriate at any time of the day.

Cooking the egg at a constant 62.5°C (144.5°F) for an hour, gives it an extraordinary texture. The white is quivering and velvety and the yolk is neither runny nor hard, but rather soft, creamy, and bright colored.

It's a good idea to test a few eggs to see the way you like them. We think 1 hour is perfect, but if you want them very soft, cook them for 45 minutes. Or you might also cook them for 1 hour and 15 minutes for a firmer white.

FOR THE SAUCE: Put the crème fraîche in a small bowl and stir in the minced herbs and then the water. Season to taste with salt and pepper. Chill until ready to serve.

FOR THE EGGS — 62.5°C (144.5°F); 1 HOUR
Using a skimmer, gently lower the eggs into 62.5°C (144.5°F) water. Cook for 1 hour, or to your preference (see headnote).

FOR THE ASPARAGUS: Bend each spear to break off the tough ends. Peel the asparagus from just below the tip to the bottom. Trim the bottoms so the spears are of equal length.

Divide the asparagus into 4 piles of 7, with the tips facing the same way. Cut 4 pieces of kitchen twine about 2 feet long and tie the spears into bundles.

To complete: About 6 minutes before serving, blanch the asparagus (see Big-Pot Blanching, page 268) until just tender. Chill in an ice bath. Remove from the water, untie the bundles, and dry on C-fold towels.

FOR THE CROUTONS: Heat 15 grams butter in a sauté pan just large enough to hold the brioche cubes in a single layer. When the butter begins to foam, add the brioche and season with salt. Keep the cubes moving in the pan so they brown evenly. If the butter begins to brown, add another 5 grams butter to stop the butter from browning and darkening the croutons. When the croutons are golden brown, drain on a C-fold towel.

AT SERVICE: Spread the sauce on the serving plates. Arrange 7 asparagus spears on each plate to form a bed for the poached egg. Crack each egg over an empty plate, as you would a raw egg, and, with a spoon, gently lift the egg, letting a towel absorb any excess water, and place over the asparagus. Sprinkle with the croutons, herb leaves, and fleur de sel and pepper. **MAKES 4 SERVINGS**

FISH AND SHELLFISH

Overleaf (left): striped bass and eel; overleaf (right) and above: eel for *Anguille à la Japonaise* (page 92)

FISH IS DELICATE, BUT I DON'T VIEW IT DIFFERENTLY FROM MEATS AS FAR AS COOKING

it goes. It still has to reach a specific temperature, and you still have to be aware of it when it gets there so that you can get it out of the heat. Many of the qualities sous vide techniques bring to fish are similar to those of conventional fish cooking. We often prepare fish in liquid or oil that is scarcely hotter than we want the fish to be. But sous vide allows us to achieve textures we couldn't get using conventional means. What's particularly enticing about cooking fish sous vide is the fact that you don't have to cook it *in* anything. Before sous vide, when we wanted to cook a fish very gently and also introduce aromatic flavors, we might, say, poach salmon in a court bouillon. That's a traditional technique. But inevitably you're going to lose flavor to the cooking liquid. With sous vide, we can infuse flavors and cook the fish in a moist, gentle environment without losing any flavor to the cooking medium. This has a remarkable effect on the flavor of the fish.

Cooking fish sous vide results in very pure tastes, especially important with fish, which can be overpowered by the flavors developed in a hot sauté pan. And we continue to take fish in an increasingly subtle direction, allowing its pure flavor to come through rather than cooking it at a high temperature that would create more complex roasted flavors. But cooking fish sous vide doesn't limit you. If you want those flavors, they can be developed after the fish comes out of the bag, much as flavor is given to meat with a final sear or roast. This is especially desirable with meaty rich fish such as monkfish and salmon.

Shellfish is great cooked sous vide. You can cook lobster through at a temperature that's so low the meat will never seize up and become rubbery. Octopus, which can become very tough when cooked conventionally, is tender and delicious cooked sous vide. Shrimp and scallops cooked sous vide have a pure flavor and an unusually delicate texture.

With some preparations, we use the bag to shape the fish and combine it with other ingredients (mackerel and ham, for instance), so that the two, the fish and meat, become a single component. You do have to be somewhat careful when sealing any fish in the bag, because fish is very delicate.

For many fish, we also use a very brief salt cure, just ten minutes or so. This draws out cell moisture so that the proteins stuck behind in the cells can't flow out, preventing that unappetizing white protein from appearing on the fish as it cooks.

Whether it's mackerel melded with ham, sturgeon with beef fat, bass cooked plain, or a wild salmon cooked in olive oil at a temperature so gentle the salmon almost feels raw even though it's completely cooked, sous vide fish cooking has myriad applications with exceptional results.

"TAGLIATELLE" OF CUTTLEFISH AND HAWAIIAN HEART OF PEACH PALM, WHITE NECTARINE, SWEET PEPPER CONFETTI, AND VINAIGRETTE *À L'ENCRE DE SEICHE*

CUTTLEFISH

1 cuttlefish (about 1.5 kilograms) preferably
    Japanese (see Sources, page 282)

1 thyme sprig

1 small rosemary sprig

2 bay leaves

1 gram coriander seeds

1 gram cumin seeds

2 dried red chiles

20 grams extra virgin olive oil

Kosher salt and freshly ground black pepper

CUTTLEFISH VINAIGRETTE

20 grams strained cuttlefish ink (from above) or
    squid ink

5 grams Dijon mustard

40 grams canola oil

20 grams lemon oil

Grated zest of ¼ Meyer lemon

HEART OF PALM

One 5-inch piece fresh heart of palm
    (about 900 grams)

Kosher salt

Extra virgin olive oil

1 ripe white freestone nectarine

Grated Meyer lemon zest

Pepper Confetti (page 263)

Mizuna leaves

What makes this simple dish of cuttlefish and heart of palm special is the flavor and exquisitely tender texture of the cuttlefish cooked sous vide for ten hours with assertive herbs and spices. Hearts of palm, the soft white shoots of underdeveloped leaves of the peach palm, are grown in Hawaii by John Mood and have been a favorite ingredient of ours for more than a decade. We combine these two ingredients with a cuttlefish ink vinaigrette and garnish the dish with white nectarine.

FOR THE CUTTLEFISH—64°C (147.2°F); 10 HOURS

To clean the cuttlefish, twist and pull off the head. Pull out the cartilage and remove the innards from the cavity. Reserve any ink from the cuttlefish for the vinaigrette. Run your finger along the body, under the wing, releasing the wing and pulling it away from the body. With scissors, split the body lengthwise. Spread open and pull out any remaining innards.

Rinse and lay on the board, inner side up. Wipe with a C-fold towel to release the membrane. Turn over and repeat. Trim the edges so they are straight and cut off the flap. Refrigerate until very cold.

Make an herb sachet (see page 269) with the thyme, rosemary, bay leaves, coriander, cumin, and chiles. Place the cuttlefish in a bag. Whisk the oil with a pinch each of salt and pepper and add to the bag, along with the sachet. Vacuum-pack on medium.

Cook at 64°C (147.2°F) for 10 hours. Chill the bag in an ice bath.

To complete: Remove the cuttlefish from the bag; strain and reserve the cooking liquid. Lay the cuttlefish flat on the work surface. Trim the edges as needed to straighten, then cut crosswise into "tagliatelle" about ⅛ inch wide. Toss with a drizzle of the cooking liquid.

FOR THE VINAIGRETTE: Put the ink in a small heatproof bowl and hold over a burner, whisking constantly, for a few seconds, just to heat and thicken it. Whisk in the mustard. Whisking constantly, drizzle in the canola oil, followed by the lemon oil. Whisk in the lemon zest.

MAKES ABOUT 85 GRAMS

FOR THE HEART OF PALM: Cut a slice off one side of the heart of palm to create a flat surface. Put the flat side against the blade of a meat slicer and slice on the thinnest setting possible. Cut the slices lengthwise into ⅛-inch-wide strips. Put in a bowl and separate the strips.

FOR THE NECTARINE: Cut the nectarine flesh away from the two flatter sides of the pit. Place the pieces flat side down on a cutting board and cut crosswise into thin slices.

AT SERVICE: Add the cuttlefish to the heart of palm and toss together with a sprinkle of salt and a drizzle of olive oil.

Spread the vinaigrette on the serving plates and arrange the tagliatelle and the nectarine slices. Garnish with lemon zest, pepper confetti, and mizuna.

MAKES 6 SERVINGS

Grilled Octopus Tentacles, Chorizo, Fingerling Potatoes, Green Almonds, and Salsa Verde (page 78)

GRILLED OCTOPUS TENTACLES, CHORIZO, FINGERLING POTATOES, GREEN ALMONDS, AND SALSA VERDE

OCTOPUS

1 octopus (about 1.15 kilograms),
    preferably Japanese or Mediterranean
    (see Sources, page 282)

Kosher salt

20 grams extra virgin olive oil,
    plus more for grilling

Freshly ground black pepper

1 thyme sprig

1 small rosemary sprig

2 bay leaves

1 gram coriander seeds

1 gram cumin seeds

2 dried red chiles

POTATOES

20 medium fingerling potatoes

2 rosemary sprigs

6 thyme sprigs

3 garlic cloves, peeled

3 bay leaves

Kosher salt to taste

Extra virgin olive oil

SALSA VERDE

50 grams basil leaves

15 grams tarragon leaves

40 grams cilantro leaves

45 grams flat-leaf parsley leaves

About 145 grams extra virgin olive oil

Kosher salt

About 0.2 gram cumin seeds

About 0.2 gram coriander seeds

Lemon juice

Minced capers

25 grams chorizo, cut into ¼-inch slices

24 green almonds (see Sources, page 282),
    peeled (see Note), or Marcona almonds,
    split in half

Cilantro shoots or leaves

The sous vide technique is perfect for octopus. It not only allows us to infuse the flesh with other flavors, it also cooks it so gently that it becomes very tender. And the flavors—the fish, the spicy chorizo sausage, the salsa verde, lemons, and capers—close your eyes and you're on the coast of the Mediterranean. We use Japanese or Mediterranean octopus because they are the highest quality. **PHOTOGRAPH ON PAGE 76**

FOR THE OCTOPUS—77°C (170.6°F); 5 HOURS

Put the octopus on a cutting board. You will feel a ball just above the eyes; cut off the head just below the ball. Put the tentacles in a bowl and cover liberally with salt. Using a stiff brush, scrub the tentacles to remove any slime. Rinse and drain.

Spread out the octopus, sucker side down, and cut off the 8 complete tentacles. Cut away the webbed skin that hangs from the sides of the tentacles and discard. Trim the tentacles, rinse them in cold water, and drain on C-fold towels.

Whisk together the olive oil and salt and pepper to taste in a bowl. Toss in the octopus, and chill.

Make an herb sachet (see page 269) with the thyme, rosemary, bay leaves, coriander, cumin, and chiles. Place the octopus in a bag in a single layer and add the sachet. Vacuum-pack on medium.

Cook at 77°C (170.6°F) for 5 hours. Let the octopus cool just enough so you can handle it.

To trim the tentacles, put each tentacle sucker side down on a work surface and, with a paring knife, scrape away the top flesh. Then work the knife in both directions, using the tip of the knife to peel and scrape away the membranes, including the suckers. You will be left with very clean, smooth pieces of octopus.

To complete: Heat a cast-iron grill pan over high heat. Toss the pieces of octopus with olive oil to coat and sprinkle with salt and pepper. Add to the grill pan and cook, turning once to mark both sides of the pieces, about 2 minutes total.

Remove from the grill pan and cut the tentacles into ⅛-inch slices. Set aside.

FOR THE POTATOES: Put the potatoes in a large saucepan, add the rosemary, thyme, garlic, and bay leaves, cover with cold water by about 1 inch, and season with salt. Bring to a boil, then simmer for about 25 minutes, or until tender.

Drain the potatoes and scrape away the skin with a paring knife. Cut into ⅛-inch slices and toss with a light coating of olive oil.

FOR THE SALSA VERDE: Bring a large pot of salted water to a boil (see Big-Pot Blanching, page 268). Blanch the herbs, one type at a time, each for about 3 minutes. Drain each herb and submerge in an ice bath to chill. Once they are cold, wring out the herbs in a kitchen towel to remove as much moisture as possible.

Transfer the herbs to a Vita-Prep and add enough of the olive oil to puree the leaves. Strain through a chinois or fine-mesh conical strainer into a metal bowl placed over an ice bath. Whisk in enough additional oil to make a smooth, slightly thickened sauce. Season to taste with salt. Leave over the ice bath to help preserve the vivid color. (The salsa verde should be made the day it is served.)

To complete: Grind the cumin and coriander seeds together. Just before serving, add a few drops of lemon juice, the coriander-cumin powder, and capers to taste to the salsa. MAKES ABOUT 150 GRAMS

AT SERVICE: Put the tentacles in a bowl. Add the potatoes, chorizo, almonds, additional olive oil, and salt and pepper to taste. Spread the salsa verde on the serving plates. Arrange the salad in the center of the plates and garnish with cilantro shoots. MAKES 20 SERVINGS

NOTE TO PEEL GREEN ALMONDS

Run a paring knife around the seam of the almond's shell, then insert the tip of the knife into the seam and twist the knife to pop open the shell; be careful not to pierce the almond. Open the shell and remove the almond. Put the peeled almonds into a bowl of acidulated water (see page 269) to keep them from discoloring.

BUTTER-POACHED MAINE LOBSTER, TOMATO *PAIN PERDU*, CELERY, AND "RUSSIAN DRESSING"

TOMATO MARMALADE

75 grams minced shallots

40 grams minced red onion

30 grams water

15 grams red wine vinegar

36 grams granulated sugar

825 grams canned San Marzano tomatoes, drained, seeded, and chopped

PAIN PERDU

500 grams whole milk

500 grams heavy cream

6 large eggs

10 grams kosher salt

2 loaves Brioche (page 262), crust trimmed

About 325 grams Tomato Marmalade (above)

Canola oil

CELERY

3 long celery stalks, trimmed

15 grams unsalted butter

Kosher salt

6 grams Vegetable Stock (page 260) or water

LOBSTER

Beurre Monté bath (page 261)

4 uncooked lobster tails (from 500-gram lobsters; see page 270)

RUSSIAN DRESSING

3 large egg yolks

50 grams cornichon juice

100 grams Clarified Butter (page 261), at 38°C (about 100°F)

10 grams finely minced horseradish

3 grams cornichon brunoise

2 grams minced tarragon

3 grams tomato brunoise

50 grams Tomato Marmalade (above), at room temperature

Kosher salt

Celery micro greens

Celery leaves

Extra virgin olive oil

Fleur de sel

Tomato Powder (page 263)

This is our take on an American classic, the lobster roll, first made by per se sous chef Josh Schwartz. The lobster is cooked so gently in a beurre monté bath—the butter heated by the circulator—that it remains extraordinarily tender. We serve it with a tomato *pain perdu,* or French toast, made by layering slices of brioche with a custard base and a marmalade made with San Marzano tomatoes. The sauce, our take on Russian dressing, starts with a choron sauce base—béarnaise with tomato—to which we add cornichons, cornichon juice, and tarragon, and we finish the plate with a small composed celery salad.

FOR THE TOMATO MARMALADE: Combine the shallots, onion, and water in a saucepan, bring to a simmer, and cook for 7 to 8 minutes, until the shallots and onion are tender. Add the vinegar and sugar and bring to a simmer, stirring to disssolve the sugar. Add the tomatoes and cook over medium-high heat, stirring frequently, until the mixture is very dry. Remove from the heat and let cool.

Vacuum-packed, the marmalade will keep, refrigerated, for up to a week.   MAKES ABOUT 375 GRAMS

FOR THE PAIN PERDU: Spray a quarter sheet pan lightly with non-stick spray. Line with parchment paper and spray the paper.

Combine the milk and cream in a saucepan and bring to a simmer.

Put the eggs and salt in a Vita-Prep. With the machine running, pour in the hot liquid, blending until well combined. Strain through a chinois or fine-mesh conical strainer.

Cut the brioche lengthwise into slices about ⅝ inch thick. *Trim the slices of brioche:* line the bottom of the sheet pan with enough slices to make a solid layer of brioche slices running lengthwise, trimming them as necessary to fit. Remove from the pan and trim the remaining brioche as necessary to make a crosswise layer; remove it from the pan as well.

Coat the bottom of the pan with some custard base and then reinsert the lengthwise layer of brioche slices. Begin to add more custard to the pan, coating the bread as evenly as possible; use your fingers to press on the bread and allow the custard to soak in. Continue to add custard, moistening the corners as well, until the bread has absorbed as much custard as it can without floating.

Reserve 50 grams of the tomato marmalade for the sauce, and spread a thin layer of the remaining marmalade evenly over the bread. Cover with the crosswise layer of bread. Add custard to soak in as before; you may not need all the custard. Spray a piece of aluminum foil with cooking spray and place it sprayed side down over the pan.

Bake the pain perdu in the center of a 300°F oven for about 55 minutes. Remove the foil: the bread should be puffed. If you press on one section, you will see the bread rise in another spot because of the air that is trapped inside. Return the uncovered pan to the oven for 3 to 4 minutes to allow some of the trapped air to escape. The top should feel dry.

Remove the pan from the oven. Cut a piece of parchment paper the same size as the pan and place on top of the pain perdu. Put another quarter sheet pan on top and weight it to gently compress the pain perdu and ensure that the custard is distributed evenly. Refrigerate, with the weight, until completely cold.

To complete: Cut the pain perdu into 2-by-2½-inch pieces and bring to room temperature.

Heat a film of canola oil in a sauté pan over medium-high heat. Add the pain perdu and brown on each side to heat through.

MAKES 20 SERVINGS

FOR THE CELERY: Peel the celery stalks. Cut the celery into twelve 1¾-inch pieces. Stand one piece on the cutting surface and trim off about ¼ inch from each long edge to make a flatter piece of celery with only a very slight curve. Repeat with the remaining pieces.

Blanch the celery (see Big-Pot Blanching, page 268). Drain, chill in an ice bath, and drain on C-fold towels.

To complete: Combine the celery with the butter, a pinch of salt, and the vegetable stock or water in a medium saucepan. Bring to a simmer and reduce to glaze the celery.

FOR THE LOBSTER—59.5°C (139.1°F); 15 MINUTES
Heat the beurre monté to 59.5°C (139.1°F). Add the lobster tails and cook for 15 minutes. Remove from the butter and reserve the beurre monté.

FOR THE RUSSIAN DRESSING: Whip the eggs and cornichon juice in a large bowl set over a saucepan of simmering water to the ribbon stage. Slowly whisk in the clarified butter to emulsify. Gently whisk in the horseradish, cornichons, tarragon, tomato, and tomato marmalade. Whisk in salt to taste.

Serve immediately, or hold for just a short time in a warm place away from direct heat; if the sauce overheats, it will break. MAKES 220 GRAMS

AT SERVICE: Trim the ends of the lobster tails slightly, so they can sit curved side up without tipping. Place the celery, pain perdu, and lobster tails on a C-fold-towel-lined sheet pan. Glaze the top of the celery with some of the reserved beurre monté.

Toss the celery greens and celery leaves with a drizzle of olive oil and a sprinkling of fleur de sel. Arrange 3 celery pieces side by side on each serving plate and top with a lobster tail and a stack of greens. Add a piece of pain perdu. Top with some Russian dressing and sprinkle the plates with tomato powder. MAKES 4 SERVINGS

BUTTER-POACHED MAINE LOBSTER TAIL, HEN-OF-THE-WOODS MUSHROOMS, BONE MARROW, SWEET CARROTS, AND PEARL ONIONS

BONE MARROW

Four 1½-inch pieces marrow bones

Canola oil

All-purpose flour

SAUCE

350 grams dry red wine,

    such as Cabernet Sauvignon

50 grams diced carrot

25 grams sliced shallot

100 grams sliced button mushrooms

25 grams sliced onion

1 bay leaf

1 thyme sprig

185 grams lobster bodies (see page 270)

1 kilogram Veal Stock (page 255), hot

LOBSTER

Beurre Monté bath (page 261)

4 uncooked lobster tails (from 500-gram lobsters;

    see page 270)

MUSHROOMS

Canola oil

4 clusters hen-of-the-woods mushrooms,

    trimmed and cleaned

Kosher salt

8 Glazed Red Pearl Onions (page 266)

8 Glazed White Pearl Onions (page 266)

8 rounds Glazed Carrots (page 267)

Sel gris

Maldon salt

Chervil leaves

A rustic classic, coq au vin, is reimagined for an elegant lobster dish. For a traditional coq au vin, a rooster is marinated in red wine and aromatics and then braised. In this case, we marinate the lobster bodies that will be used to make the sauce in red wine with aromatics, then sear the shells, add the clarified marinade and veal stock (almost as if it were a braise), and reduce the liquid. The result is a deep, rich lobster sauce. The lobster is cooked in a beurre monté bath and the dish is completed with the classic components of a rich braise—onions, carrots, mushrooms, and bone marrow.

FOR THE BONE MARROW: Soak the bone marrow in a bowl of ice water for 20 minutes; drain. Remove the marrow from the bones by pushing it out with your finger. If it doesn't come out easily, soak the bones briefly in warm water, just long enough to loosen the marrow.

Soak the pieces of marrow in a bowl of ice water for 36 to 48 hours, changing the water every 6 to 8 hours. (It is important to change the water, because as the blood is extracted from the marrow, the water will become saturated with blood and the marrow could spoil.)

Drain the marrow and cut into ½-inch pieces. You will need 8 slices of marrow; reserve any extra marrow for another use.

To complete: Heat a film of canola oil in a sauté pan over high heat. Dust the bone marrow with flour, either in the palm of your hand or in a strainer, and sear quickly until light golden.

FOR THE SAUCE: Place a metal container large enough to hold the lobster bodies and marinade over an ice bath. Combine the red wine, vegetables, and herbs in a saucepan and bring to a boil over medium-high heat. Carefully ignite the wine and let it boil for a minute after the flames subside, then strain the marinade into the metal container to cool. Reserve the vegetables.

Cut the lobster bodies into quarters and add to the marinade. Add the reserved vegetables, and refrigerate for at least 12 hours, or overnight.

Strain the marinade, reserving the shells and vegetables, and pour into a saucepan. Bring to a boil, continually skimming to remove all the impurities and to clarify. Strain through a chinois or fine-mesh conical strainer.

Place the reserved vegetables and lobster bodies in a rondeau and cook to evaporate any liquid and slightly roast them. Add the clarified marinade and reduce until the pan is dry. Strain the veal stock through a chinois or fine-mesh conical strainer into the pan and reduce by about half, to a sauce consistency.

Strain the sauce again through a chinois or fine-mesh conical strainer; do not press on the solids, or you will push through any remaining impurities, which would cloud the sauce. Discard the solids, rinse the chinois, and repeat the straining until nothing remains in the strainer (this could take up to 8 strainings). MAKES ABOUT 400 GRAMS

FOR THE LOBSTER—59.5°C (139.1°F); 15 MINUTES
Heat the beurre monté to 59.5°C (139.1°F). Add the lobster tails to the butter and cook for 15 minutes. Remove from the butter.

FOR THE MUSHROOMS: Heat a film of canola oil in a medium sauté pan. Add the mushrooms, sprinkle with salt, and cook, turning to brown on all sides, about 5 minutes. Drain on C-fold towels.

AT SERVICE: Trim the ends of the lobster tails slightly so that they sit curved side up without tipping. Spoon some sauce onto each plate and top with a lobster tail. Arrange the pearl onions, carrots, mushrooms, and bone marrow around the lobster. Sprinkle sel gris on the pieces of bone marrow and Maldon salt on the lobster. Garnish with chervil leaves.

MAKES 4 SERVINGS

Above: St. Peter's fish curing in salt; opposite: St. Peter's Fish with Black Truffle Mousse, White Asparagus, and Mousseline (page 86)

ST. PETER'S FISH WITH BLACK TRUFFLE MOUSSE, WHITE ASPARAGUS, AND MOUSSELINE

FISH AND MOUSSE

One 2.25- to 2.75-kilogram St. Peter's fish
   (John Dory), skin removed

3 sea scallops (85 grams), muscles removed

80 grams crème fraîche

28 grams heavy cream

0.5 gram polyphosphate
   (see Sources, page 282)

Kosher salt

6 grams minced black truffles

Beurre Monté (page 261)

ASPARAGUS

12 medium spears white asparagus

Granulated sugar

Kosher salt

55 grams milk, cold

15 grams water

Beurre Monté (page 261)

MOUSSELINE

10 grams thinly sliced shallot

1 tarragon sprig

64 grams champagne vinegar

3 black peppercorns

15 grams water

1 large egg yolk

85 grams Clarified Butter (page 261),
   melted and warm

¼ lemon

Kosher salt

20 grams whipped cream

12 thin black truffle rounds

Baby mâche

Fleur de sel

St. Peter's fish, also known as John Dory, is a mild white fish; although it is not a true flatfish, it has two fillets per side, so one large fish will serve four. We puree the belly and the trim from its fillets for the mousse, a way to use all of the valuable fish.

This dish couldn't be more traditional seeming, yet it would be impossible to cook so precisely without the technology of the immersion circulator. A classic mousseline filling has egg in it, so it must reach about 65°C (149°F) before it sets up, higher than the delicate fish needs. We use an eggless "mousse" on the fillets instead. We lay them on rigid plastic, to maintain a uniform shape (we use the covers for our one-third pans), and seal in the bag. Because there's no egg in the filling, we don't need to cook the fish at as high a temperature as is traditional (just 60°C [140°F] for 10 minutes).

The remaining components are very traditional—white asparagus and a mousseline, a hollandaise enriched with cream. PHOTOGRAPH ON PAGES 84-85

FOR THE FISH: Fillet the fish; cut away and reserve the belly. Separate each fillet at the "seam" to make 4 pieces. Trim the pieces to make 4 rectangles, about 60 to 85 grams each. Reserve 145 grams of the trimmings and belly for the mousse. Refrigerate the fillets.

FOR THE MOUSSE: —60°C (140°F); 10 MINUTES

Combine the scallops, fish trimmings and belly, and crème fraîche in a food processor and puree, scraping down the sides as necessary, until smooth, about 2 minutes. Stop the machine and scrape down the sides. While pulsing the machine, drizzle in the cream, just to incorporate.

Scrape the puree through a tamis into a metal bowl, and place the bowl over an ice bath. Stir in the polyphosphate. Beat the mixture well with a sturdy spoon to dissolve and thoroughly incorporate the polyphosphate. Season the mousse with a bit of salt. Stir in the truffles, and refrigerate until cold.

Season both sides of the fish with a sprinkling of salt. Let the fillets sweat for 3 to 4 minutes, then dry with C-fold towels. Place the fillets on a Plexiglas board that will fit into a bag (this will help maintain the shape of the fragile fillets).

Transfer the mousse to a pastry bag with a plain tip and pipe the mousse over the top of the fillets. Use a small offset spatula to spread the mousse evenly. Refrigerate to chill completely.

Place the fish fillets, still on the plastic, into a large bag. Vacuum-pack on low to medium, being careful not to distort the shape of the mousse. Refrigerate until ready to cook.

To complete: Cook at 60°C (140°F) for 10 minutes. Transfer the fillets to a cutting surface and trim the sides of each fillet to make a perfect rectangle.

Line a small baking tray with C-fold towels and place the fillets on them. Nap the tops with beurre monté and heat in a 350°F oven for 1 minute, or until hot.

FOR THE ASPARAGUS—85°C (185°F); 30 MINUTES
Bend the spears to break off the tough ends. Peel the asparagus. Trim the ends to make the spears the same size. Line up the asparagus in a single layer in a bag, tips up. Add a pinch each of sugar and salt and the milk. Refrigerate until cold.

Vacuum-pack the asparagus on medium-high.

Cook at 85°C (185°F) for 30 minutes. Chill the bag in an ice bath.

Remove the asparagus from the bag and rinse well with cold water. Trim the ends of the spears on the bias.

To complete: Add the water and enough beurre monté to cover the bottom of a large sauté pan, then add the asparagus in one layer. Simmer over medium heat for about 30 seconds to heat through. Drain on C-fold towels.

FOR THE MOUSSELINE:
Combine the shallot, tarragon, vinegar, and peppercorns in a small saucepan, bring to a simmer over medium heat, and simmer to reduce the liquid to a glaze; the pan should be almost dry. Swirl in the water, then strain into a small bowl.

Pour half the strained liquid into a small saucepan, add the egg yolk, and cook over very low heat, whisking constantly. Move the sauce on and off the heat as necessary to control the temperature so the sauce doesn't get too hot; after about 2 minutes, the mixture will be light and thickened, and as you whisk, you will see the bottom of the pan. Remove the pan from the heat and slowly begin drizzling in the butter, whisking constantly. Once you have added about 28 grams of butter, whisk in the remaining strained reduction, then continue to add the butter. If the sauce begins to break at any point, whisk in 5 to 10 grams of hot water to recombine it. Add a squeeze of lemon juice and season with salt to taste. Gently fold in the whipped cream.   **MAKES ABOUT 150 GRAMS**

AT SERVICE: Spoon some mousseline onto each serving plate. Add the fish and garnish with the asparagus spears, truffle rounds, and baby mâche. Sprinkle with fleur de sel.   **MAKES 4 SERVINGS**

SPANISH MACKEREL AND SERRANO HAM *EN BRIOCHE*, CAPERS, PIQUILLO PEPPERS, AND LEMON CONFIT

MACKEREL

1 side Spanish mackerel (455 grams), skin on,
    bones removed

Kosher salt

1 to 2 paper-thin slices serrano ham
    (about 20 grams)

0.7 gram Ajinomoto RM transglutaminase
    (see Sources, page 282)

Eight ⅛-inch-thick slices Brioche (page 262),
    crusts removed

Clarified Butter (page 261)

CAPER VINAIGRETTE

10 grams Spanish capers, drained and chopped

1 gram minced flat-leaf parsley

2 grams minced shallot

23 grams extra virgin olive oil

Kosher salt

LEMON CONFIT

70 grams water

70 grams granulated sugar

12 lemon suprêmes

30 grams small dice piquillo peppers

Fleur de sel

Parsley shoots

This dish is packed with big, harmonious flavors—ham, capers, lemon, and peppers—that contrast with the assertive mackerel and create a vivid plate. It's kind of a sandwich in a sandwich. Dry-cured ham is placed between two fillets, which are cooked sous vide, then sandwiched in brioche, like a grilled sandwich.

The Spanish capers, lemon suprêmes, and piquillo are not only bold accompanying flavors, they're dynamic visual counterpoints to the mackerel. Piquillos are fruity, sweet, and slightly spicy; they come charred over fire and so have a roasted flavor to them as well. **PHOTOGRAPH ON PAGE 91**

FOR THE MACKEREL—61°C (141.8°F); 12 MINUTES

Cut off the sinewy tail end of the mackerel and trim the sides to even the fillet. It should be about 10 inches long and 1½ to 2 inches wide. Cut the fillet lengthwise in half down one side of the bloodline. Cut away the bloodline and discard. Cutting with the grain, trim the top of each piece of fillet to create an even surface. Trim the edges as necessary to make the fillets of even thickness and width. Season with a sprinkle of salt on each side. Let the pieces rest at room temperature, flesh side up, for 4 to 5 minutes, or until the fish starts to sweat. Pat dry with C-fold towels.

Trim any excess fat as well as any very firm dark areas from the ham. Cut the ham into pieces large enough to cover and just slightly overlap the top of one fillet and reserve.

Sprinkle the transglutaminase through a small basket strainer over the tops of the fillets. Lay the ham over one fillet. Place the other fillet skin side up over the ham. Put the "sandwich" in the refrigerator to chill completely.

Place the fish in a bag and vacuum-pack on medium-high. Refrigerate for 6 hours to allow the transglutaminase to bond the fillets.

To complete: Cook at 61°C (141.8°F) for 12 minutes. Remove the mackerel from the bag. Trim away the ends. Cut the mackerel crosswise into 4 equal rectangles. Trim the sides as necessary.

The mackerel can be prepared ahead to this point and refrigerated; bring to room temperature before proceeding.

Line up 4 slices of the brioche and top with the mackerel (see photograph, page 90). Trim the pieces of bread so that the bread is slightly larger than the mackerel.

Heat a film of clarified butter in a sauté pan over medium-low heat. Add the mackerel, brioche side down. Cook for about 2 minutes to brown the brioche, pressing down lightly on the fish so that it adheres to the bread.

Meanwhile, lay out the remaining 4 slices of brioche. When the first pieces of brioche are browned, remove the mackerel and brioche and invert onto the remaining brioche so that the browned side is up. Trim the bottom brioche to the size of the fish and return to the heat to brown the second side. Remove and drain on C-fold towels. Trim the edges as necessary to even them.

FOR THE VINAIGRETTE: Mix the capers, parsley, shallot, and olive oil with a small pinch of salt. MAKES ABOUT 35 GRAMS

FOR THE LEMON CONFIT: Combine the water and sugar in a saucepan and bring to a simmer, stirring to dissolve the sugar. Pour over the lemon suprêmes and allow to cool to room temperature.

AT SERVICE: Drizzle the vinaigrette over the serving plates. Arrange the sandwich, lemon suprêmes, and piquillo peppers on the plates and sprinkle with fleur de sel. Garnish with parsley shoots. **MAKES 4 SERVINGS**

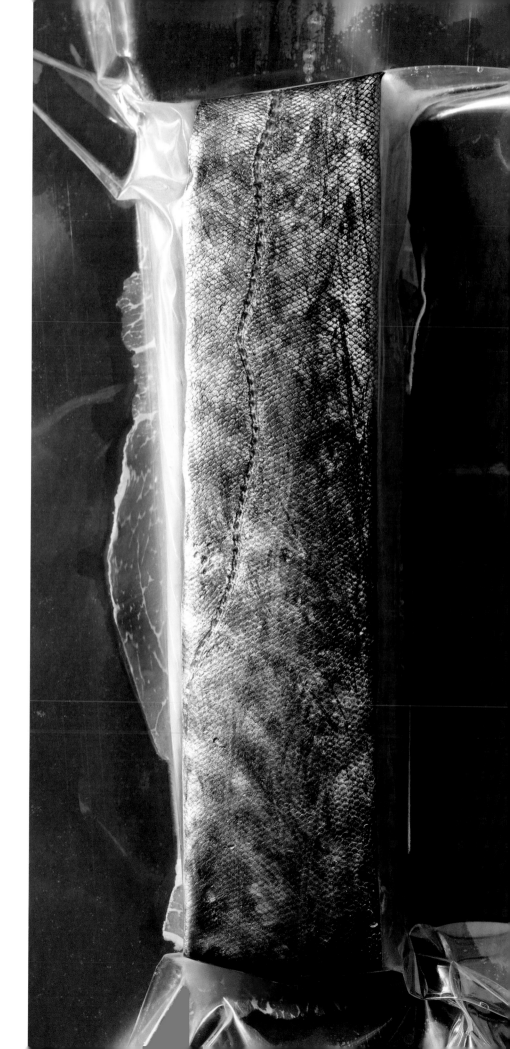

Above: The cooked mackerel before the brioche is trimmed; opposite: Spanish Mackerel and Serrano Ham *en Brioche,* Capers, Piquillo Peppers, and Lemon Confit (page 88)

ANGUILLE À LA JAPONAISE

MARINADE

37 grams granulated sugar

75 grams rice wine vinegar

12 grams mirin

38 grams water

12 grams white sesame oil

25 grams tamari

2 grams kanzuri paste (see Sources, page 282)

1 gram bonito

6 grams grated fresh ginger

25 grams sliced shallot

EGGS

1 Jidori egg (see Sources, page 282)

1 Jidori egg yolk

AVOCADO COULIS

15 grams water

30 grams lemon juice

160 grams chopped peeled avocados (about 2)

25 grams canola oil

Kosher salt

EEL

1 anago (about 285 grams), butterflied through
    the belly

1 to 2 red French breakfast radishes

Pinch of toasted nori

RICE

23 grams mirin

6 grams champagne vinegar

5 grams grapeseed oil

255 grams cooked Akita Komachi rice
    (see Sources, page 282), hot

8 sea urchin tongues

Perilla sprouts

Anago, a sea eel, is similar to unagi, freshwater eel, but it has a more delicate flavor and is a little smaller, shorter, and leaner. Its bones are so small and fine they do not need to be removed. We cut the flesh of the eel in a crosshatch pattern to help the bones break down, but even without that, they're scarcely noticeable. To prepare the eel, we make a sweet-sour marinade with mirin, rice vinegar, and tamari sauce, which are heated together and then cooled; we cook the eel sous vide in the marinade.

The numerous accompaniments include a simple avocado puree that forms a base on each plate, along with red radish, chopped nori, perilla (or shiso, an herb in the mint family), and sea urchin tongues (or roe). Jidori hens are a wild Japanese breed. The yolks of their eggs are deeply colored, almost orange. They're not imported into the United States, but there's a farm in Modesto, California, that raises a similar breed, and their eggs are what we use. We scramble the eggs until they're dry and beginning to form beads, then chop them fine and add them to the rice. **PHOTOGRAPH ON PAGE 94**

FOR THE MARINADE: Combine all the ingredients in a saucepan and slowly bring to a boil. Strain and let cool. Refrigerate until cold.

MAKES 180 GRAMS

FOR THE EGGS: Put the egg and yolk into a small saucepan and whisk constantly over medium heat for 5 to 6 minutes; the eggs should dry out completely and become granular in texture. Transfer to a cutting board and chop very fine. Set aside.

MAKES ABOUT 55 GRAMS

FOR THE AVOCADO COULIS: Combine the water, lemon, and avocado in a Vita-Prep. While blending on high speed, drizzle in the oil. Season to taste with salt. Pass through a small chinois or fine-mesh conical strainer and refrigerate until cold.

MAKES ABOUT 225 GRAMS

FOR THE EEL—59°C (138.2°F); 10 MINUTES

Cut the eel crosswise in half. Trim the long sides and tail end. Trim away the small flap and any blood spots. Score the flesh in a shallow crosshatch pattern. Refrigerate the eel until chilled.

Place the eel in a bag, add the marinade, and vacuum-pack on medium. Cook at 59°C (138.2°F) for 10 minutes. Remove the bag from the water and let sit for about 20 minutes to cool to room temperature.

To complete: Remove the eel from the bag and strain the liquid into a saucepan. Reduce the liquid for about 15 minutes, to a glaze consistency.

Cut the eel pieces lengthwise in half, then trim into 4 serving pieces about 4 inches long. Use a pair of tweezers to pull away the skin from the fillets. Remove the skin, cut the remaining eel and trimmings into a fine dice, and set aside.

FOR THE GARNISHES: Slice the radishes into very thin rounds. You will need 12 perfect rounds that are equal in size. Place in a bowl of ice water and refrigerate until serving.

Grind the nori to a fine powder in a spice grinder.

FOR THE RICE: About 20 minutes before serving, stir the mirin, champagne vinegar, and grapeseed oil into the hot rice.

AT SERVICE: Heat the diced eel with about 30 grams of the glaze in a sauté pan. Meanwhile, place the serving pieces of eel skin side down in the remaining glaze in another pan. Bring to a simmer, basting the fish with the glaze to reheat.

Stir half the rice into the diced eel. Divide the egg between the two rice mixtures. Spread the avocado coulis on the serving plates. Arrange the rice on the plates and sprinkle with the nori. Place the eel and the sea urchin on the rice. Garnish with the radishes and sprouts, and drizzle the plates with some of the glaze, if desired. **MAKES 4 SERVINGS**

Opposite: *Anguille à la Japonaise* (page 92); above: Columbia River Wild Sturgeon Confit à la Minute, Herb Spaetzle, Heirloom Beets, Dill "Mousse," and Borscht Sauce (page 96)

COLUMBIA RIVER WILD STURGEON CONFIT À LA MINUTE, HERB SPAETZLE, HEIRLOOM BEETS, DILL "MOUSSE," AND BORSCHT SAUCE

SPAETZLE

94 grams all-purpose flour

1 large egg

63 grams whole milk

0.5 gram minced chives

0.8 gram minced flat-leaf parsley

Kosher salt

Extra virgin olive oil

CABBAGE

80 grams ¼-inch-wide strips green cabbage

Canola oil

14 grams unsalted butter

ROASTED BEETS

2 medium red beets

Kosher salt

Granulated sugar

56 grams unsalted butter

BORSCHT SAUCE

Canola oil

135 grams beef short blade ribs, cut into 1-inch
    pieces

80 grams sliced onions

Kosher salt

60 grams 1-inch pieces green cabbage

350 grams beet juice
    (from 8 to 10 medium beets)

120 grams Beef Stock (page 257)

Red wine vinegar

Granulated sugar

3.5 grams minced shallot

7 grams unsalted butter

DILL MOUSSE

200 grams crème fraîche

2.5 grams minced dill

STURGEON

250 grams trimmed skinless sturgeon loin,
    1½ inches thick

Kosher salt

40 grams Rendered Beef Fat (page 270)

40 grams canola oil

We wanted to make a play on borscht and began to think about what would go with this beet and beef broth preparation. It evokes Eastern European and Russian cuisine, of course—thus the spaetzle. Sturgeon, which we get from the Columbia River in Washington, is a big meaty fish that can carry these robust components without relinquishing any of its delicate flavor, especially cooked sous vide, to which it's supremely suited. As with so much of the fish we serve, the sturgeon is given a brief cure to draw out moisture from the surface cells so they don't leak proteins during the gentle cooking.

The dill crème fraîche that tops the sturgeon, a traditional garnish for borscht, is a perfect way to finish the dish. **PHOTOGRAPH ON PAGE 95**

FOR THE SPAETZLE: Put the flour in a large bowl, make a well in the center, and add the egg. Use a sturdy spoon to begin to beat the egg and then to bring in and incorporate the flour. Once it is incorporated, beat in the milk until the batter is smooth, about 5 minutes. Stir in the chives, half the parsley, and 10 grams salt. Refrigerate the batter for 1 hour.

Bring a large pot of salted water to a boil. Place a spaetzle maker over the pot and push the batter through the machine, into the water. Cook for 45 seconds. Transfer to a strainer and submerge in an ice bath to chill. Drain well and toss with a light coating of olive oil. Set aside.

MAKES 250 GRAMS

FOR THE CABBAGE: Blanch the cabbage in boiling salted water for a few seconds just to wilt it. Drain in a strainer and submerge in an ice bath to chill, then drain and dry on C-fold towels.

To complete: Heat a film of canola oil in a sauté pan large enough to hold the spaetzle and cabbage in a single layer. Add the spaetzle and cook for about 1 minute, until lightly golden. Add the cabbage and a sprinkling of salt and sauté for another 1½ minutes. Stir in the butter to coat the spaetzle. Add the remaining parsley.

FOR THE ROASTED BEETS: Place the beets on a piece of foil large enough to enclose them. Sprinkle with a pinch of salt and a large pinch of sugar, dot with the butter, and wrap in the foil.

Put the beets on a sheet tray and roast in a 400°F oven for about 1½ hours, until tender. Remove the beets from the oven and allow them to cool enough to handle. Unwrap the beets and rub off the skin with a C-fold towel. Cut the beets into brunoise; set aside.

FOR THE SAUCE: Heat a film of canola oil in a wide saucepan. Add the beef and brown it on all sides, about 4 minutes. Add the onions and a sprinkling of salt and sauté for about 3 minutes. Add the cabbage and sauté for about 1½ minutes, until just wilted. Add a little of the beet juice to deglaze the pan, then add the remaining juice and boil vigorously, skimming often, to reduce to a glaze, about 15 minutes. Reducing it quickly will help maintain the vivid color of the beet juice.

Strain into a small saucepan, pressing on the solids to extract all the glaze. Add the beef stock and reduce to a sauce consistency, skimming as necessary.

To complete: Add the brunoise of beets and season with vinegar, sugar, and salt to taste. Stir in the shallot and butter.   **MAKES 180 GRAMS**

FOR THE CRÈME FRAÎCHE: Whip the crème fraîche until thickened. Fold in the dill.

Refrigerate until serving.

FOR THE STURGEON—61°C (141.8°F); 16 MINUTES
Season the fish with salt and place in a bag with the beef fat and oil. Refrigerate until cold.

Vacuum-pack on medium-high.

Cook at 61°C (141.8°F) for 16 minutes. Remove the bag from the water and let it rest at room temperature for 5 minutes.

Remove the sturgeon from the bag, blot on C-fold towels, and cut on the diagonal into 4 pieces.

AT SERVICE: Spoon the borscht sauce onto the serving plates. Top with the spaetzle and fish. Garnish with the crème fraîche.

MAKES 4 SERVINGS

Double Chop of Striped Bass Belly *en Persillade*, Black-Eyed Peas, and Whole-Grain Mustard Sauce (page 100)

DOUBLE CHOP OF STRIPED BASS BELLY *EN PERSILLADE*, BLACK-EYED PEAS, AND WHOLE-GRAIN MUSTARD SAUCE

BLACK-EYED PEAS

210 grams fresh black-eyed peas

470 grams Chicken Stock (page 257)

470 grams water

145 grams slab bacon, cut into 4 strips

A 50-gram piece of carrot

A 60-gram piece of peeled onion

A 35-gram piece of leek (white and light green

    parts only)

2 thyme sprigs

1 flat-leaf parsley sprig

43 grams unsalted butter

1 medium tomato, peeled, seeded,

    and cut into ¼-inch dice (54 grams)

3.5 grams minced shallot

1 gram minced flat-leaf parsley

Champagne vinegar

7.5 grams Brunoise (page 269)

Kosher salt

BASS

2 striped bass bellies (350 to 375 grams each)

Rib bones from 1 striped bass

Kosher salt

2 large eggs

11 grams Roasted Garlic Puree (page 266)

130 grams Dijon mustard

125 grams fresh bread crumbs (see page 263)

2 grams minced flat-leaf parsley

Freshly ground black pepper

Clarified Butter (page 261)

MOUSSE

40 grams sea scallops (muscles removed)

70 grams reserved bass trimmings

35 grams crème fraîche

15 grams heavy cream

0.1 gram polyphosphate

    (see Sources, page 282)

Kosher salt

3 grams Preserved Lemons

    (page 264; use Meyer lemons), finely chopped

40 grams whole-grain mustard

80 grams Quick Veal Sauce (page 260), warmed

A large bass belly is a substantial cut, and trimming it to size for this dish gives us enough leftover meat to make a mousse for stuffing the belly. The belly is wrapped around the mousse and shaped into a roulade that is cooked sous vide. The roulade is then treated something like a rack of lamb *en persillade,* coated with bread crumbs, parsley, and seasonings and browned. It is served with earthy black-eyed peas and a mustard sauce. **PHOTOGRAPH ON PAGE 99**

FOR THE PEAS: Put the peas in a stockpot and add the chicken stock, water, bacon, carrot, and onion.

Cut the piece of leek lengthwise in half. Wash the leek under cold water. Sandwich the thyme and parsley sprigs between the two pieces of leek and tie with a piece of kitchen twine. Add to the pot.

Bring to a simmer over medium-high heat. Cover with a parchment lid (see page 270) and simmer for about 15 minutes, or until the peas are tender. Turn off the heat and let the peas cool to room temperature in their liquid.

Remove the vegetables and bouquet garni and discard. Drain the beans over a bowl. Strain the cooking liquid through a chinois or fine-mesh conical strainer into a small saucepan, and reduce over medium heat to about 250 grams.

To complete: Bring the beans and about 35 grams of the reduced cooking liquid to a boil. Add 30 grams of the butter and bring to a simmer. When the beans are hot and creamy, add the tomato, shallot, minced parsley, a few drops of champagne vinegar, and the brunoise. Stir in the remaining butter and season to taste with salt.

MAKES ABOUT 530 GRAMS

FOR THE BASS: Trim the bellies. Cut each belly crosswise in half, creating 4 pieces 5½ to 6 inches long by 1½ inch thick by about 2 inches wide. Reserve the trimmings for the mousse.

Season the fish with a sprinkling of salt on both sides and let sit for 10 minutes to sweat. You'll see moisture on the top of the bellies. Dry with C-fold towels and refrigerate while you make the mousse.

FOR THE MOUSSE: Combine the scallops and fish trimmings with the crème fraîche in a food processor. Puree, scraping down the sides as necessary, until smooth, about 2 minutes. Stop the machine and scrape down the sides. Pulsing the machine, drizzle in the cream, just to incorporate.

Set a tamis over a large bowl. Scrape the puree through the tamis and place the bowl over an ice bath. Stir in the polyphosphate. Beat well with a sturdy spoon to dissolve and thoroughly incorporate the polyphosphate. Season the mousse with a bit of salt. Stir in the preserved lemon.

FOR THE CHOPS—62°C (143.6°F); 11 MINUTES

Spread the mousse evenly over 2 of the pieces of bass belly. Top with the other two pieces. Cut 2 pieces of cheesecloth about 14 inches long and about 12 inches wide. Dampen the cheesecloth. Put one assembled belly in the center of each piece of cheesecloth, leaving about 4 inches on each side. Rolling it away from you, roll each belly up in the cheesecloth into a tight log. Tie the ends with kitchen twine and tie once in the center. Refrigerate until cold.

Place the bass in two separate bags and vacuum-pack on medium-high.

Cook at 62°C (143.6°F) for 11 minutes. Transfer the bags of bass to an ice bath to chill.

To complete: Remove the rolls from the bags and dry well on C-fold towels. Cut off the ends of the rolls and unroll the cheesecloth. The fish will be set but still feel undercooked.

Whisk the eggs with the garlic puree and mustard in a shallow bowl. Mix the crumbs, parsley, and salt and pepper to taste in another shallow bowl. Dip each piece of fish into the egg mixture, then roll in the crumbs, coating the ends as well. Repeat.

Coat the bottom of a medium nonstick sauté pan with clarified butter and heat until hot. Add the bass and place in a 350°F oven. After 5 minutes, remove the pan and turn the fish to coat evenly in the butter. Return to the oven for another 5 minutes.

Remove the pan from the oven and return to medium heat. Turn the fish to brown any areas that did not brown in the oven. Drain on C-fold towels.

FOR THE RIB BONE GARNISH: Cut the 4 longest bones from each section of rib bones; discard the rest. Cut between the bones to separate them. With a paring knife, scrape the bones to remove as much skin and flesh as possible.

Put the bones in a small pot, cover with cold water, and bring to a boil over high heat. Cook for about 20 minutes, or until any remaining meat can be pulled easily from the bones. Drain the bones, strip off the meat, and discard it. Rinse the bones under cold water and dry on C-fold towels. With a pair of kitchen shears, trim about 1 inch from the thicker end of each bone. Set the bones aside.

AT SERVICE: Whisk the mustard into the warm veal sauce. Push 4 of the reserved bones, evenly spaced, into each piece of bass to resemble the bones on a rack of lamb. Trim the ends of the rolls, and cut each piece in half.

Spoon the sauce onto the plates. Top with the peas and stand a "chop" in each portion.   **MAKES 4 SERVINGS**

Torchon of monkfish liver (see page 105)

TORCHON OF MONKFISH LIVER
WITH GREEN APPLE JELLY AND OSSETRA CAVIAR

APPLE JELLY

1.25 grams ascorbic acid

2 to 3 Granny Smith apples (450 grams)

2 gelatin sheets, 2 grams each, soaked in
    cold water to soften

MONKFISH LIVER

61.3 grams kosher salt, plus extra for seasoning

23.3 grams Hobbs' Curing Salt
    (see Sources, page 282)

8 grams granulated sugar

8 grams freshly ground white pepper, plus extra
    for seasoning

1 kilogram water, cold

1 small monkfish liver (about 380 grams)

3.5 grams powdered gelatin

APPLESAUCE

2 Granny Smith apples (about 495 grams)

10 grams granulated sugar

10 grams lemon juice

56 grams Caspian Sea ossetra caviar
    (see Sources, page 282)

The texture of the monkfish liver is the real highlight of this dish. Although the liver is often compared with foie gras, it is light and creamy and less dense. Here it's rolled like a traditional foie gras torchon after being cured in a brine and cooked gently sous vide, resulting in a very mild, delicious taste. The cure draws out impurities and blood and enhances the color and flavor.

The apples for the applesauce are also cooked sous vide to maintain a very bright appearance, then pureed and strained. The apple juice for the jelly is clarified not by cooking but by freezing, a way to clarify the liquid without high heat, resulting in a purer flavor. It's jelled and then cut into slices that top the disks of monkfish liver, which are finished with a layer of caviar. The apple bridges the flavors of the liver and caviar and brings the dish together.

Be aware that monkfish liver can become fishy if it's overcooked or not pristinely fresh.

FOR THE APPLE JELLY: Set up a juicer. Put the ascorbic acid in a liquid measuring cup with at least a 350-milliliter capacity to catch the juice. Core the apples and cut them into 1-inch pieces (the apple peel will color the apple juice). Run the apples through the juicer until you have 250 milliliters of juice. Stir to combine with the ascorbic acid, then pour into a container and freeze until solidly frozen.

Line a fine-mesh basket strainer with 4 layers of dampened cheese-cloth and set over a bowl. Transfer the frozen juice to the strainer and let it melt at room temperature (or let it melt in the refrigerator for several hours, or overnight). As the juice melts, any sediment will stay in the cloth; it should be discarded.

Heat about 125 grams of the apple juice until warm. Stir in the softened gelatin sheets to dissolve them, then stir in the remaining juice.

Line an 8-by-12 inch container (such as a baking pan) with plastic wrap. Pour in the juice: the layer of juice will be about ⅛ inch thick. Refrigerate for several hours or overnight to firm.

To make the brine, combine the kosher salt, curing salt, sugar, and white pepper in a container that will just hold the liver once the water has been added. Bring about 250 grams of the water to a boil. Pour into the container and stir to dissolve the salt and sugar. Then stir in the remaining water. Chill completely. Place the monkfish in the brine and refrigerate for 3 hours.

Remove the liver from the brine, rinse under cold water, and dry on a C-fold towel. Place the liver bottom side up on a work surface. Cut out and discard the large vein that runs lengthwise through the liver. Cut away any imperfections, veins, or discolored areas from both sides of the liver. Turn the liver bottom side up. Fold it crosswise in half and cut a slash ¼ inch deep into the fold to mark the center of the liver. Unfold it and season both sides with salt and pepper.

Turn the liver bottom side up. Put the gelatin in a small basket strainer and sprinkle it over the liver. Cut a 24-by-14-inch piece of doubled cheesecloth, dampen it, and lay it on the work surface with a short end toward you. Fold the liver in half, so the gelatin is on the inside, and place it lengthwise across the bottom center of the cheesecloth. Rolling it away from you, roll it up in the cheesecloth into a tight log, twisting the ends as you roll to force the liver into a compact log; if possible, have another person hold the far end of the cheesecloth flat on the work surface as you roll.

Loop a length of string around your index finger. With the same hand, hold one end of the cheesecloth tightly and wind the string around the end of the liver. Continue wrapping the string about ¼ inch into the liver; this will help compress the liver into a tight roll. Tie a knot around the cheesecloth. Repeat the procedure on the other end. If you have rolled and tied it tightly enough, you will see bits of the liver being forced through the cheesecloth. Tie 3 pieces of string, equally spaced, around the log. Place in a bag and refrigerate until cold.

Vacuum-pack the liver on medium-high. Refrigerate for at least 30 minutes before cooking.

Cook at 64°C (147.2°F) for 3 hours and 15 minutes. Transfer the bag to an ice bath and refrigerate the liver in the ice water.

Peel and core the apples. Cut into 1-inch pieces and put them in a bowl. Lightly sprinkle the apples with the sugar and lemon juice; tossing to coat. Refrigerate for about 30 minutes to chill.

Spread the apples in a single layer in a bag and vacuum-pack on high.

Cook at 85°C (185°F) for 25 minutes. The apples should be completely softened; if not, return to the water and continue to cook. Put the bag in an ice bath to cool the apples.

Transfer the cooled apples to a Vita-Prep. Begin to puree them on low speed, scraping down the sides as necessary, then increase the speed and puree until completely smooth. Pass the puree through a chinois or fine-mesh conical strainer into a container and refrigerate.

MAKES ABOUT 255 GRAMS

AT SERVICE: Remove the monkfish from the ice water. Leaving it in the cheesecloth, cut away the ends (see photograph, page 102), then cut the liver into 4 slices about ½ inch thick. Remove the cheesecloth and drain on a C-fold towel.

Turn the apple jelly out onto a piece of plastic wrap and cut 4 squares slightly larger than the monkfish pieces, wide enough to come slightly down the sides, cutting through the plastic wrap (discard the excess jelly). Drape each piece of jelly over a slice of liver by lifting the jelly on the plastic wrap and inverting it over the liver, then carefully remove the plastic wrap.

Set a bowl of hot water at your side. Dip a round cutter slightly smaller than the diameter of the monkfish in the hot water, dry it with a C-fold towel, and cut through one portion of jelly and liver to make a smooth round. Remove and discard the trimmings. Leave the cutter in position to serve as a guide, wipe the edges, and place the monkfish round on a serving plate. Spoon one-quarter of the caviar onto the center of the round and smooth to the edges. Lift away the cutter very carefully, and repeat with the remaining portions.

Alternatively, cut the rounds of torchon and jelly, then place the cutter on each plate, spoon one-quarter of the caviar into the cutter, and smooth it to the edges. Lift away and place a round of liver on the top of the caviar.

Serve with a spoonful of applesauce on the side.   MAKES 4 SERVINGS

OLIVE-OIL-POACHED BLUEFIN TUNA, JACOBSEN'S FARM TOMATOES *EN VIERGE*, TOASTED PINE NUTS, NIÇOISE OLIVES, AND BASIL SEEDS

TUNA

A 220-gram block of Atlantic bluefin tuna top loin, about 5 by 2 by 1 inch, cold

40 grams canola oil

40 grams extra virgin olive oil

GARNISHES

One 250-milligram package organic basil seeds

1 large Italian eggplant

Extra virgin olive oil

Kosher salt

10 grams pine nuts

12 Niçoise olives

150 grams peeled heirloom tomatoes, at room temperature

Balsamic vinegar

Fleur de sel

Small sweet basil leaves

This dish is all about a specific cut of bluefin tuna. It comes from the top loin, near the skin of the fish, where there are large concentrations of both fat and the sinew that holds it together. The fat is what makes the dish so good, but the sinew would be unpleasantly tough if raw or rare. So, if we were to sauté or roast this cut, we'd have to overcook it in order to tenderize the sinew. But with the low temperatures available to us when we cook sous vide, we can soften that sinew without overcooking the fish, resulting in tuna that is rich and luxurious, almost in the same way Wagyu beef is. It's extraordinary in flavor and color.

Here we use a combination of a neutral oil, canola, and olive oil for poaching because we've chosen Mediterranean flavors, including olives, for the garnish (straight olive oil would overpower the fish). But on another occasion we take this dish in more meaty directions, changing the garnish, and when we do, we change the fat, using rendered beef fat instead of olive oil.

We often use tomatoes from Peter Jacobsen, who grows some of the most wonderful produce I know of. I realize everyone can't buy from Peter, but I mention him here to underscore the importance of chefs finding, and working with, excellent local purveyors.

This is a very easy dish that feels light and tastes rich at the same time, perfect for summer.

FOR THE TUNA—59.5°C (139.1°F); 13 MINUTES

Place the tuna in a bag and add the oils. Vacuum-pack on medium. Cook at 59.5°C (139.1°F) for 13 minutes. Remove the tuna from the bag and put on a rack set over a sheet pan to drain.

FOR THE GARNISHES: Put the basil seeds in a bowl, cover with 250 grams of room-temperature water, and soak for 1 hour.

With a knife, cut the skin away from the eggplant with ¼ inch of the flesh attached to each piece of skin; reserve the remaining eggplant for another use. Trim the edges of the pieces to even them. Lay each section skin side down and trim the flesh to an even thickness. Cut into a brunoise. You need about 30 grams.

Heat a film of olive oil in a sauté pan, add the eggplant, and sauté for a minute or so to cook the eggplant without browning. Season with salt and spread on C-fold towels to drain.

Heat about ⅛ inch of olive oil in a small saucepan until hot. Add the pine nuts and cook for a few seconds, until golden brown. Drain and sprinkle with salt.

Cut the flesh of each olive away in 2 pieces, cutting from top to bottom on opposite sides of the pit. Cut the tomatoes into a variety of shapes: some can be sliced, others cut into wedges.

AT SERVICE: Sprinkle the tomatoes with olive oil, balsamic vinegar, and fleur de sel to taste. Gently toss in the eggplant and olives. Arrange on serving plates, leaving the center free for the tuna. Drain the basil seeds and add to the plates.

Slice the tuna into 1-inch slices. Brush both sides of each slice with olive oil and arrange on the plates. Sprinkle the tuna with fleur de sel, basil, and the pine nuts. **MAKES 4 SERVINGS**

POULTRY AND MEAT

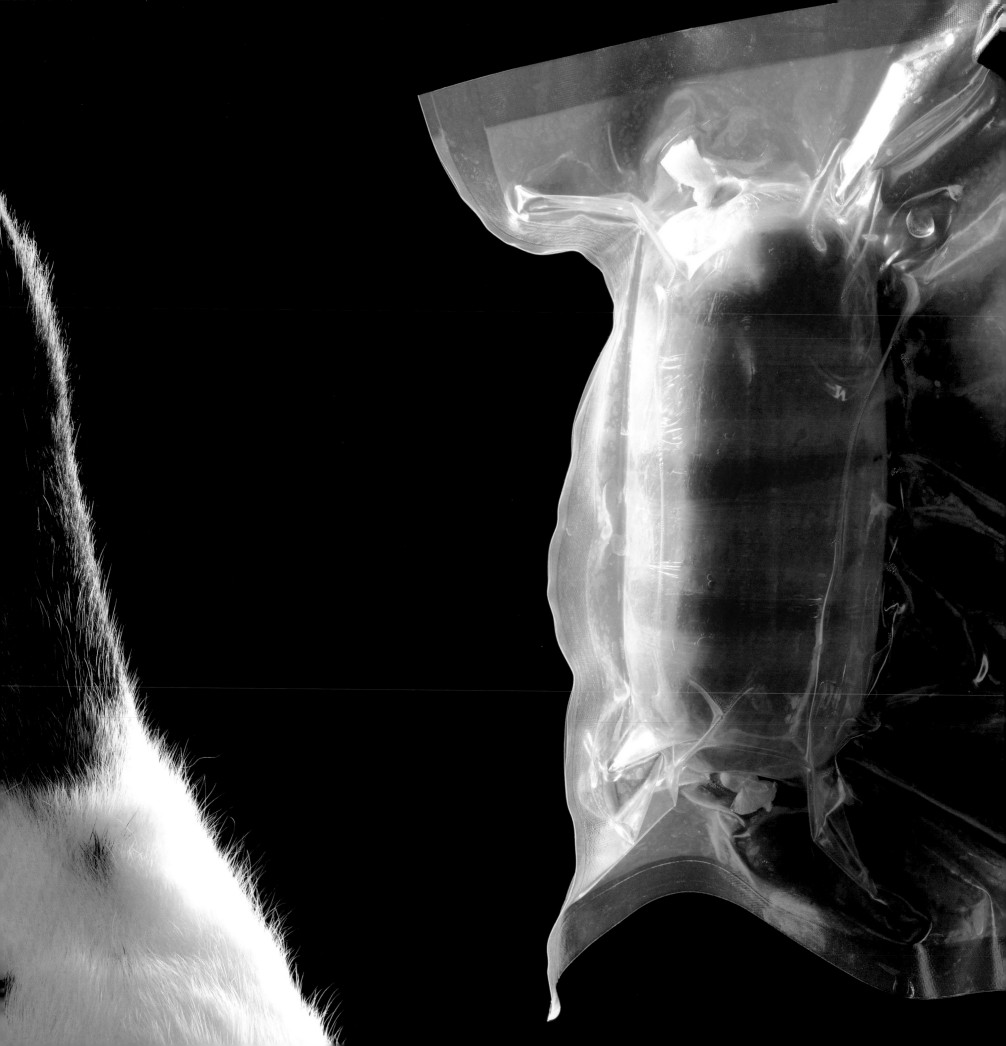

Overleaf (right) and above: rabbit for Rabbit and Bacon *Pressé*, Slow-Poached Royal Blenheim Apricots, Rabbit Liver Mousse, and Green Pistachios (page 134)

COOKING MEAT MAY REPRESENT THE PINNACLE OF SOUS VIDE TECHNIQUE; IT'S A

category where sous vide really soars. I've talked a lot about my love of braising because there are so many enjoyable phases of the braising process and because it's kind of magical in that it transforms an inexpensive cut of meat into something tender and succulent. Sous vide takes the braise cut one step further. With the traditional braising technique, the meat is cooked to well above the point at which the muscle fibers contract and squeeze out their juices, in order to melt the connective tissues that make them tough. With sous vide, we can cook these meats at temperatures below the point at which the muscle fibers contract, but long enough for the connective tissue to melt into gelatin. The result is braised meat of extraordinary tenderness and juiciness.

Braised cuts are often first marinated. We can also marinate them sous vide—a technique that is faster, cleaner, easier, and, because less marinade is required, more efficient.

Confiting meat sous vide is also easier, more efficient, and less costly. Here again, sous vide is better in every way than the conventional technique. You need far less fat, the aromatics have a more powerful effect, and the gentle heat ensures a perfect texture every time—furthermore, you don't have a big pot taking up oven space for fourteen hours. Confited meats are also cured first, and, of course, the meat can be cured sous vide as well.

Sometimes we use sous vide for combining and shaping meats, rather than for cooking them. We might vacuum-pack a rabbit loin and cook it sous vide just long enough to set the shape before it is cooked conventionally. Or we might layer a *farce* on a poultry breast and package it so that the two ingredients cook together and can be sliced easily and neatly, as though the solid meat and the pureed *farce* were one thing.

The sous vide technique also works well with cuts of meat that are naturally tender and don't require long cooking. Sous vide will bring a lamb loin to a perfect medium-rare, and it will be uniformly cooked from the edges to the center—again, something impossible to achieve in any other way. Squab breast should be cooked just to medium-rare, or its flavor can become too strong and the texture dry; cooked sous vide, it's uniform and consistent every time. And if you add some foie gras fat to the bag, its flavor is enhanced even more.

Whether long cooking for tough cuts and confits, or short cooking for tender cuts, sous vide techniques are extraordinary on many levels.

ROUELLE OF FOUR STORY HILLS FARM POULARDE WRAPPED IN SWISS CHARD WITH HOBBS' APPLEWOOD SMOKED BACON AND *PRUNEAUX D'AGEN*

POULARDE

1 Four Story Hills poularde (about 1.75 kilograms; see Sources, page 282) or 2 large boneless, skinless poularde breast halves

Kosher salt and freshly ground white pepper

Ajinomoto RM transglutaminase (see Sources, page 282)

3 to 4 large Swiss chard leaves

POACHED PRUNES

130 grams dry red wine, such as Cabernet Sauvignon

130 grams granulated sugar

130 grams water

4 pitted prunes

Canola oil

Extra virgin olive oil

Sel gris

BACON GARNISH

4 slices thin-sliced Hobbs' Applewood Smoked Bacon (see Sources, page 282)

BACON EMULSION

100 grams Hobbs' Applewood Smoked Bacon (see Sources, page 282)

75 grams canola oil, plus additional for the shallot

12 grams thinly sliced shallot

125 grams White Veal Stock (page 255)

10 grams sherry vinegar, plus more for finishing

23 grams unsalted butter

Kosher salt

This dish and many others at The French Laundry and per se use products raised by or made available by two special people, Sylvia and Stephen Pryzant. They raise poultry on their Pennsylvania farm, with extraordinary care for the animals. We buy their chicken, poularde (a chicken fattened for roasting), and squab, among other fowl. But more than just raising animals, the Pryzants also work with nearby farmers who raise different animals, and help them distribute their products.

FOR THE POULARDE—62°C (143.6°F); 1½ HOURS

Cut away the legs and wings from the poularde; reserve for another purpose. Cut out and discard the wishbone. Cut away each breast half from the bone. Remove the skin and trim away any fat, sinew, and rough edges from the pieces. Remove the tenderloins from the breast halves and reserve for another use.

Place one breast underside up on the work surface. Sprinkle with salt and white pepper. Using a small basket strainer, sprinkle with a light dusting of the transglutaminase, as you would with confectioners' sugar. Place the second breast half underside down on top, with the thicker end over the thinner end of the bottom piece. Tear off a piece of 18-inch-wide food-safe plastic wrap about 20 inches long and lay it on the work surface with a short end toward you. Lay the poularde across the center of the bottom of the plastic wrap and roll it up in the plastic, keeping it in the center and rolling as tightly as possible. Holding the poularde, twist one end of the plastic wrap several times against the meat, then repeat on the other end, twisting in the opposite direction, to make a perfect cylinder. Tie the ends of plastic, keeping them tight against the poularde. Refrigerate for 6 hours to allow the transglutaminase to bond the breast pieces together.

Trim the large ribs from the leaves of Swiss chard. Blanch the leaves (see Big-Pot Blanching, page 268) until they wilt, then transfer to an ice bath to chill. Drain and dry on C-fold towels.

Lay a 20-inch-long piece of plastic wrap on the work surface, with a short end toward you. Lay out the chard in a single layer to make a rectangle large enough to enclose the poularde. Remove the poularde from the plastic wrap and lay across the chard. Roll up to enclose the poularde in the chard and twist the ends of the plastic to tighten and shape the poularde into a log as before, then knot the plastic at both ends. Refrigerate until cooking.

To complete: Cook the poularde at 62°C (143.6°F) for 1½ hours. Remove from the water and let rest for several minutes.

FOR THE POACHED PRUNES: Bring the wine to a boil and flambé to burn off the alcohol. Add the sugar and water, stirring to dissolve the sugar. Pour the liquid over the prunes and let sit for about 20 minutes, until the liquid cools to room temperature and the prunes have softened.

Lay 4 small pieces of plastic wrap on the work surface and rub each with a light coating of canola oil. Roll up a prune in each one, twist the ends to compress and shape the prunes, and tie the ends. Set aside.

To complete: Reheat the prunes in the plastic in warm water. Carefully cut off one end of each plastic packet and press from the other side to remove the prune. Brush each prune lightly with olive oil and sprinkle with a pinch of sel gris.

FOR THE BACON GARNISH: Lay the bacon on a Silpat-lined sheet pan. Cover the bacon with another Silpat and another sheet pan. Bake at 325°F for 25 minutes, then rotate the pan and cook for about 25 minutes longer. Check the bacon from time to time—it should be cooked but still malleable, not crisp.

Remove the slices from the pan and trim each slice into a rectangle that is about 4 inches by ½ inch. Return the bacon to the pan, cover and weight as before, and return to the oven. Cook for another 15 minutes. Uncover and cook until crisp, about 5 minutes. The pieces may be crisp at different times, so remove them as they are done. Trim the ends if needed for a clean cut.

FOR THE BACON EMULSION: Grind the bacon. Put in a small saucepan over low heat and allow the bacon fat to render. Pour off and reserve 30 grams of the bacon fat. Reserve the bacon and any additional fat for another use, if desired.

Heat a film of oil in a small saucepan. Add the shallot and sweat over low heat for about 2 minutes. Add the stock and the 10 grams vinegar and simmer to reduce the liquid by half.

Whisk in the butter, then transfer to a Vita-Prep. With the machine running on low speed, drizzle in the 75 grams of oil, followed by the bacon fat. Season to taste with salt and a few drops of vinegar. Blend at medium speed just until the sauce has emulsified; do not overblend, or it will break. Strain through a chinois or fine-mesh conical strainer.

AT SERVICE: Unwrap the poularde, trim the edges, and slice into 4 equal rounds. Spoon some of the emulsion onto each plate. Place a slice of poularde on the emulsion, and garnish with a prune and strip of bacon.

MAKES 4 SERVINGS

CHESTNUT-STUFFED FOUR STORY HILLS FARM CHICKEN
WITH CELERY AND HONEY-POACHED CRANBERRIES

CHICKEN

1 Four Story Hills Farm chicken
(1.33 to 1.5 kilograms; see Sources, page 282)

Kosher salt

1 gram polyphosphate (see Sources, page 282)

0.2 gram quatre-épices

30 grams Chicken Stock (page 257) or water

75 grams crème fraîche

Freshly ground white pepper

7.5 grams Brunoise (page 269)

3 grams finely chopped chives

10 peeled fresh medium chestnuts (see Note)

Ajinomoto RM transglutaminase
(see Sources, page 282)

Clarified Butter (page 261)

CELERY

2 celery stalks

Canola oil

Beurre Monté (page 261)

8 light green to yellow celery leaves,
from the heart

Extra virgin olive oil

Champagne vinegar

Kosher salt

CELERY ROOT PUREE

170 grams coarsely chopped peeled celery root

100 grams heavy cream, cold

Kosher salt

GLAZED CHESTNUTS

25 grams Quick Chicken Sauce (page 260)

10 grams honey

10 grams unsalted butter

Kosher salt

8 peeled fresh medium chestnuts (see Note)

About 250 grams Chicken Stock (page 257)

CRANBERRIES

60 grams honey

22 grams Banyuls vinegar

50 grams cranberries

55 grams Quick Chicken Sauce (page 260),
warmed

Fleur de sel

Micro celery

This dish was developed by Devin Knell, a longtime French Laundry chef, as a way to turn flavorful chicken thighs into a refined dish. It's an exciting preparation for that reason, and it's also a dish that would be impossible without sous vide. The concept is simple, classical even: we make a mousse from the breast meat, enriched with crème fraîche and mixed with chestnuts and aromatics. This *farce* is spread on a boned chicken thigh, covered with a second thigh, and sealed sous vide, then cooked very gently for an hour. The bag maintains the shape of the chicken and the gentle heat cooks the thigh and the *farce* all the way through without overcooking them, leaving both very juicy.

Just before serving, we crisp the skin in the pan. The chicken is sliced and served with a garnish of celery, glazed chestnuts, and cranberries.

PHOTOGRAPH ON PAGE 117

FOR THE CHICKEN: Cut between one thigh and breast to remove the leg and thigh in one piece, keeping as much skin as possible attached. It is important to leave enough skin attached to the leg to encompass the meat; it will shrink back as it cooks. Repeat on the other side. Refrigerate the legs while you make the mousse.

To make the mousse: Remove the breasts from the bone. Remove the skin and trim away any fat, sinew, and rough edges. You will need 150 grams breast meat or tenders. The meat must be cold to make the mousse; refrigerate if needed. Reserve the remaining chicken for another use.

Combine the breast meat, 2 grams salt, the polyphosphate, and quatre-épices in a food processor and process to the consistency of a thick paste. With the processor running, slowly add the chicken stock, then continue to mix, scraping the sides as needed. When the mixture begins to look wet and shiny, it means the polyphosphate is absorbing the liquid; the mixture will feel tacky to the touch. With the processor running, add the crème fraîche. The mousse will be dense.

Pass the mousse through a tamis. Add a few turns of white pepper, the brunoise, and chives. Stir in the chestnuts. MAKES ABOUT 200 GRAMS

FOR THE LEGS—64°C (147.2°F); 1 HOUR

The legs need to be boned, leaving the skin in one piece without tears or cuts. Place one leg skin side down on the work surface. Make a cut through the center of the skin down the drumstick and then the thigh, going deep enough to hit the bone. Gently pull back the skin and meat. Cut off the end of the drumstick, then remove the bones, using your knife to work up one side of the bones and then the other. Be especially careful at the knee joint not to rip the skin that is against the work surface. Lift out the bones and pat the meat and skin into as even a layer as possible. Cut out the tendons and veins; scrape any excess fat from the meat or skin (smaller pieces of fat do not need to be removed). The surface of the meat will be uneven. Butterfly the thicker areas to create an even rectangular layer. Trim the excess skin, leaving a ½- to ¼-inch border of skin extending past the meat on all sides. Repeat with the second leg.

Season the meat side of both pieces of chicken with a light sprinkling of salt and white pepper. Using a small basket strainer, sprinkle enough transglutaminase over each piece to resemble a dusting of confectioners' sugar. Be certain to reach all the edges.

Place one piece of chicken skin side down on a parchment-lined sheet pan. Spread about half the mousse over the meat. With a small offset spatula, gently work the mousse across the surface, making sure the chestnuts are evenly distributed, and filling in any thinner spots of meat with mousse. Add the remaining mousse, spreading it to create a layer that is about ⅓ inch thick and tapered along the edges. Top with the second leg, skin side up. Refrigerate for 6 hours to allow the transglutaminase to bond the meat and mousse together.

Carefully position the chicken in the bottom of a bag, without disturbing the layers. Smooth the skin to the edges of the meat to remove any wrinkles. Vacuum-pack on medium-low.

Using a stiff scraper, gently push on the edges of the chicken through the plastic to straighten the rectangular shape. Fold the empty part of the bag over the meat and tape it to maintain the shape of the chicken; do not wrap too tight or create wrinkles in the skin.

Cook at 64°C (147.2°F) for 1 hour. Let the chicken rest at room temperature for 5 minutes.

To complete: Remove the chicken from the bag and pat dry on C-fold towels. Melt about a ⅛-inch layer of clarified butter in a nonstick sauté pan. When it is hot, add the chicken and cook until the first side is golden, about 2 minutes. Turn and brown on the second side, tilting the pan to collect the butter and basting the chicken as it cooks, about 2 minutes. Transfer to a cutting board.

Carefully trim the edges, and cut the chicken into slices or cubes. Brush the top with additional melted clarified butter.

FOR THE CELERY: Trim the ends of the celery stalks. Stand one stalk on a cutting board and trim off about ¼ inch from each long edge to make a flatter piece with only a very slight curve. Repeat with the other stalk. Cut 8 pieces of celery on the bias, each about 2 inches long. Chill in ice water until cold.

Drain the celery and blanch (see Big-Pot Blanching, page 268) until tender. Transfer to an ice bath.

To complete: Drain and dry the celery. Heat a film of canola oil in a small sauté pan over medium heat. Add the celery and enough beurre monté to warm and glaze the celery.

Just before serving, lightly dress the celery leaves with oil, vinegar, and a sprinkle of salt.

FOR THE CELERY ROOT PUREE—85°C (185°F); 1½ HOURS

Place the celery root in a bag with the cream and a pinch of salt. Vacuum-pack on high.

Cook at 85°C (185°F) for 1½ hours, or until the celery root is completely tender.

Transfer the celery root to a Vita-Prep and add enough of the cream to begin to puree it. Slowly add the remaining cream, blending until the mixture is very smooth. Season to taste with salt.   MAKES 175 GRAMS

FOR THE CHESTNUTS: Combine the chicken sauce, honey, butter, and a sprinkle of salt in a small saucepan. Add the chestnuts and enough stock to cover them. Cook over medium heat for 30 to 40 minutes, or until tender, spooning the liquid over chestnuts from time to time, particularly toward the end, to glaze them.

FOR THE CRANBERRIES: Combine the honey and vinegar in a small sauté pan or saucepan that will hold the cranberries in a single layer. Heat over medium heat until the mixture reaches 107.2°C (225°F), the thread stage. Remove from the heat and let cool to 21.1°C (70°F).

Add the berries to the syrup. The heat of the syrup will be enough to heat and plump the cranberries, but not hot enough to pop them. If any do pop, discard. Using a small spoon, gently turn the berries to coat them. The berries can be kept warm, loosely covered so that they do not steam.

AT SERVICE: Spoon some sauce onto each plate and arrange the chicken on top. Sprinkle with fleur de sel. Garnish the chicken with the glazed celery, chestnuts, and cranberries, and arrange the celery leaves and micro celery around the dish.   MAKES 4 SERVINGS

NOTE TO PEEL CHESTNUTS

Pour about 1½ inches canola oil into a small saucepan and heat to 137°C (278.6°F).

Trim off the sharp point from each chestnut and, with the tip of a paring knife, score the flat side with an X. Remove the pan of oil from the heat, add 3 chestnuts, return to the heat, and cook for several seconds, until the X opens up enough to peel away the shell. Adjust the heat as necessary. Peel the chestnuts. If there is a dark skin attached to the chestnuts, use a paring knife to remove it. Repeat with the remaining chestnuts, returning the pan of oil to the heat briefly if it cools too much.

Chestnut-Stuffed Four Story Hills Farm Chicken with Celery and Honey-Poached Cranberries (page 114)

"PASTRAMI"
LIBERTY PEKIN DUCK BREAST, COLESLAW,
RYE MELBA TOAST, AND 1000 ISLAND *GASTRIQUE*

BRINE

100 grams granulated sugar

100 grams kosher salt

1 large garlic clove, peeled

1.5 grams yellow mustard seeds

1.5 grams powdered ginger

1 small fresh bay leaf

7 cloves

10 juniper berries

3.5 grams cracked black peppercorns

1.5 grams cracked coriander seeds

2 grams Hobbs' Curing Salt
   (see Sources, page 282)

1 kilogram water

DUCK

1 whole skinless Liberty Pekin duck breast
   (about 300 grams; see Sources, page 282),
   split

50 grams Rendered Duck Fat (page 270), cold

COLESLAW

500 grams water

250 grams champagne vinegar

250 grams granulated sugar

29 grams yellow mustard seeds

25 grams caraway seeds

6 black peppercorns

1 bay leaf

1 thyme sprig

4 grams brown mustard seeds

350 grams savoy cabbage chiffonade

150 grams julienned carrots (about 2)

100 grams sliced red onion

1000 ISLAND GASTRIQUE

30 grams Banyuls vinegar,
   plus additional for finishing

18 grams honey

115 grams Quick Duck Sauce (page 260)

6 grams minced shallot

10 grams minced Duck Tongue (page 265)

8 grams cornichon brunoise

6 grams unsalted butter

Kosher salt and freshly ground black pepper

10 grams tomato brunoise

2 grams minced tarragon

6 grams Brunoise (page 269)

RYE MELBA

1 small loaf rye bread

Clarified Butter (page 261), melted

Kosher salt

Caraway seeds

For many years now, I've been using Liberty ducks, raised by Jim Reichardt at Sonoma County Poultry. They're a strain of Pekin developed in Denmark that are suited to slower growing, which results in a big and flavorful breast.

For this dish, the duck breast is brined using traditional pastrami seasonings—mustard, bay, coriander, pepper, ginger, and juniper, with a little Hobbs' Curing Salt to keep it a natural color—and then poached sous vide with duck fat. As with other poultry, the gentle heat is the ideal cooking environment for the duck breast. It is served with coleslaw, rye melba toast, and confit of duck tongue that's diced into a "1000 Island *Gastrique*" made with duck sauce, Banyuls vinegar, honey, cornichons, tarragon, and tomato.

FOR THE BRINE: Combine all the ingredients except the water in a large bowl. Bring about 250 grams of the water to a boil. Pour into the bowl and stir to dissolve the salt and sugar. Then stir in the remaining water. Chill completely.

FOR THE DUCK—60.5°C (140.9°F); 25 MINUTES

Add the duck breast to the brine and refrigerate for 3 hours.

Remove the duck from the brine, pat it dry, and place it on a rack set over a sheet pan. Refrigerate, uncovered, to dry for an hour.

To complete: Put the duck in a bag with the cold duck fat. Vacuum-pack on medium.

Cook at 60.5°C (140.9°F) for 25 minutes. Let rest at room temperature for 10 minutes.

Remove the duck from the bag and dry on C-fold towels. Cut on the diagonal into thin slices.

FOR THE COLESLAW: Combine the water, vinegar, and sugar in a saucepan and bring to a boil, stirring to dissolve the sugar. Add 25 grams of the yellow mustard seeds, the caraway seeds, peppercorns, bay leaf, and thyme. Remove from the heat and let steep for 30 minutes.

Strain the liquid into a saucepan and return to a simmer.

Put the remaining 4 grams yellow mustard seeds and the brown mustard seeds in a small bowl. Pour in just enough pickling liquid to cover the seeds. Let the seeds cool to room temperature and pickle in the liquid, then cover and refrigerate.

Meanwhile, put the cabbage, carrots, and red onion in three separate bowls. Strain the hot pickling liquid over the vegetables. The vegetables will wilt in the hot liquid. Once they are wilted, the liquid should just cover them. Let the vegetables cool to room temperature, then refrigerate overnight. The vegetables can be refrigerated for up to 2 days.

MAKES ABOUT 600 GRAMS

FOR THE DRESSING: Combine the vinegar and honey in a medium saucepan and simmer over medium heat until reduced by slightly more than half and thickened to a glaze. Add the duck sauce and simmer for about 5 minutes, or until reduced to a sauce consistency. Add the shallot, duck tongue, and cornichons and bring to a simmer over medium-high heat. Add the butter, salt and pepper to taste, and a few drops of vinegar. Remove from the heat.

Just before serving, stir in the tomato, tarragon, and brunoise.

MAKES ABOUT 150 GRAMS

FOR THE MELBA TOAST: Freeze the bread until it is firm enough to cut into thin slices on a meat slicer. Cut 4 slices and reserve additional bread for another use. Cut an oval about 2¾ by 2¼ inches from each piece of bread.

Place a Silpat on a sheet pan and brush with clarified butter. Lay down the slices of bread and sprinkle lightly with salt and caraway seeds. Butter another Silpat and place butter side down over the bread. Top with another sheet pan.

Bake at 300°F for about 18 minutes, turning the pan around halfway through the cooking, until the toasts are crisp and golden brown. Set aside.

AT SERVICE: Drain the cabbage, carrots, red onions, and pickled seeds. Toss together. Place a mound of the slaw on each serving plate. Drape each mound with overlapping slices of duck. Spoon the dressing over the duck and top each with a Melba toast. MAKES 4 SERVINGS

CONFIT OF LIBERTY PEKIN DUCK LEG, *POMMES SARLADAISE*, FRIED HEN EGG, AND FRISÉE SALAD

DUCK

1.33 kilograms kosher salt

20 black peppercorns

3 bay leaves

6 thyme sprigs

6 garlic cloves, crushed and peeled

4 Liberty Pekin duck legs
    (1.86 kilograms; see Sources, page 282)

400 grams Rendered Duck Fat (page 270),
    at room temperature or cold

Canola oil

POTATOES

4 thin slices garlic

2 thyme sprigs

2 small bay leaves

10 black peppercorns

24 Yukon Gold potato rounds about ⅜ inch thick

Kosher salt

150 grams Rendered Duck Fat (page 270)

Canola oil

25 grams unsalted butter

10 grams minced shallot

Minced flat-leaf parsley

4 medium eggs

FRISÉE SALAD

250 grams red wine vinegar

20 grams granulated sugar

20 grams Rendered Duck Fat or
    Rendered Foie Gras Fat (page 270)

Frisée leaves

Canola oil for deep-frying

All-purpose flour

Beaten eggs

Potato starch

Fleur de sel

Freshly ground black pepper

---

wo confit preparations, both done sous vide, are the focus of a dish that takes ingredients common on French bistro menus to an elegant extreme: duck confit, golden brown sautéed potatoes, fried eggs, and frisée salad. Here, as ever, sous vide is a means for achieving a perfect duck confit. It requires less fat and aromatics than traditional confits and results in a consistently succulent and tender product. Pommes Sarladaise are traditionally cooked in duck fat, then browned in a pan and finished with parsley. Here, they too are cooked sous vide in the fat until tender, then crisped just before serving.

FOR THE DUCK—82.2°C (180°F); 8 HOURS

Mix together the salt, peppercorns, bay leaves, thyme, and garlic. Pack the duck legs in the salt mixture, covering them completely, and refrigerate to cure for 6 hours.

Remove the legs from the salt mixture, rinse with cold water to remove the salt, and pat dry with C-fold towels. Remove 2 garlic cloves, 4 thyme sprigs, 1 bay leaf, and 10 peppercorns from the salt mixture (rinse and dry with C-fold towels) and make into an herb sachet (see page 269). Place in a bag with the duck fat. Add the duck to the bag.

Vacuum-pack on medium.

Cook at 82.2°C (180°F) for 8 hours. Let sit at room temperature until the duck has cooled enough to handle.

Drain the duck. Cut through the joint of each leg to separate the thigh and drumstick. Reserve the drumsticks for another use. Place one thigh meat side up on the work surface. Use a paring knife and your fingers to lift up the thigh bone, and twist the bone to remove it; discard the bone. Repeat with the remaining thighs. Place the thighs skin side up on a parchment-lined sheet pan. Top with another piece of parchment paper and another sheet pan. Place a medium weight over the top and refrigerate for at least 2 hours. (The weight should be enough to compress the duck slightly, to an even thickness.)

To complete: Trim each of the 4 thighs into pieces about 2 by 2½ inches.

Heat a film of canola oil in a sauté pan. Add the duck skin side down and cook to brown and crisp, about 5 minutes. Transfer to a plate, skin side up.

FOR THE POTATOES—85°C (185°F); 20 TO 25 MINUTES

Make 2 herb sachets (see page 269) with the garlic, thyme, bay leaves, and peppercorns. Using a cutter, trim the potato slices to make 1¼-inch rounds. Divide the potatoes between two bags, keeping them in a single layer. Stir a sprinkling of salt into the duck fat, then add half the fat and a sachet to each bag

Vacuum-pack on medium.

Cook at 85°C (185°F) for 20 to 25 minutes, until tender.

To complete: Heat about ¼ inch of canola oil in a sauté pan. Add the potatoes and cook until golden brown, about 1½ minutes on each side. Pour off the oil. Add the butter and shallot to the pan and swirl to coat the potatoes. Swirl in parsley to taste.

FOR THE EGGS: Cook the eggs in a pot of boiling water for 5 minutes, and then shock in an ice bath.

FOR THE SALAD: Bring the vinegar and sugar to a simmer in a small saucepan and reduce until the pan is almost dry. With a spoon, stir in the fat to taste to create a broken vinaigrette.

Toss the frisée with a light coating of the vinaigrette.

AT SERVICE: Heat the canola oil to 325°F. Dry the eggs, carefully peel them, then coat in flour, beaten eggs, and, finally, potato starch. Deep-fry the eggs until they are a light golden brown, about 3 minutes. Remove from the oil and drain on C-fold towels.

With a serrated knife, cut off the bottom ¼ inch of each egg to create a flat surface so the egg will stand upright. Stand each egg on a serving plate and quickly cut down through the middle of the egg. Arrange a piece of the duck on each plate. Sprinkle the eggs with fleur de sel and pepper. Overlap slices of the potatoes around the duck. Drizzle any remaining vinaigrette around the duck. Garnish with frisée salad.

MAKES 4 SERVINGS

SQUAB WITH PIQUILLO PEPPERS, MARCONA ALMONDS, FENNEL, AND MEDJOOL DATE SAUCE

SQUAB

2 squab (330 to 380 grams each)

About 200 grams kosher salt

14 grams Rendered Duck Fat (page 270)

Canola oil

65 grams Rendered Foie Gras Fat (page 270)

Sel gris

Freshly ground black pepper

18 grams ground Marcona almonds

PIQUILLO PEPPER COULIS

40 grams extra virgin olive oil

10 grams thinly sliced shallot

Kosher salt

Cayenne pepper

400 grams red bell pepper juice

225 grams whole piquillo peppers

FENNEL

1 medium fennel bulb

Extra virgin olive oil

Kosher salt

Granulated sugar

30 grams Chicken Stock (page 257)

14 grams unsalted butter

DATE PUREE

220 grams dry white wine,
  such as Sauvignon Blanc

220 grams water

210 grams granulated sugar

10 coriander seeds

10 black peppercorns

4 cloves

1 star anise

10 Medjool dates

67 grams Quick Squab Sauce (page 260)

14 grams unsalted butter, at room temperature

Dash of sherry vinegar

Kosher salt

Squab breast can be difficult to sauté because you have to cook it precisely to medium-rare—beyond that, it takes on a liver flavor and becomes dry. With sous vide, the entire cut is cooked perfectly medium-rare throughout. Sous vide is great for squab breast for this reason, and the resulting texture is far more delicate than when squab is cooked conventionally. The breast is cooked on the bone in the bag, then the meat is removed from the bone, and the tenderloin is separated from the breast and rolled in crushed almonds. The legs are given a brief cure and are confited sous vide with duck fat, then seared and crisped just before serving.

PHOTOGRAPH ON PAGE 126

FOR THE SQUAB—68°C (154.4°F); 2 HOURS

To cure and cook the legs: Lift up one of the legs of one squab and cut between the thigh and breast to remove the leg in one piece; repeat on the other side. Repeat with the remaining squab. Crack the joint between each thigh and drumstick and cut off the bottom of the drumstick so that the meat will contract and "french," exposing the bone as it cooks. Pack the legs in kosher salt to cover completely and refrigerate to cure for 30 minutes.

Remove the legs from the salt and rinse with cold water. Pat dry. Spread the duck fat in a medium bag, add the legs in one layer, and refrigerate until cold.

Vacuum-pack on medium-high.

Cook at 68°C (154.4°F) for 2 hours. Submerge the bag in an ice bath.

When the legs are cold, remove them from the bag. Cut out and remove the thigh bones. Trim the legs of excess skin, for smooth, rounded edges.

To complete: Heat a film of canola oil in a small nonstick sauté pan over medium heat. Add the squab legs skin side down and sauté gently for 2 to 3 minutes to heat through and crisp the skin.

TO PREPARE THE BREASTS: Turn one squab breast side down and make an incision through the skin just under the wings on each side of the backbone. You want to keep the wings attached to the breasts. Peel the skin off the breasts and discard. You will see a line of fat running along the bottom of each breast. With scissors, cut along the fat lines, leaving the wing bone attached to the breast. With a paring knife, remove the wishbone from the squab breast. Lift the wing up and use a sharp paring knife to cut around the first joint. Pull down the skin and flesh to reveal the bone. Using scissors, cut the bone at the top of the first joint. The bone is soft before the joint and will cut cleanly, leaving just the bone nearest the breast. Trim the breast of any remaining skin and excess fat. Repeat with the remaining squab.

Sprinkle the breasts with salt and pepper. Brush each breast with a coating of foie gras fat and refrigerate until the fat sets (reserve the remaining fat). Brush again and return to the refrigerator until very cold.

TO COOK THE BREASTS—59.5°C (139.1°F); 30 MINUTES
Place each breast in a separate bag. Vacuum-pack on medium-high.

Cook at 59.5°C (139.1°F) for 30 minutes. Let cool slightly.

To complete: Once the breasts are cool enough to handle, remove the breasts from the carcass: cut away each breast half from the bone in one piece. Remove the tenderloins and set aside. Trim a small piece off each side of the breast to bring the bottom of the breast to a point. Sprinkle the meat with sel gris and pepper.

Add a pinch of sel gris to the almonds. Roll the tenders in the almonds.

FOR THE PEPPER COULIS: Heat 13 grams of the oil in a medium saucepan over medium heat. Add the shallot and a pinch each of salt and cayenne and cook until the shallot is translucent but has not colored, about 2½ minutes. Add the pepper juice and cook over medium to medium-high heat to reduce the liquid by about three-quarters. Add the peppers and heat through.

Transfer to a Vita-Prep, add another pinch of salt, and puree. With the Vita-Prep running, drizzle in the remaining 27 grams oil. Transfer to a container, cover, and refrigerate.   MAKES ABOUT 250 GRAMS

FOR THE FENNEL—85°C (185°F); 40 MINUTES
Trim the root end and remove the stalks and outer layers from the fennel. Cut into ½-inch wedges. You will need 4 wedges for this recipe; reserve the remaining fennel for another use. Toss the fennel wedges with a drizzle of olive oil and a sprinkle of salt and sugar.

Place in a bag and vacuum-pack on medium. Cook at 85°C (185°F) for 40 minutes, or until tender. Chill the bag in an ice bath.

To complete: Combine the fennel, stock, and butter in a small saucepan; the liquid should come halfway up the fennel. Bring to a simmer over high heat. Reduce the heat to medium and simmer for 4 to 5 minutes to glaze the fennel.

FOR THE DATE PUREE: Combine the wine, water, sugar, and spices in a medium saucepan and bring to a boil over high heat, stirring to dissolve the sugar.

Put the dates in a medium bowl. Strain the hot liquid over the dates and let sit until cooled to room temperature, then drain. (The poaching liquid can be refrigerated and used again for poaching.)

Rub the skin from the dates and remove the pits. Put the dates in a Vita-Prep. The dates can be cooked and pureed ahead, but don't add the butter until just before serving. The puree should not be refrigerated.

Bring the squab sauce to a boil. Begin to puree the dates, slowly adding the sauce. Scrape down the sides. Add the butter and puree on high speed. Strain through a chinois or fine-mesh conical strainer and season to taste with sherry vinegar and salt.   MAKES ABOUT 150 GRAMS

AT SERVICE: Spoon some of the date puree and pepper coulis onto each serving plate. Arrange a wedge of fennel and a squab breast and leg on each plate. Top each piece of breast with a nut-coated tender.

MAKES 4 SERVINGS

NOTE

The foie gras fat should be at a consistency just below solidifying (like that of a soft paste) when you coat the breasts. If it is solid, warm it briefly in a bowl set in warm water.

Above: Squab with Piquillo Peppers, Marcona Almonds, Fennel, and Medjool Date Sauce (page 124);
opposite: *Pigeon aux Truffles Noires,* Candele Pasta Gratin, Brussels Sprouts, and *Sauce Périgourdine* (page 128)

PIGEON AUX TRUFFLES NOIRES, CANDELE PASTA GRATIN, BRUSSELS SPROUTS, AND SAUCE PÉRIGOURDINE

SQUAB

4 squab breast halves

1 boneless duck breast (180 grams)

Kosher salt

1 large egg yolk

5 grams minced black truffle, plus thin black
    truffle rounds (to cover the squab breasts)

7 grams white truffle oil, plus more for brushing

75 grams crème fraîche

Fleur de sel

TRUFFLE SAUCE

110 grams Veal Stock (page 255)

6 grams finely minced black truffle

Champagne vinegar

8 grams unsalted butter

3 grams white truffle oil

Kosher salt and freshly ground white pepper

BRUSSELS SPROUTS

4 small Brussels sprouts

Beurre Monté (page 261)

PASTA

2 kilograms White Veal Stock (page 255)

12 grams canola oil

62 grams unsalted butter

Kosher salt

500 grams candele pasta, handmade
    (see Pasta Dough for Extruding page 263), or
    store bought (see Sources, page 282)

Mornay Sauce (page 261)

Fleur de sel

This preparation would be very difficult to do were it not for sous vide. Squab breasts are coated with a *farce* made from duck breast, truffle, and crème fraîche, then vacuum-sealed to maintain the shape and help the *farce* to adhere to the squab. The squab is cooked *à la minute,* just before service, and it is consistent every time, so beautiful and vivid red.

The French Laundry makes its own candele, the tubular pasta used here.

PHOTOGRAPH ON PAGE 127

FOR THE SQUAB—60.7°C (141.3°F); 20 MINUTES

Remove the squab breasts from the bone. Remove and discard the skin, fat, and sinew from both the squab and the duck breasts. Lightly salt the skinned side of the squab and let it sit to sweat and release moisture that might keep the mousse from adhering to the meat.

Cut the duck into pieces and transfer to a food processor. Add the egg yolk and puree. Pass the puree through a tamis into a bowl set over an ice bath. Stir in the minced truffle and truffle oil. Stirring vigorously, add 50 grams of the crème fraîche and stir until the mousse is smooth and shiny.

Pat the squab breasts dry. Pipe the mousse in a dome onto each squab breast, or, using a small palette knife, spread the mousse over the squab in an even layer. Arrange overlapping truffle slices over the mousse on each breast to cover it.

Tear off 4 pieces of food-safe plastic wrap, each about 12 inches long, and lay on the work surface with a short end toward you. Brush each piece lightly with truffle oil. Lay one breast across the center of the bottom of one sheet of plastic wrap. Carefully roll up in the plastic so as not to disturb the layers. Gently twist one end of the plastic wrap a few times against the meat; do the same thing on the other end. Repeat with the remaining squab. Refrigerate until completely cold.

To complete: Transfer the chilled breasts to the freezer for 10 minutes to firm them and help maintain the shape of the mousse when it is sealed. Place each squab breast, still in the plastic wrap, in a bag. Vacuum-pack on medium-low.

Cook at 60.7°C (141.3°F) for 20 minutes. Remove from the water and let rest for 10 minutes.

FOR THE TRUFFLE SAUCE: Combine the veal stock, truffles, and a drop or two of vinegar in a small saucepan—you shouldn't taste the vinegar, just use it as you would use salt to enhance the other flavors. Bring to a simmer and simmer for 3 to 4 minutes, until reduced to a sauce consistency; it should coat the back of a spoon.

Swirl the butter and truffle oil into the sauce and season to taste with salt and white pepper. **MAKES ABOUT 90 GRAMS**

FOR THE BRUSSELS SPROUTS: Remove 24 whole leaves from the sprouts, and blanch (see Big-Pot Blanching, page 268). Transfer the leaves to an ice bath to chill, then drain and dry on C-fold towels.

To complete: Glaze the leaves in a little beurre monté in a sauté pan.

FOR THE PASTA: Bring the veal stock to a simmer. Heat the oil, butter, and a pinch of salt in a large roasting pan until the butter foams. Add the pasta and toss to coat. Cover the pasta with the veal stock and bring to a gentle boil. Cover with a sheet of parchment and cook until the pasta is al dente.

Remove the pasta and lay them side by side on a parchment-lined sheet pan. Gently press the pasta together.

Reduce the veal stock to a glaze and spoon over the pasta to bind the strands together. Let cool, then cut into 2- to 3-inch-squares. You will need 4 squares for this recipe; reserve the remaining pasta for another use.

To complete: Nap the surface of the 4 pasta squares with Mornay sauce. Run under the salamander to brown just before serving.

AT SERVICE: Remove the squab from the bags and plastic wrap. Carefully turn the pieces mousse side down and drain on a C-fold towel.

Trim away the two long edges of each breast. Cut each breast lengthwise in half and arrange on the serving plates. Spoon the sauce around the breasts and arrange the Brussels sprout leaves around the squab. Place a portion of pasta on each plate. Sprinkle the squab breasts with fleur de sel. **MAKES 4 SERVINGS**

"QUAIL IN A JAR"
QUAIL STUFFED WITH MOULARD DUCK FOIE GRAS, CIPOLLINI, FIGS, AND PORT WINE GLAZE

QUAIL

1 semiboneless quail (about 340 grams; see Sources, page 282)

A 185-gram pieces Grade A foie gras

Foie Gras Cure (page 267)

About 500 grams Duck Consommé (page 259)

365 grams port

2 gelatin sheets (2 grams each), soaked in cold water to soften

GARNISHES

4 cipollini (about 1½ inches in diameter), peeled

Extra virgin olive oil

Kosher salt

Granulated sugar

4 fresh figs

Baby mâche

Red wine vinegar

Sel gris

Freshly ground black pepper

Several years ago, we were participating in a benefit at the Atlanta restaurant of Gunter Seeger, one of the best French chefs in the country, and he served quail stuffed with foie gras. This is my interpretation of that idea. The stuffed quail—we get our quail from Brent Wolfe at Wolfe Ranch Quail in Dixon, California—is shaped using cheesecloth and poached in consommé, then cooled in the cooking liquid, glazed, sliced, and served cold. The quail is not sealed in a bag, so technically it's not cooked sous vide, but it is cooked in a jar with liquid whose temperature is regulated by the immersion circulator and so takes advantage of the benefits of sous vide. (The jar also serves as an intriguing presentation piece.) The glaze, made with some of the reduced consommé, both adds flavor and gives the quail an appealing lacquered finish. It is served with a sauce made from more of the reduced cuisson, fortified with a port reduction.

FOR THE QUAIL—64°C (147.2°F); 1 HOUR

Very gently, so as not to tear the skin, turn the quail body inside out, working from the neck end. Season both the inside of the quail and the foie gras with a sprinkling of the foie gras cure.

Trim the foie gras as necessary so it will fit inside the quail, keeping the piece as large as possible. Place the foie gras on the inside of the quail, and reshape the quail around the foie gras, taking care to align the breasts; the cooked quail will be sliced crosswise, so it is important to keep the shape as symmetrical as possible.

Cut a piece of cheesecloth about 24 inches long and 12 inches wide. Lay the quail across the center of the short end of the cheesecloth closest to you and, rolling it away from you, roll it up in the cheesecloth into a tight log, twisting the ends as you roll to force the quail into a compact log. If possible, have another person hold the end of the cheesecloth flat against the work surface as you roll.

Loop a length of string around your index finger. With the same hand, hold one end of the cheesecloth tightly and wind the string around the end of the quail. Continue wrapping the string about ¼ inch into the quail; this will help compress the quail into a tight roll. Tie a knot around the cheesecloth. Repeat the procedure on the other end. Tie 3 pieces of string equally spaced around the log.

Place the quail in a 1-quart Mason jar and add consommé to cover. Seal the jar. Refrigerate until cold.

Cook in the jar at 64°C (147.2°F) for 1 hour. Transfer the jar to an ice bath to chill.

Refrigerate the quail in the jar for at least a day, or up to 1 week (see photograph, page 133).

To complete: Remove the fat that has risen to the top of the jar. Carefully remove the quail from the jar, scraping the jelled consommé around the quail back into the jar. Then strain the consommé and any remaining fat through a chinois or fine-mesh conical strainer into a small saucepan. Bring to a simmer, skimming any fat from the surface of the consommé, and reduce by about half. Remove from the heat.

Meanwhile, unwrap the quail, wipe away any consommé, and trim the ends slightly. Put the quail on its end on a rack over a quarter sheet pan and refrigerate.

Pour the port into a saucepan, bring to a simmer, and reduce to a glaze. Add 50 grams of the reduced consommé and reduce again to a glaze. Set aside.

Squeeze the gelatin to remove excess water. Add the softened gelatin to the remaining consommé and stir to dissolve. Refrigerate until the consommé has set to a coating consistency.

Spoon some of the glaze over the quail and refrigerate to set. Continue to coat the quail with glaze, returning it to the refrigerator to set each time, until all the glaze is used. There will probably be enough for about 6 coatings. Let the quail sit for at least 3 more hours in the refrigerator to set completely.

FOR THE GARNISHES—85°C (185°F); 1 HOUR
Toss the onions with a drizzle of olive oil, a sprinkle of salt, and a pinch of sugar. Place in a bag and vacuum-pack on high.

Cook at 85°C (185°F) for 1 hour. Remove and chill in an ice bath.

Remove the onions from the bag, cut off the top and bottom of each one, and separate the layers into rings. Put the rings in a small bowl.

Cut 2 figs in half and quarter the remaining 2 figs. Put in a small bowl. Put the mâche in another small bowl. Toss the onions, figs, and mâche separately with a sprinkling of red wine vinegar, a pinch of salt, and a drizzle of olive oil.

AT SERVICE: Cut the quail crosswise into slices. Drizzle some glaze on each plate and top with a slice of the quail. Arrange the garnishes on the plate, and sprinkle the quail with sel gris and pepper.   **MAKES 2 SERVINGS**

Above: fig; opposite: quail being refrigerated in a jar (see page 131)

RABBIT AND BACON *PRESSÉ*, SLOW-POACHED ROYAL BLENHEIM APRICOTS, RABBIT LIVER MOUSSE, AND GREEN PISTACHIOS

RABBIT PRESSÉ

30 pieces rabbit flank

Kosher salt and freshly ground black pepper

Ajinomoto RM transglutaminase
   (see Sources, page 282)

280 grams Hobbs' Applewood Smoked Bacon,
   cut into 32 slices about 1/16 inch thick
   (setting #1½ on a slicer)

Canola oil

LIVER MOUSSE

100 grams Foie Gras Cure (page 267)

1 kilogram water, cold

4 to 5 rabbit livers (350 to 375 grams),
   excess fat removed

Canola oil

1 garlic clove, crushed and peeled

1 thyme sprig

30 grams sliced shallots

20 grams unsalted butter

120 grams dry white wine,
   such as Sauvignon Blanc

30 grams crème fraîche

APRICOTS

100 grams dry white wine,
   such as Sauvignon Blanc

105 grams granulated sugar

200 grams water

8 whole dried apricots (see headnote)

PISTACHIO BREAD CRUMBS

10 grams water

30 grams granulated sugar

8 grams liquid glucose

13 grams raw green Sicilian pistachios
   (see Sources, page 282)

25 grams fresh bread crumbs (see page 263)

Fleur de sel

Small frisée leaves

Extra virgin olive oil

Champagne vinegar

Kosher salt

This dish grew out of our desire to use every part of the animal when possible—in this case, the rabbit flank, which is somewhat tough, thin, and irregularly shaped. We end up with a lot of them because we serve other cuts of rabbit, so we wanted to find a way to turn them into something special and elegant. We first used them to make what we called rabbit andouille, rolling the flank up with bacon, tying it, and cooking it. Here we simply layer it with bacon and cut it into slices, which works beautifully. It is a perfect sous vide dish, because sealing the flanks layered with the bacon shapes the meat and holds the layers together as the meat cooks; the result almost resembles slab bacon. We can cut it into many shapes and sizes, to use as a first course or a garnish.

We make a rich mousse from the rabbit liver to complement the lean rabbit and add creaminess. The pistachio bread crumbs add textural contrast and a nutty flavor. The apricots, plumped in a syrup of white wine and sugar, give the dish sweetness and another distinct texture. We prefer a variety called Royal Blenheim, which is available in early summer and is especially sweet.

PHOTOGRAPH ON PAGE 136

FOR THE RABBIT PRESSÉ—74°C (165.2°F); 12 HOURS

Remove any sinew or cartilage from the rabbit flanks and dry them well. With a sharp paring knife, score the outside (smoother side) of each flank in a ½-inch crosshatch pattern. This will help the flanks absorb the seasoning and cook better. Season the scored side with salt and pepper. Refrigerate until very cold.

Arrange 6 rabbit flanks on a large piece of parchment paper, overlapping them slightly, to form a rectangle about 7 by 9 inches. Sprinkle with transglutaminase powder through a small basket strainer, as you would use confectioners' sugar over a soufflé. Top with a layer of 8 overlapping slices of bacon. Sprinkle again with transglutaminase powder. Continue the layering process until you have 5 layers of rabbit and 4 layers of bacon. Refrigerate until very cold.

Place the rabbit in a large bag and vacuum-pack on high (see photograph, page 137). Refrigerate for 6 hours to allow the transglutaminase to bond the layers.

Cook at 74°C (165.2°F) for 12 hours. Remove from the water and let stand just until the rabbit is almost room temperature; it is important to weight the rabbit before the bacon begins to firm. Line a sheet pan with parchment paper. Place the meat in the bag on the parchment. Top with another piece of parchment and another sheet pan. Place a heavy weight over the pan and refrigerate to chill completely.

To complete: Trim the edges of the rabbit *pressé*. Cut 8 slices about ⅛ inch thick. Cut small cubes from the remaining block.

Heat a film of canola oil in a sauté pan. Add the rabbit slices and sauté over medium-high heat for about 3 to 4 minutes to brown each side, including the edges, until rich golden brown and hot throughout. Add the cubes and brown them as well. Remove from the heat.

FOR THE LIVER MOUSSE: To make the brine, place the cure in a container that will just hold the livers. Bring about 250 grams of the water to a boil. Pour into a container and stir to dissolve the salt. Stir in the remaining cold water. Chill completely. When it is cool, submerge the livers in the brine and refrigerate for 3 hours.

Drain the livers, rinse with cold water, and dry well on C-fold towels. Heat a film of canola oil in a sauté pan over high heat. Add the livers and cook for about a minute to caramelize them on the first side. Turn, add the garlic and thyme, reduce the heat to medium, and cook until the liver is medium, a total of 2 to 4 minutes.

Remove the thyme and transfer the livers to a Vita-Prep. Add the shallots and butter to the pan and cook over gentle heat to soften the shallots, about 2 minutes. Add the wine and simmer to reduce by two-thirds. Strain the liquid through a chinois or fine-mesh conical strainer onto the livers, pressing on the solids to extract as much liquid as possible. Begin to puree the livers. Add the crème fraîche and continue to blend, scraping down the sides as necessary. When the puree is smooth,

strain through a chinois or fine-mesh conical strainer. Refrigerate the mousse until completely cold. MAKES ABOUT 300 GRAMS

FOR THE APRICOTS: Heat the wine in a saucepan until it comes to a simmer. Add the sugar and water and return to a simmer, stirring to dissolve the sugar. Add the apricots and remove from the heat.

Cover the pan with food-safe plastic wrap and run a strip of tape around the pan to seal the plastic wrap tightly. Let the pan sit in a warm area for 12 hours.

FOR THE BREAD CRUMBS: Combine the water, sugar, and glucose in a small saucepan and heat to 143°C (290°F), stirring to dissolve the sugar. Stir in the pistachios, coating them completely and evenly with the syrup. Spread the mixture on a Silpat and let cool completely and harden.

Break the sheet of praline into smaller pieces, transfer to a food processor, and pulse to chop fine.

To separate the small (bread-crumb size) pistachio crumbs, hold a coarse strainer over a chinois or fine-mesh conical strainer, add the pistachio pieces, and shake the strainers. The smaller pieces and the fine powder will fall into the fine-mesh strainer. Process the large pieces again. You need 15 grams of the pieces that fall into the fine strainer. The fine dust can be used in tuiles or as a garnish.

Toss the 15 grams of pistachios with the bread crumbs and a pinch of fleur de sel.

AT SERVICE: Drain the apricots. Toss the frisée with a few drops of olive oil, a drop of so of vinegar, and a small pinch of salt. Spread some of the bread crumb mixture on each serving plate. Top with a slice of rabbit *pressé*, a few rabbit cubes, and some mousse. Garnish each plate with frisée and an apricot. MAKES 8 SERVINGS

Above: Rabbit and Bacon *Pressé*, Slow-Poached Royal Blenheim Apricots, Rabbit Liver Mousse,
and Green Pistachios (page 134); opposite: alternating layers of rabbit and bacon

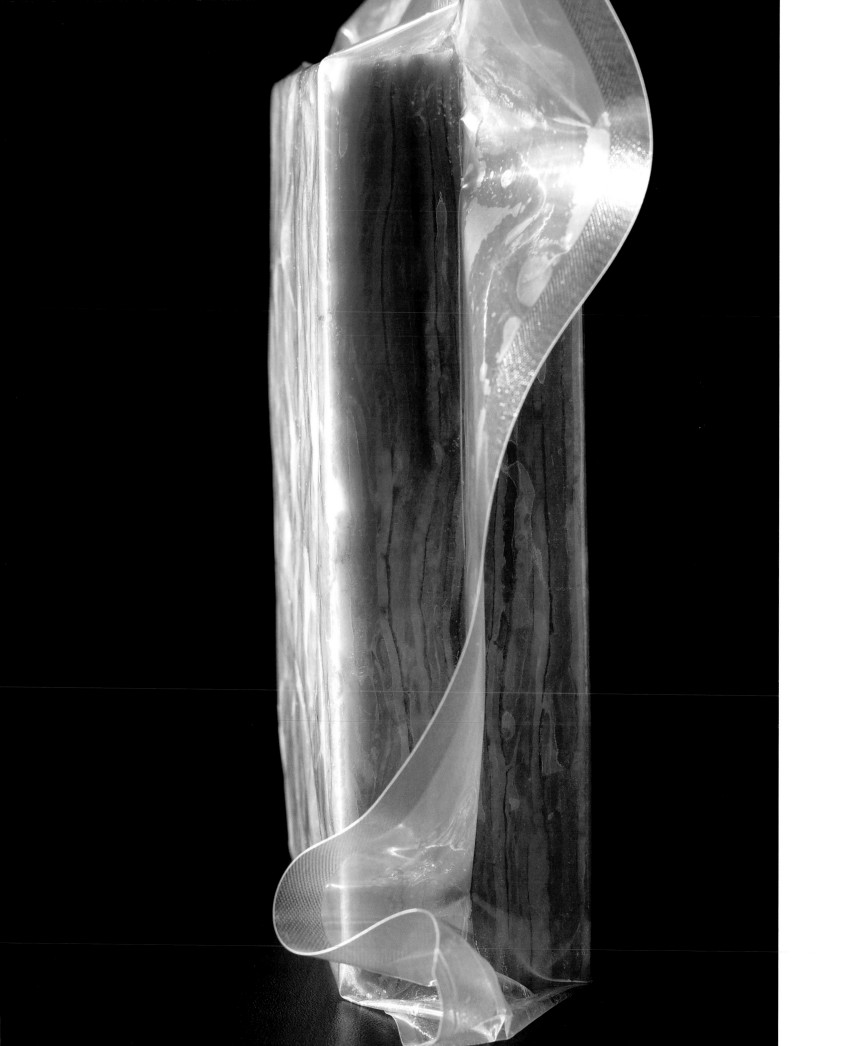

SIRLOIN OF DEVIL'S GULCH RANCH RABBIT
WRAPPED IN HOBBS' APPLEWOOD SMOKED BACON
WITH SUMMER SUCCOTASH AND CORN "PUDDING"

RABBIT

1 whole rabbit saddle, racks attached

Kosher salt and freshly ground black pepper

12 thin slices Hobbs' Applewood Smoked Bacon
(see Sources, page 282)

Canola oil

Quick Rabbit Sauce (page 260), warmed

CORN PUDDING AND SUCCOTASH

60 grams small lima beans or peeled fava beans,
germs removed

60 grams Hobbs' Applewood Smoked Bacon,
cut into ¼-inch dice

60 grams corn kernels, cold

Granulated sugar

Kosher salt

15 grams unsalted butter

380 grams corn juice (from about 8 ears of corn)

60 grams diced (¼-inch) peeled red bell pepper

60 grams diced (¼-inch) peeled yellow bell
pepper

20 Roasted Cherry Tomatoes (page 266)

Canola oil

15 grams unsalted butter

15 grams Vegetable Stock (page 260) or water

Roast rabbit loin wrapped in bacon and served with a little rack of rabbit is a classic preparation, but our version shows sous vide's power. The boneless loin is wrapped in bacon and plastic wrap and compressed into the torchon shape before it is vacuum-packed and cooked sous vide, then sliced and reheated at service. Sous vide ensures that every rabbit loin is cooked exactly the same.

The rabbit—we use rabbit from Mark Pasternack's Devil's Gulch Ranch (see Sources, page 282) in northern California—is served with a corn succotash and a corn "pudding" made from thickened corn juices. Corn is extraordinary cooked sous vide; no flavor is lost to the cooking medium.

PHOTOGRAPH ON PAGE 140

FOR THE RABBIT—64°C (147.2°F); 12 MINUTES

Remove the kidneys from the saddle and peel off the outer membrane. Refrigerate.

Separate the racks from the saddle, but leave the last rib from each rack attached to the saddle. Using kitchen shears or a sharp heavy knife, split each rack crosswise in half. Refrigerate until cold.

Use a sharp boning knife to remove the loins from the saddle, leaving the flank (flap) attached to one of the loins. The other flank can be trimmed away and used for another purpose or discarded. Clean the attached flank of excess fat and trim it to be the same length as the loin. Score the flank in a ¼-inch crosshatch pattern. Season the loins with salt and pepper. Lay the loins side by side with the trimmed loin lying on the flank. Roll the flank around both loins to form a compact cylinder.

Lay the strips of bacon side by side on a piece of parchment paper, overlapping the slices by about ¼ inch. Lay the rabbit cylinder over the bacon, running crosswise to the strips of bacon, and roll up. Trim off any excess bacon. Lay a 20-inch-long piece of food-safe plastic wrap on the work surface with a short side toward you. Lay the wrapped loins across the center and roll up in the plastic to form a compact cylinder. Tie the ends of the plastic, keeping them tight against the loin. Refrigerate until cold, then place in a bag. Vacuum-pack on medium high.

Cook the rabbit at 64°C (147.2°F) for 18 minutes. (The rabbit will be finished cooking as the bacon is crisped.) Place in an ice bath to chill. Refrigerate until 30 minutes before you are ready to complete the dish.

To complete: Heat a film of canola oil in a sauté pan over medium-high heat. Remove the rabbit loins from the plastic and add to the pan, seam side down. Cook, turning to brown the bacon well on all sides, for a total of about 5 minutes; tilt the pan occasionally and baste the rabbit with the accumulated fat. Drain on C-fold towels, then slice the loins.

Season the racks with salt and pepper, and wrap the bones in aluminum foil. Heat 15 grams oil in a sauté pan over high heat. Place the racks meat side down in the pan and brown quickly, lowering the heat if necessary to cook to medium. Add the kidneys to the pan, and cook for 3 to 4 minutes, turning the kidneys to cook evenly. Drain on C-fold towels. Slice the racks into individual chops.

FOR THE CORN PUDDING AND SUCCOTASH—85°C (185°F); 1 HOUR

Blanch the lima or fava beans (see Big-Pot Blanching, page 268). Chill in an ice bath. If the beans are larger than ¼ inch, cut them into ¼-inch brunoise.

Sauté the bacon until it is richly browned. Drain on C-fold towels.

Place the corn in a bag with a pinch of sugar, a pinch of salt, and the butter; spread the corn out in an even layer. Vacuum-pack on medium-high.

Cook at 85°C (185°F) for 1 hour.

Meanwhile, heat the corn juice in a saucepan over medium-high heat until it comes to a simmer and the starch in the juice begins to thicken it. Reduce the heat and simmer for about 7 minutes, until thickened. Add salt to taste and cook for another minute. Strain the pudding and keep warm.

To complete: Reserve 16 pieces each of the red and yellow peppers, corn, limas or favas, and tomatoes for garnish.

Heat a film of oil in a saucepan. Add the remaining red pepper and sauté for about 1 minute, or until the oil begins to take on a bit of color from the peppers. Add the bacon, the remaining yellow peppers, corn, beans, and tomatoes, the butter, and vegetable stock and heat through. Season with salt.

AT SERVICE: Spoon some of the corn pudding and rabbit sauce onto each plate. Sprinkle the kidneys with salt and pepper. Arrange the rabbit loin, chops, and kidneys on the plates and scatter the reserved vegetables around them. Serve the succotash on the side. **MAKES 4 SERVINGS**

Opposite: Sirloin of Devil's Gulch Ranch Rabbit Wrapped in Hobbs' Applewood Smoked Bacon with
Summer Succotash and Corn "Pudding" (page 138); above: *Blanquette de Veau* (page 142)

BLANQUETTE DE VEAU

SWEETBREADS

340 grams sweetbreads

Canola oil

Kosher salt and freshly ground black pepper

40 grams ¼-inch dice carrot

40 grams sliced leek
   (white and light green parts only)

40 grams ¼-inch dice onion

4 flat-leaf parsley sprigs

2 thyme sprigs

1 bay leaf

80 grams dry vermouth

440 grams White Veal Stock (page 255)

All-purpose flour

VEAL

2 veal calottes (about 350 grams each)

Kosher salt and freshly ground black pepper

100 grams sweetbread cuisson (from above)

Minced flat-leaf parsley

SAUCE

½ yellow onion, studded with 2 cloves

500 grams sweetbread cuisson (from above) or
   White Veal Stock (page 255)

50 grams Beurre Manié (page 261)

100 grams heavy cream

Kosher salt and freshly ground white pepper

Lemon juice

GARNISHES

200 grams carrot juice

2 large king trumpet mushrooms

Canola oil

20 grams unsalted butter

8 Glazed Thumbelina Carrots (page 267),
   quartered

Minced flat-leaf parsley

4 Glazed Red Pearl Onions (page 266)

4 Glazed White Pearl Onions (page 266),
   cut in half

Parsley shoots

Traditionally a blanquette is made with tough shoulder meat that is simmered in stock. For this preparation, we use the calotte, so we can serve it medium or *à point*. Sous vide is a perfect technique for this cut because it gives you a great amount of control and the capacity to introduce additional flavors from the cuisson, or cooking liquid. We use the cuisson from the sweetbreads, made with white veal stock, vermouth, and aromatics. The veal and sweetbreads are served with traditional blanquette garnishes: glazed pearl onions and carrots. **PHOTOGRAPH ON PAGE 141**

FOR THE SWEETBREADS: Soak the sweetbreads in cold water to cover for 6 hours, or overnight, changing the water at least 2 or 3 times.

Fill a large pot with lightly salted water and bring to a boil (using a large volume of water will help maintain the boil when the sweetbreads are added). Add the sweetbreads, reduce the heat slightly, and simmer for 2 minutes. Drain the sweetbreads and put them in an ice bath to cool, then drain again.

Remove any excess membrane or fat from the sweetbreads. Place them on a C-fold towel-lined baking sheet and cover with another C-fold towel, another baking sheet, and a light weight. You want the sweetbreads to compress to about ¼ inch thick, no more. Refrigerate overnight.

Heat ⅛ inch oil in a large heavy sauté pan. Lightly season the sweetbreads with salt and pepper and place them smooth side down in the hot oil. Sauté until lightly browned. Turn them and cook for an additional 2 minutes. Transfer to a plate.

Add the carrot, leek, and onion to the pan and sweat for 5 minutes. Add the parsley, thyme, bay leaf, vermouth, and stock and bring to a simmer. Return the sweetbreads to the pan and simmer for 5 minutes.

Remove the sweetbreads from the cooking liquid, and strain the liquid into a tall narrow container; discard the solids. Let the cooking liquid sit for 5 to 6 minutes to allow the fat to rise to the top. Remove the fat, add the sweetbreads to the liquid, and refrigerate until ready to finish the dish, or up to 2 days.

To complete: Remove the sweetbreads from the liquid (reserve it) and dry on C-fold towels. Separate the sweetbreads along the natural breaks into nuggets approximately 25 grams in size. Season with salt and pepper. Heat about ⅛ inch of canola oil in a small sauté pan. Dredge the sweetbreads in flour and place in the hot oil. Sauté over medium heat for about 4 to 5 minutes, until golden brown; turn and sauté on the second side for 4 to 5 minutes.

FOR THE VEAL—60.5°C (140.9°F); 15 MINUTES

Place one cap on the board fat side up. Cut away any fat, sinew, and silverskin from the surface. There is a small triangle of meat at one end of the cap that should be cut away and reserved for another use. Flip the meat over, and cut away the chain of meat that runs the length of the cap. Trim the ends of the cap to even them. Repeat with the other cap. Cut each cap in half. Refrigerate to chill completely.

To complete: Season the meat with salt and pepper. Place in a single layer in a large bag and add the sweetbread cuisson. Vacuum-pack on medium.

Cook at 60.5°C (140.9°F) for 15 minutes.

Remove the meat from the bag and drain on C-fold towels. Place the meat on a tray and heat in a 350°F oven until hot, about 3 minutes. Remove from the oven.

FOR THE SAUCE: Combine the onion and cuisson in a saucepan, bring to a simmer, and reduce by half. Strain into another saucepan and bring to a simmer, then whisk in the beurre manié. Simmer for 15 to 20 minutes to eliminate any raw flour taste and to thicken the sauce. The consistency should be like a light roux, and as you whisk, you will see the bottom of the pan.

Add the cream and reduce until the sauce is a napping consistency, about 225 to 250 grams. Season to taste with salt and white pepper.

To complete: Just before serving, rewarm if necessary and whisk in lemon juice to taste.   MAKES 225 TO 250 GRAMS

FOR THE GARNISHES: Bring the carrot juice to a boil in a small saucepan and reduce to a glaze.

Meanwhile, cut the mushrooms lengthwise in half or into quarters if very large. Score the cut sides.

To complete: Heat a film of canola oil in a sauté pan. Sauté the mushrooms until golden brown on all sides and tender. Drain on C-fold towels.

Bring the reduced carrot juice to a simmer. Whisk in the butter and strain. Stir in the glazed carrots.

AT SERVICE: Arrange a piece of veal and a piece of sweetbread on each plate. Nap the top of each piece of veal with the sauce and sprinkle with minced parsley. Garnish with the mushrooms, carrots, pearl onions, and parsley shoots.   MAKES 4 SERVINGS

TENDERLOIN OF NATURE-FED VEAL, ARTICHOKES BARIGOULE, CARAMELIZED GARLIC, PICHOLINE OLIVES, TOMATO "MARMALADE," AND BARIGOULE EMULSION

VEAL TENDERLOIN

1 veal tenderloin (about 1.2 kilograms)

Kosher salt and freshly ground black pepper

25 grams Ajinomoto FP transglutaminase
  (see Sources, page 282)

75 grams water

Canola oil

75 grams unsalted butter

2 garlic cloves, crushed and peeled

2 thyme sprigs

BARIGOULE EMULSION

Canola oil

20 grams thinly sliced shallot

50 grams dry white wine, such as Sauvignon
  Blanc

50 grams liquid from Artichokes Barigoule
  (page 266)

90 grams unsalted butter

Kosher salt

ARTICHOKES

3 Artichokes Barigoule (page 266)

Canola oil

GARLIC

6 garlic cloves, peeled, halved lengthwise,
  and germ removed

Granulated sugar

55 grams Quick Veal Sauce (page 260), warmed

60 grams Tomato Marmalade (page 80)

Picholine olive halves

Sel gris

Freshly ground black pepper

Small basil leaves

---

t's always preferable to cook larger cuts of meat whole rather than portioned, but it would be hard, for example, to roast a veal tenderloin ahead of time for service. With sous vide, we can cook the veal uniformly rare and then finish it, portion by portion, in a pan with butter, garlic, and thyme when we're ready to serve. It's simply seasoned with salt and pepper, wrapped in plastic wrap to ensure uniformity of presentation, then sealed, and cooked sous vide for a half hour.

For this dish, the veal is combined with artichokes, cooked *à la barigoule* sous vide; olives, which are a piquant counterpoint to the artichokes and veal; tomato marmalade for color, sweetness, and acidity; and caramelized garlic. The sauce is made from the barigoule poaching liquid and butter, with good acidity from the wine.

Note that there are two types of transglutaminase, RM and FP, and they're not interchangeable. For preparations that call for sprinkling it over the meat, RM must be used. For preparations in which a slurry is made, such as this one, FP must be used.

FOR THE TENDERLOIN—61°C (141.8°F); 30 MINUTES

Trim all sinew and fat from the tenderloin, being sure to remove all of it from the larger end. Generously sprinkle the tenderloin with salt and pepper on all sides. Let stand for about 10 minutes, until the meat starts to sweat.

Dry the tenderloin with C-fold towels. Mix the transglutaminase with the water to make a slurry. Lay a piece of food-safe plastic wrap about 24 inches long on the work surface with a short end toward you. Lay the tenderloin across the bottom of the plastic wrap. Rub the slurry over the surface of the meat, making sure to coat all the uneven pieces that resulted from trimming the larger end, so that they will adhere to one another. Fold the thinner end over itself to create an even piece. Roll the veal up in the plastic, keeping it in the center and rolling as tightly as possible. Holding the veal, twist one end of the plastic wrap several times against the meat, then repeat on the other end, twisting in the opposite direction, to make a perfect cylinder. Tie the ends of the plastic, keeping them tight against the veal. Refrigerate for 6 hours.

Place in a bag and vacuum-pack on medium.

Cook at 61°C (141.8°F) for 30 minutes.

To complete: Heat a generous film of canola oil in a medium sauté pan over medium-high heat until just beginning to smoke. Unwrap the veal, add to the pan, and brown on all sides, about 7 minutes. Add the butter, garlic, and thyme to the pan and cook, turning the meat and basting it on all sides, for about 2 minutes. Let the meat rest for a few minutes.

Trim off the ends of the veal, then cut the veal crosswise into thirds. Cut each piece lengthwise in half and trim as necessary to make neat rectangles.

FOR THE BARIGOULE EMULSION: Heat a film of oil in a medium saucepan. Add the shallot and sweat for about 2 minutes. Add the wine and reduce until the pan is almost dry. Add the barigoule liquid and cook until reduced by about half.

Slowly and gradually, whisk in the butter to emulsify, about 2 minutes. Strain the sauce. Season to taste with salt, and keep warm.

MAKES ABOUT 100 GRAMS

FOR THE ARTICHOKES: Cut each of the artichoke hearts into 6 equal wedges. Heat a film of oil in a small sauté pan over medium heat. Add the artichokes and lightly brown on all sides, about 5 minutes.

FOR THE GARLIC: Put the garlic in a small saucepan, cover with cold water, and bring to a boil over medium heat. Drain. Return the garlic to the pan, cover with cold water, and bring to a boil; drain. Repeat a third time, but simmer until the garlic is tender; drain.

To complete: Put the garlic in a pan with a pinch of sugar and about 25 grams of water. Bring to a simmer and simmer until the water has evaporated and the garlic has caramelized to a golden brown.

AT SERVICE: Spoon some barigoule sauce onto each plate and add a piece of veal. Garnish with the tomato marmalade, artichokes, olives, and garlic. Add a small spoonful of veal sauce and sprinkle with sel gris and pepper. Scatter over some basil leaves.
MAKES 6 SERVINGS

Opposite: apple balls; above: Glazed Breast of Pork with Swiss Chard, White-Wine-Poached Granny Smith Apples, and Green Mustard Vinaigrette (page 148)

GLAZED BREAST OF PORK WITH SWISS CHARD, WHITE-WINE-POACHED GRANNY SMITH APPLES, AND GREEN MUSTARD VINAIGRETTE

PORK

1 thyme sprig

1 bay leaf

5 black peppercorns

1 brined Pork Belly (page 265)

265 grams Chicken Stock (page 257),
   plus more if needed

Canola oil

75 grams Quick Pork Sauce (page 260)

30 grams unsalted butter

APPLE BALLS

25 grams water

25 grams dry white wine,
   such as Sauvignon Blanc

25 grams granulated sugar

1 to 2 large Granny Smith apples

CHARD STEMS

1 large red rainbow chard stem
   (or several smaller stems)

1 large white rainbow chard stem
   (or several smaller stems)

1 large yellow rainbow chard stem (or several
   smaller stems)

3 bay leaves

3 thyme sprigs

3 small garlic cloves, peeled

15 grams olive oil, plus more for finishing

Kosher salt and freshly ground white pepper

Champagne vinegar

CHARD GREENS

A 30-gram piece of carrot

A 20-gram piece of celery

4 grams thyme sprigs

1 fresh bay leaf

30 grams canola oil

A 50-gram chunk of slab bacon

40 grams minced sweet onion

8 grams minced garlic

5 grams unsalted butter

275 grams rainbow chard greens,
   cut into 2-inch squares

125 grams Vegetable Stock (page 260)

Kosher salt

VINAIGRETTE

50 grams green apple mustard
   (see Sources, page 282)

10 grams Dijon mustard

10 grams honey

60 grams extra virgin olive oil

5 grams cider vinegar

50 grams Quick Pork Sauce (page 260), warmed

Sel gris

Freshly ground black pepper

Pork belly is one of the very best cuts to cook sous vide because you can cook it long enough at a low temperature that the fat, one of the great pleasures of this cut, remains intact but the belly becomes exquisitely tender. We take a brined pork belly, with its enhanced color and flavor, and cook it sous vide, then remove the skin, and cook the pork in pork sauce until the stock is reduced to a glaze, which gives the meat a beautiful lacquered sheen.

The Swiss chard greens are braised with onion and bacon, and the stems are cooked sous vide. In a sous vide bag, the stems absorb flavor like a sponge, so you have to be careful not to add too many aromatics. Granny Smith apple balls cooked sous vide in a poaching liquid become tender but not at all mushy, another advantage of using sous vide for fruit. To complete the dish, a simple Dijon vinaigrette. PHOTOGRAPH ON PAGE 147

FOR THE PORK—82.2°C (180°F); 12 HOURS

Make an herb sachet (see page 269) with the thyme, bay leaf, and peppercorns. Place the pork in a bag and add 250 grams of the chicken stock and the herb sachet. Vacuum-pack on medium.

Cook at 82.2°C (180°F) for 12 hours. Submerge the bag in an ice bath. Once it is cooled, refrigerate until chilled.

Drain the pork and cut off and discard the skin and excess fat from the top of the slab, leaving a thin layer of fat. Trim the belly into a straight-edged block; it should have a finished weight of about 285 grams.

To complete: Cut the slab of pork lengthwise into 4 pieces. Heat a film of oil in a sauté pan over medium-high heat. Add the slices of pork and sauté for about 3 to 4 minutes, until a rich golden brown on all sides and edges. Drain on C-fold towels.

Bring the pork sauce and the remaining 15 grams chicken stock to a simmer in a small sauté pan. Add the pork and bring the liquid to a simmer. Simmer, spooning the liquid over the pork pieces as it reduces to glaze the pork, until the glaze has thickened and the pork is hot. (If the sauce becomes too thick, add more chicken stock.) Swirl the butter into the pan until melted, and remove from the heat.

FOR THE APPLES—85°C (185°F); 30 MINUTES

Combine the water, wine, and sugar in a medium saucepan and bring to a boil over medium heat, stirring to dissolve the sugar. Pour into a metal bowl set over an ice bath to chill. Making the poaching liquid first means you can put the apple balls directly into the cold syrup and you will not have to hold them in acidulated water as you cut them.

Cut off both ends from each apple and peel the apples. Using a #18 melon baller, cut 12 balls and add to the cold poaching liquid.

Transfer the poaching liquid and apples to a bag. Vacuum-pack on high.

Cook at 85°C (185°F) for 30 minutes. Place the bag in an ice bath to chill completely.

FOR THE CHARD STEMS—85°C (185°F); 1¼ HOURS

Cut all the stems into matchsticks about 2¼ inches long and ½ inch wide. You will need 4 matchsticks of each color. Place each color in a separate small bag. Make 3 herb sachets (see page 269) with the bay leaves, thyme, and garlic cloves and add one to each bag. Mix the oil with a little salt and white pepper and divide among the bags.

Vacuum-pack on medium-high.

Cook at 85°C (185°F) for 1¼ hours. Place the bags in an ice bath to chill completely.

To complete: Trim the pieces of chard stem so that they are all the same size, about 2 inches long by ⅜ inch wide. Put the stems of each color of chard in a separate small pan with a pinch each of salt and white pepper, a drizzle of olive oil, and a few drops of champagne vinegar. Warm over low heat.

FOR THE CHARD GREENS:

Tie the carrot, celery, thyme, and bay leaf together with a piece of kitchen twine to make a bouquet garni. Heat a large pot over medium-high heat and add the oil. Add the bacon and onion to the pot and stir, then add the garlic and bouquet garni and stir to keep the onion and garlic from browning. After about 30 seconds, when the vegetables are fragrant, add the butter, stirring constantly as it melts and foams. Add the chard, reduce the heat, and cook the chard gently, stirring constantly, until it has wilted, 1 to 2 minutes.

Add the stock, cover with a parchment lid (see page 270), and transfer to a 350°F oven. After about 15 minutes, stir the greens, then continue to cook, for a total of 30 minutes.

Set the pot on a burner, bring the liquid to a boil, and cook, uncovered, to reduce the liquid and coat the chard.

Line a sheet pan with parchment paper and spread the chard on it. Let cool, then finely chop.

To complete: Reheat the greens in a saucepan and season to taste with salt.

FOR THE VINAIGRETTE:

Whisk the apple mustard and Dijon mustard together. Whisk in the honey, followed by the olive oil and vinegar.

MAKES 135 GRAMS

AT SERVICE: Spoon some pork sauce and vinaigrette onto each plate. Place a piece of the pork belly on each plate and spoon some of the glaze from the pan over the top. Arrange the apple balls and chard around the pork. Sprinkle the pork with sel gris and pepper. **MAKES 4 SERVINGS**

Opposite: white peaches; above: *Saucisson à l'Ail,* Shaved Cornichons, Compressed White Peach, Pickled Pearl Onions, and Dijon Mustard (page 152)

SAUCISSON À L'AIL, SHAVED CORNICHONS, COMPRESSED WHITE PEACH, PICKLED PEARL ONIONS, AND DIJON MUSTARD

SAUCISSON À L'AIL

700 grams lean pork

300 grams fatback

12 grams Hobbs' Curing Salt

    (see Sources, page 282)

5 grams kosher salt

2 grams freshly ground white pepper

2 grams quatre-épices

0.6 grams freshly grated nutmeg

3 grams polyphosphate (see Sources, page 282)

40 grams minced garlic

Dijon mustard

Finely ground panko crumbs

    (ground in a food processor)

Minced flat-leaf parsley

Canola oil

PICKLED PEARL ONIONS

16 white pearl onions, peeled

200 grams water

100 grams champagne vinegar

100 grams granulated sugar

4 grams yellow mustard seeds

1 bay leaf

6 black peppercorns

Extra virgin olive oil

Kosher salt

COMPRESSED PEACH

110 grams granulated sugar

110 grams water

1 large peach

30 grams Dijon mustard

10 to 15 grams water

4 cornichons

Baby mustard greens

Extra virgin olive oil

Kosher salt

Fleur de sel

This is a classic garlic sausage, made with plenty of fat to give it flavor and succulence. It's cooked in what is more or less a block, cooled, and then sliced (though it could be diced or cut into another shape, depending on how you wanted to serve it). To finish, we give it a brushing of mustard and coat it with panko, for additional flavor and texture. The sausage is cooked sous vide at what is the desired final temperature, so it loses very little moisture and fat, and it remains juicy.

We serve it with typical accompaniments—pickled onions and cornichons—but also with a peach that has been compressed sous vide in a simple syrup. The peach adds vibrancy, a fresh fruity flavor, and an intriguing color to the dish, and it's an excellent flavor pairing with mustard. **PHOTOGRAPH ON PAGE 151**

FOR THE SAUCISSON—70°C (158°F); 2 HOURS

Cut the pork and fatback into ½-inch dice and place in a bowl. Add both salts, the pepper, quatre-épices, and nutmeg, toss, and refrigerate overnight.

Set up a grinder with a ⅜-inch die. Add the polyphosphate to the pork and mix well. The pork should be very, very cold. Run it through the grinder. (The red meat and white fat should remain separate as the mixture comes through the die; if the fat begins to smear and melt, the ingredients were not cold enough.) Refrigerate the sausage until very cold.

Run some ice through the grinder to clean it and chill it. Replace the die with an ⅛-inch die. Run the cold sausage through the grinder as before into a mixer bowl. Refrigerate until very cold.

Put the garlic in a small saucepan, cover with cold water, and bring to a boil. Drain. Repeat 2 more times, simmering the garlic until tender the last time. Drain.

Fit the mixer with the paddle attachment and attach the mixer bowl of sausage. Mix the garlic with the sausage just until incorporated; the meat should have an almost elastic quality to it. Refrigerate to chill completely.

Place the sausage into a large bag and press on the sausage, through the bag, to work out any air bubbles. Lay the bag flat on the table and, using a pastry scraper, scrape the sausage downward through the plastic to clean the inside of the bag and compress the sausage into a block about 6 by 9 by 1¼ inches. Refrigerate until cold.

Vacuum-pack on medium-high. If there are still a lot of air bubbles, scrape the sausage with a pastry scraper as before. Use the tip of a paring knife to poke holes through the bag, and slightly into the meat, wherever any air bubbles remain. Remove the sausage from the bag and pack into a clean bag. (It will be easier to place with one of the short sides of the sausage rectangle resting on the bottom of the bag.) Vacuum-pack on medium.

Cook at 70°C (158°F) for 2 hours. Submerge the bag in an ice bath and refrigerate until serving time.

To complete: Remove the sausage from the bag and cut into 5-by-1¼-by-⅝-inch slices, weighing about 55 grams. (You need 8 slices for this recipe; there will be extra sausage for another use.) Brush the top and bottom of each slice with a light coating of Dijon mustard. Mix together the panko crumbs and parsley. Dip the top and bottom of each slice of sausage into the mixture.

Heat a film of canola oil in a nonstick sauté pan over medium-high heat. Add the sausage and cook for 2 to 2½ minutes per side, or until golden brown and heated through. Drain on C-fold towels.

FOR THE PICKLED ONIONS: Bring a small saucepan of water to a boil. Add the onions and simmer until they are tender. Drain and transfer to a container.

Combine the 200 grams water, the vinegar, sugar, mustard seeds, bay leaf, and peppercorns in another small saucepan and bring to a simmer, stirring to dissolve the sugar. Pour over the onions. Refrigerate for several hours or longer.

To complete: Drain the pickled onions and dry. Cut the onions in half and remove the centers, leaving a shell of the outer layers of onion. (Discard the centers or reserve for another use.) Toss the shells with a few drops of olive oil and a sprinkling of salt.

FOR THE COMPRESSED PEACH: Combine the sugar and water in a small saucepan and bring to a simmer, stirring to dissolve the sugar. Chill over an ice bath or in the refrigerator until cold.

Peel the peach, cut it in half, and remove the pit. Place the peach halves and syrup in a bag and vacuum-pack at medium. Set aside at room temperature for 2 hours.

AT SERVICE: Mix the mustard with the water to thin it as desired. Slice the cornichons on a Japanese mandoline lengthwise into thin ribbons. Drain and dry the peach and cut into shapes. Toss the baby mustard greens with a few drops of olive oil and a little salt.

Brush the thinned mustard down one side of each serving plate. Place a slice of sausage on each plate and sprinkle with fleur de sel. Arrange the pickled onions, peach pieces, and cornichon slices around, and garnish with the mustard greens.　　　　**MAKES 8 SERVINGS**

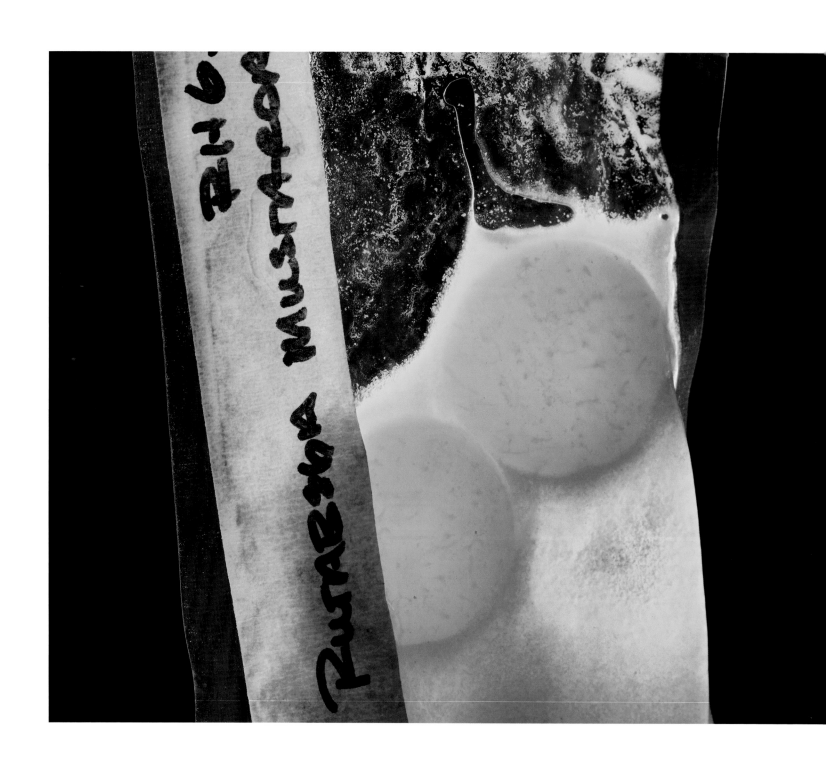

Dégustation de Porcelet, Rutabaga Mostarda, Wilted Mustard Greens, and Potato "Mille-Feuille" (page 156)

DÉGUSTATION DE PORCELET, RUTABAGA MOSTARDA, WILTED MUSTARD GREENS, AND POTATO "MILLE-FEUILLE"

RUTABAGA MOSTARDA

500 grams Simple Syrup (page 267)

5 grams Colman's dry mustard

1 gram turmeric

4 grams yellow mustard seeds

4 grams brown mustard seeds

60 grams grated fresh horseradish

5 small dried red chiles

24 rounds of peeled rutabaga, about 1⅛ inches in
    diameter and ¼ inch thick

15 grams unsalted butter

PORK BELLY

1 brined baby Pork Belly (about 225 grams),
    (see page 265; double the quantities for
    the brine)

Canola oil

PORK LEG AND SHOULDER CONFIT

2 baby pork legs (about 1.2 kilograms each)

2 baby pork shoulders (about 1.2 kilograms each)

3 kilograms kosher salt

60 grams garlic cloves, smashed, skin left on

4 grams bay leaves

4 grams thyme sprigs, plus 2 additional sprigs

20 grams black peppercorns

6 grams juniper berries

8 grams coriander seeds

1 kilogram lard or Rendered Duck Fat
    (page 270)

Caul fat, soaked in cold water for 30 minutes

Kosher salt and freshly ground black pepper

Canola oil

30 grams unsalted butter

2 rosemary sprigs

PORK RACKS AND SADDLE

2 baby pork racks, frenched

1 baby pork saddle, flaps still attached

Kosher salt and freshly ground black pepper

Ajinomoto RM transglutaminase
    (see Sources, page 282)

40 grams extra virgin olive oil

2 thyme sprigs

2 garlic cloves, peeled

Canola oil

15 grams unsalted butter

POTATOES

5 large russet potatoes

Clarified Butter (page 261)

Kosher salt and freshly ground black pepper

MUSTARD GREENS

20 grams unsalted butter

100 grams mustard greens

Kosher salt

Granulated sugar

5 grams finely minced shallot

200 grams Chicken Stock (page 257)

Quick Pork Sauce (page 260), warmed

This *dégustation* involves five cuts from a baby pig: a slice of loin, a double chop, a piece of belly, and a confit of shoulder and leg. For the confit, the pork is cured for eight hours with salt and aromatics, then cooked sous vide with lard. The meat, now falling-apart tender, is shaped, covered with a piece of skin that's been scraped of excess fat, wrapped in caul fat, and sautéed until very crisp. It's paired with a mostarda, a traditional Italian condiment or preserve, defined by its sweet and spicy flavors. Here we make a syrup with Colman's mustard, mustard seed, tumeric, horseradish, and chiles and use it to cook the very porous rutabaga sous vide (this works great with turnips and pears as well). The sweet-spicy mustardy flavor is a perfect match for the various cuts of rich, savory pork and the crisp potato.

To make this dish, you need 1 baby pig weighing about 10.5 kilograms, broken down into belly, shoulders, legs, racks, and saddle. **PHOTOGRAPH ON PAGE 155**

Bring the simple syrup to a simmer. Whisk in the dry mustard and turmeric, stir in the mustard seeds, horseradish, and chiles, and return to a simmer. Remove from the heat and let the liquid cool at room temperature to infuse the flavors. Refrigerate to chill completely.

Divide the rutabaga and syrup between two bags. Vacuum-pack on medium.

Cook at 85°C (185°F) for 2 hours. Let rest at room temperature for 10 minutes, then chill the bags in an ice bath and refrigerate. The mostarda is best made 1 to 2 days ahead.

To complete: Drain the rutabaga, reserving the liquid. Strain the liquid into a saucepan, bring to a boil over high heat, and boil to reduce to a glaze.

Meanwhile, reheat the rutabaga in another pan. Add the butter to the glaze and swirl the pan to incorporate. Pour the glaze over the rutabaga. Serve warm or at room temperature.

FOR THE PORK BELLY—82.2°C (180°F); 12 HOURS

Place the brined pork belly in a bag and vacuum-pack on medium.

Cook at 82.2°C (180°F) for 12 hours. Let rest for about 10 minutes, then submerge the bag in an ice bath. Once it is cold, refrigerate until thoroughly chilled.

Drain the pork and cut off and discard the skin and excess fat from the top of the slab, leaving a thin layer of fat. Trim into a straight-edged block.

To complete: Cut the slab of pork into 8 serving pieces. Heat a film of oil in a sauté pan over medium-high heat. Add the pieces of pork belly and sauté for about 3 to 4 minutes, until a rich golden brown on all sides and edges. Drain on C-fold towels.

FOR THE PORK LEGS AND SHOULDERS—80°C (176°F); 8 HOURS

Trim away and discard any silverskin from the legs and shoulders.

To make the cure, mix the salt, garlic, bay leaves, 4 grams thyme sprigs, and spices. Transfer one-quarter of the cure to a 6-inch square or round plastic container. Add the pork legs and shoulders and cover with the remaining cure mix. Cover tightly and refrigerate for 8 hours.

Remove the legs and shoulders from the cure and rinse well.

Transfer the cure to a chinois or fine-mesh conical strainer and run under warm water to dissolve the salt; transfer the herbs and spices to a tray. Separate the garlic, bay, thyme, and spices. Reserve 4 garlic cloves and 4 bay leaves. Divide the thyme and the spices into 4 portions. Make 4 herb sachets (see page 269) with the bay leaves, garlic, thyme, and spices. Place the shoulders and legs in separate bags and add 250 grams of the lard and an herb sachet to each one. Vacuum-pack on medium.

Cook for 8 hours at 80°C (176°F). Let rest at room temperature for 15 minutes.

Remove the meat from the bags. Carefully pull away the skin from each shoulder and leg, trying to keep it in one piece. Carefully make one cut down to the bone in each piece and debone the meat, keeping it in one piece and maintaining the shape as much as possible.

Line a sheet pan with parchment paper. Place the meat on the pan, cover with another piece of parchment paper, and top with another sheet pan. Put a heavy weight on the pan to compress the meat and refrigerate overnight.

This confit will yield 25 to 30 servings, but for this dish you need only 8 portions; reserve the remaining confit for another use. Cut one of the pieces of meat in half and then cut each half crosswise into 4 squares, about 1 to 1¼ inches on each side, 55 grams each. Cut the squares as neatly as possible, but do not be worried if you need to do some patching of meat; it will be wrapped in caul fat and retain its shape.

Use a paring knife to scrape the excess fat and sinew from the underside of the pieces of skin. Place outer side down on a cutting surface, trim the edges evenly, and cut into 1½-inch-square pieces (slightly larger than the meat). Place a piece of meat on each piece of skin.

Lay a 4-inch-square piece of caul fat on the work surface. Place a piece of pork skin side down on the caul fat and wrap it in the fat, trimming the caul fat so the edges just overlap slightly. Place a piece of food-safe plastic wrap on the work surface (it should be large enough to enclose the pork, allowing an overhang on either end of the pork). Place the wrapped pork skin side down on the bottom of the piece of plastic wrap and roll it up in the wrap, pushing both ends of the pork gently toward the center from time to time as you wrap, to shape the pork. Fold the ends of the plastic underneath the pork. Repeat with the remaining pork.

Refrigerate the pork overnight, or freeze for long enough to set the shape.

To complete: Remove the plastic wrap and sprinkle the pork with salt and pepper. Heat a film of canola oil in a sauté pan over low heat. Place the pork skin side down in the pan and cook for about 3 minutes, until browned. Transfer the pan to a 350°F oven and cook for 3 minutes, then turn the meat over and cook for another 3 minutes. Remove the pan from the oven, set over medium heat, and add the butter, rosemary, and thyme. Cook, basting the meat, for about 2 minutes.

FOR THE PORK RACKS AND SADDLE—60.5°C (140.9°F); 20 MINUTES

Tie the racks: Trim any silverskin from the racks. Each bone will be tied twice, once on either side of the bone. Place the rack meat side down, with the bones toward you. Run a piece of twine under the meat, bring the twine up on one side of the bone, and tie the end of the chop. Repeat to tie the bone in one direction. Place another piece of twine on the other side of the bone and tie on the opposite diagonal. (By making one loop from left to right and then a second from right to left, you create an X, which holds the bone in place.) Repeat on all the chops. The racks will weigh about 150 grams each. Refrigerate until ready to cook.

Prepare the loins and tenderloin: Leaving the skin attached to the meat, use a sharp boning knife to remove the loins and tenderloins from the saddle. Trim any silverskin. Trim the flaps (flanks) attached to the loin to 1 inch wide (the flaps should be long enough to wrap around the loin once). Remove any muscle that would cause the meat to contract during cooking.

Trim the ends of the meat to even them. Season the loins and tenderloins with salt and pepper. Place the loins skin side down and score the interior of the flaps in a ⅜-inch crosshatch pattern. Using a small basket strainer, sprinkle the meat with the transglutaminase, as you would confectioners' sugar. Lay a tenderloin lengthwise over each loin. Roll up the tenderloins in the flaps and tie the pork with twine every ¾ inch, so it will hold its shape. The loins will weigh about 180 grams each. Refrigerate for 6 hours to allow the transglutaminase to bond the meat.

To cook: Season the loins and racks on all sides with salt and pepper. If desired, for an added measure of safety, wrap the bones in C-fold towels to prevent them from puncturing the bag. Place both racks in one large bag and both loins in another, leaving space between them. Add half the olive oil, 1 thyme sprig, and 1 garlic clove to each bag. Vacuum-pack on medium.

Cook at 60.5°C (140.9°F) for 20 minutes. Remove from the water and let rest for 5 minutes, then remove the pork from the bags and place on a cooling rack set over a sheet pan.

To complete: Wrap the bones of the racks with aluminum foil. Heat a film of canola oil in a large sauté pan over medium heat. Add the pork loins and cook gently, rolling them from time to time so they cook evenly, for about 6 minutes. Add the racks meat side down and turn up the heat to brown the meat. After 1½ minutes, add the butter to the pan and turn the racks to brown the other side. Tilt the pan and baste the meat. Remove the racks to a cooling rack to rest after they have cooked for about 3 minutes total, and continue to cook and baste the loins for about another 2 minutes. Remove to the cooling rack and spoon some of the butter over the top of all of the meat.

After the racks have rested 10 minutes, use a small pair of scissors to remove the string. Cut away and remove every other bone from the racks. Cut each rack into 4 double chops. Cut each loin crosswise into 4 pieces.

FOR THE POTATOES: Peel the potatoes. Use a "2 in 1" vegetable slicer (see Sources, page 282) to cut slices of the potatoes into long strips. Brush the bottom of a 6-by-4-inch terrine mold with clarified butter. Layer the potatoes in the mold, brushing every layer with clarified butter and seasoning every other layer with salt and pepper, until they are about 2 inches high. Brush the top with butter and season with salt and pepper.

Bake at 350°F for 1 hour. Remove from the oven and place a piece of parchment paper over the top of the potatoes, place another pan on top and weight with bricks. Refrigerate until cold.

Unmold the cold potato mille-feuille and cut into rectangles about 1½ inches long and 1 inch wide. You need 4 rectangles for this recipe; reserve the remaining potatoes for another use.

To complete: Heat about ⅛ inch of clarified butter in a sauté pan over medium heat. Add the potato batons and cook to heat through and brown on all sides. Glaze the potatoes with butter.

FOR THE MUSTARD GREENS: Melt the butter in a sauté pan over medium heat. Add the greens, sprinkle with a pinch each of salt and sugar, and cook, turning constantly with tongs, until the greens are wilted, about 2 minutes. Stir in the shallot and cook for a few seconds. Add the chicken stock, bring to a boil, and boil gently until the stock reduces and glazes the mustard greens, 8 to 10 minutes.

AT SERVICE: Spoon some pork sauce onto each serving plate. Arrange the pieces of belly, rack, loin, and the squares of confit on the plates. Place some mustard greens, a piece of potato mille-feuille, and some mostarda on each plate.

MAKES 8 SERVINGS

MEDALLIONS OF ELYSIAN FIELDS FARM LAMB SADDLE, GARDEN VEGETABLES, AND BAGNA CAUDA SAUCE

SAUCE

Canola oil

½ Meyer lemon

25 grams extra virgin olive oil

10 grams minced garlic

15 grams finely chopped shallot

10 grams flat-leaf parsley sprigs,
    cut into ½-inch pieces

Kosher salt

38 grams red wine vinegar

8 grams salt-packed anchovy, rinsed

500 grams Veal Stock (page 255)

500 grams Lamb Stock (page 256)

20 grams Roasted Garlic Puree (page 266)

50 grams unsalted butter

1 gram grated lemon zest

Sherry vinegar

Finely chopped flat-leaf parsley

LAMB SADDLE

1 split bone-in Elysian Fields Farm lamb saddle,
    flank attached (see Sources, page 282)

Kosher salt and freshly ground black pepper

Ajinomoto RM transglutaminase
    (see Sources, page 282)

15 grams extra virgin olive oil

2 garlic cloves, smashed and peeled

2 thyme sprigs

Canola oil

50 grams unsalted butter

VEGETABLES

Canola oil

25 grams cauliflower florets,
    cut into ¼-inch pieces

25 grams ¼-inch pieces carrot

25 grams ¼-inch pieces yellow bell pepper

25 grams ¼-inch pieces red bell pepper

25 grams ¼-inch pieces cardoon

25 grams ¼-inch pieces fennel

1 Artichoke Barigoule (page 266),
    cut into ¼-inch pieces

Kosher salt and freshly ground black pepper

Sel gris

B*agna cauda*, literally "hot bath," is a traditional Italian sauce of anchovies, garlic, olive oil, and butter that is served warm as a dipping sauce for various vegetables, such as cardoons and fennel. In this lamb dish, bagna cauda components become the garnish—vegetables with a sauce of olive oil, lemon juice, vinegar, shallot, garlic, and anchovy. The strong flavor of the lamb is enhanced by the strong flavors in the sauce. We cook the lamb to rare sous vide and finish it in a hot pan to caramelize, then serve it atop the sauce and vegetables.

Our lamb Is grown by Keith Martin of Elysian Fields Farm, a very special farmer and a longtime friend. Not only do we think his lamb is the best in the country, we admire him for his work generally in raising the standards of animal husbandry and in enlisting other farmers near him in western Pennsylvania to adopt his protocols.

FOR THE SAUCE: Heat a film of canola oil in a small sauté pan over medium heat. Place the lemon half cut side down in the sauté pan and cook for about 30 minutes, swirling the pan occasionally, to slowly caramelize the lemon. If the lemon begins to brown too quickly, lower the heat or place the pan on a diffuser. Set aside.

Heat 20 grams of the olive oil in a medium saucepan over medium heat. Add the garlic, shallot, and parsley, sprinkle with salt, and sweat the vegetables for 2 to 3 minutes. Add the vinegar and cook until it has reduced slightly, about 2 minutes. Add the anchovy and cook, stirring and breaking up the anchovy, until the vinegar has cooked off and only the olive oil remains in the pan.

Strain the veal and lamb stocks through a chinois or fine-mesh conical strainer onto the anchovy mixture, bring to a simmer, and simmer, skimming as necessary, for 20 minutes.

Strain the sauce, swirling the chinois, into a container; do not press on the solids. Discard the solids, rinse the chinois, and strain the sauce. Again rinse the chinois and strain a final time into a clean saucepan. Add the lemon half and simmer for about 50 minutes, until it has the consistency of a light sauce; strain the sauce into a clean saucepan every 10 to 15 minutes or whenever a ring of accumulated sauce gathers on the sides of the pan.

To complete: Bring the reduced sauce to a simmer in a small saucepan over medium heat. Whisk in the garlic puree, followed by the butter, the remaining 5 grams olive oil, the lemon zest, and a few drops of sherry vinegar. Season to taste with salt. Just before serving, sprinkle in the parsley.

MAKES ABOUT 350 GRAMS

FOR THE LAMB SADDLE—60.5°C (140.9°F); 35 MINUTES
Bone the lamb saddle, removing the loin and tenderloin. With the meat side down, cut the flank away from the fat, leaving the fat attached to the loin. Reserve the flank for another use. Trim any silverskin. Trim the fat to ⅛-inch thick. Score the outside of the fat in a ¼-inch crosshatch pattern. Season the loin and tenderloin on all sides with salt and pepper. Turn it fat side down and, using a small basket strainer, sprinkle with a dusting of transglutaminase, as if dusting with confectioners' sugar. Top with the tenderloin. Trim the fat to square off, leaving enough to enclose the meat. Roll to make an even piece and tie with twine at 1-inch intervals. Refrigerate for 6 hours to bond the pieces of meat.

Make an herb sachet (see page 269) with 1 garlic clove and 1 thyme sprig. Place the lamb in a bag with the olive oil and herb sachet. Vacuum-pack on medium.

Cook at 60.5°C (140.9°F) for 35 minutes. Remove the lamb from the bag and pat dry on C-fold towels.

To complete: Generously salt and pepper the meat. Heat a film of canola oil in a medium sauté pan over medium-high heat. Once the oil is shimmering, add the lamb and brown on all sides, for about 3 minutes total.

Drain all but about 30 grams of the fat from the pan and reduce the heat to medium. Add the butter, the remaining thyme sprig, and the remaining garlic clove and cook, turning the meat and basting on all sides, for about 2 minutes. Transfer to a rack and let rest for 5 to 10 minutes.

Cut the lamb into 4 equal medallions.

FOR THE VEGETABLES: Heat a film of canola oil in a sauté pan. Sauté the cauliflower, carrot, peppers, cardoon, and fennel individually, until tender. Combine all the vegetables, add the artichoke, and heat until warmed. Season to taste with salt and pepper.

AT SERVICE: Spoon some sauce onto each plate. Top with a bed of the vegetables and a medallion of lamb. Sprinkle the lamb with sel gris.

MAKES 4 SERVINGS

Left: Sirloin of Prime Beef, Spring Garlic Cloves, Glazed Carrots, Cèpes, Bone Marrow, and Bordelaise Syrup (page 164); right: the finished pommes maxim (see page 165)

SIRLOIN OF PRIME BEEF, SPRING GARLIC CLOVES, GLAZED CARROTS, CÈPES, BONE MARROW, AND BORDELAISE SYRUP

BEEF

400 grams trimmed prime beef sirloin, cold

Kosher salt and freshly ground black pepper

Canola oil

15 grams unsalted butter

2 garlic cloves, peeled

1 thyme sprig

POMMES MAXIM

325 grams Yukon Gold potato, peeled

Kosher salt

6 grams cornstarch

Clarified Butter (page 261)

BONE MARROW SAUCE

500 grams White Veal Stock (page 255)

10 grams thinly sliced shallot

5 black peppercorns

1 thyme sprig

2 grams xanthan gum (see Sources, page 282)

34 grams crème fraîche

55 grams Rendered Bone Marrow Fat
    (page 270), warm

Champagne vinegar

Kosher salt

BORDELAISE SYRUP

100 grams Bordelaise Sauce (page 261)

50 grams liquid glucose

25 grams granulated sugar

25 grams red wine vinegar

SPRING GARLIC

20 spring garlic cloves

25 grams White Veal Stock (page 255)

Granulated sugar

Kosher salt

CÈPES

8 medium cèpes

Canola oil

20 grams unsalted butter

4 grams minced shallot

Minced flat-leaf parsley

8 small turned Glazed Carrots (page 267)

Sel gris

Although beef is the centerpiece here, paired with robust mushrooms, carrots, and potatoes, one of the more interesting components is a sauce flavored with bone marrow fat. It's very rich and luxurious, with a texture like a thick mayonnaise. We first served this dish at a benefit for the Starlight Children's Foundation in Australia. We'd arrived in the early spring when beautiful spring garlic was available along with cèpes, which went naturally with the beef. We love to use spring garlic, and we can also use different parts of it—for this dish, we use the cloves, but in another we might use the stalk. The sauce is a reinterpretation of a classic bordelaise. PHOTOGRAPH ON PAGE 163

FOR THE BEEF—59.5°C (139.1°F); 45 MINUTES

Generously season the meat on all sides with salt and pepper. Place in a bag and vacuum-pack on medium.

Cook at 59.5°C (139.1°F) for 45 minutes. Remove from the water and let rest for 10 minutes.

To complete: Heat a film of canola oil in a sauté pan. When the pan is hot, add the beef and brown on all sides, turning the meat to brown the ends as well, about 5 minutes. Add the butter, garlic, and thyme. Continue to cook, tilting the pan and basting with the butter from time to time, for a total of about 10 minutes. Remove the meat and let rest before slicing.

FOR THE POMMES MAXIM: Slice the potatoes about ¹⁄₁₆ inch thick on a Japanese mandoline. With a round cutter, cut a disk from each slice about 1⅝ inches in diameter.

Bring a large pot of salted water to a boil. Blanch the potatoes for 20 seconds, then immediately transfer to an ice bath. Blanching them will keep the potatoes from oxidizing.

Drain the potatoes and dry on C-fold towels. Put in a bowl and season with salt. Sprinkle in the cornstarch and toss the potatoes with the cornstarch, rubbing the potato slices between your fingers to separate them and coat with a light layer of starch.

Cut four 5-inch squares of parchment paper. Overlap about 10 potato slices in a circle to make a pinwheel about 3½ inches across on each square of parchment. Refrigerate.

To complete: Heat a film of clarified butter in a large nonstick sauté pan. Carefully invert each potato pinwheel into the pan and lift off the parchment. Cook over medium heat, turning carefully from time to time, until evenly browned, about 10 to 12 minutes (see photograph, page 163).

FOR THE SAUCE: This sauce should be made right before serving. Combine the veal stock, shallot, peppercorns, and thyme in a saucepan, bring to a simmer, and simmer until the stock is reduced by half.

Strain the reduced stock into a Vita-Prep. Blend in the xanthan gum, followed by the crème fraîche. With the machine running on high speed, drizzle in the warm bone marrow fat. Add a few drops of vinegar and a sprinkle of salt. Keep in a warm spot. MAKES ABOUT 325 GRAMS

FOR THE BORDELAISE SYRUP: Combine the bordelaise sauce, glucose, sugar, and vinegar in a saucepan and simmer to reduce by about half, to a syrupy consistency. MAKES ABOUT 125 GRAMS

FOR THE GARLIC: Put the garlic cloves in a small saucepan, cover with water, and bring to a boil. Drain and rinse with cold water. Return the garlic to the saucepan and add the stock and a pinch each of sugar and salt. Bring to a simmer and cook until the garlic is tender and glazed.

FOR THE CÈPES: Cut off one side of each mushroom to make a smooth flat side. (Reserve the rest for another use.) With the tip of a paring knife, score the cut side of the mushrooms in an ⅛-inch crosshatch pattern.

Heat a film of canola oil in a small nonstick sauté pan. Add the mushrooms cut side down and brown for about 2 minutes. Add the butter, turn the mushrooms, and continue to cook, tilting the pan and basting the mushrooms with butter, until tender. Toss with the shallot and parsley.

AT SERVICE: Spoon some bone marrow sauce onto each plate. Add a drizzle of bordelaise syrup. Arrange the beef, potatoes, garlic, carrots, and mushrooms on the plates. Sprinkle the meat with sel gris.

MAKES 4 SERVINGS

AIR-CURED WAGYU, TREVISO LEAVES, COMPRESSED ASIAN PEAR, AND WHIPPED PINE NUT OIL

CURED BEEF

40 grams kosher salt

6 grams Hobbs' Curing Salt
    (see Sources, page 282)

24 grams granulated sugar

1 kilogram Wagyu boneless beef

COMPRESSED PEAR

1 firm Asian pear

Juice of ½ lemon

9 grams granulated sugar

WHIPPED PINE NUT OIL

1 gelatin sheet (2 grams), soaked in cold water to
    soften

100 grams boiling water

0.4 gram xanthan gum (see Sources, page 282)

57 grams pine nut oil

3 grams champagne vinegar

Granulated sugar

Kosher salt

4 Treviso radicchio leaves

8 grams ground toasted pine nuts

We cure Wagyu, this expensive, fat-rich beef, because the result is so good—the protein becomes dense and the mild flavor becomes more concentrated and beefy, and the fat becomes supple, almost lardo-like, and melts in your mouth. And, the yield is higher—we don't lose valuable fat or juices to cooking. Here we pair the sliced beef with the bitter notes of Treviso and the sweetness of balsamic and compressed Asian pear.

We specify boneless Wagyu beef in this dish because beef from Wagyus raised in Japan can be imported into the United States only that way.

FOR THE BEEF: Mix together both salts and the sugar. Rub half the cure into the beef; reserve the remaining cure. Refrigerate the beef to cure for 1 week.

Rub half the remaining cure into the meat. Refrigerate and cure for 1 more week. Repeat a final time with the remaining cure and refrigerate for a final week.

Rinse the beef in ice water to remove the excess surface salt and pat dry. Tie the meat crosswise every ¾ inch with butcher's twine. Wrap another piece of twine lengthwise around the meat, running this piece under the other pieces of twine. Leave a long end of twine for hanging the beef.

Hang in a well-ventilated area at 55°F (12.8°C) and 65 percent humidity for approximately 3 months. The length of time will vary with the hanging conditions.

The aged beef can be sliced, placed on parchment paper, and vacuum-packed for storage.

FOR THE PEAR: Peel the pear and cut it in half. Cut out the core.

Toss the pear with the lemon juice and sugar. Place in a bag and vacuum-pack on high. Refrigerate for a few hours, or overnight.

Remove from the bag and cut into a variety of shapes.

FOR THE PINE NUT OIL: Combine the softened gelatin and boiling water in a Vita-Prep and blend on low speed. With the machine running, very slowly sprinkle in the xanthan gum. Very slowly drizzle in the oil. Add the vinegar and a pinch each of sugar and salt. Refrigerate for at least 2 hours. **MAKES ABOUT 160 GRAMS**

AT SERVICE: Cut the Treviso leaves on the diagonal. Thinly slice the beef.

Whisk the whipped pine nut oil, and spread it over the plates. Coat some of the pieces of pear with the ground pine nuts, and arrange on the plate with the Treviso and beef. **MAKES 4 SERVINGS**

VARIETY MEATS

for sous vide: the soft organ meats (kidneys, liver, sweetbreads) and the tough muscles and "extreme" cuts (calf's heart, tongue, pig's tail).

For the tougher cuts, sous vide allows you to break down the connective tissues without overcooking the meat, the importance of which can't be overstated. And for the softer organs, the techniques are more varied.

The sous vide kidney, a preparation Jonathan Benno defined—manipulating this cut, wrapping it in solid fat, bagging it, and cooking it very gently— was a revelation. Liver also works well. Corey Lee's Confit of Moulard Duck Foie Gras (page 192) is so pure and succulent it feels even more decadent than foie gras is normally. For sweetbreads, which have the capacity to absorb flavors, we create a flavorful cuisson of white veal stock, vermouth, and aromatics. The cuisson, further enhanced by the sweetbread juices, can then be used for cooking and enhancing other cuts such as the veal for the *Blanquette de Veau* (page 142).

VEAL CHEEKS *ZINGARA*
BRAISED VEAL CHEEKS, PUREE OF YUKON GOLD POTATOES, SERRANO HAM, AND BLACK TRUFFLES

VEAL CHEEKS

12 veal cheeks (about 1.35 kilograms untrimmed
   weight)

Kosher salt and freshly ground black pepper

Canola oil

All-purpose flour

60 grams chopped leek (white and light green
   parts only)

60 grams 1-inch dice carrots

60 grams 1-inch dice onions

3 thyme sprigs

2 garlic cloves, peeled

2 bay leaves

450 grams Veal Stock (page 255)

45 grams unsalted butter

TRUFFLE SAUCE

175 grams Quick Veal Sauce (page 260)

10 grams chopped black truffle
   (pieces or peelings are fine)

A few drops of champagne vinegar

Kosher salt and freshly ground black pepper

Dry Madeira

POTATO PUREE

1 kilogram Yukon Gold potatoes

Kosher salt

200 grams heavy cream, plus more for
   finishing, hot

200 grams Chicken Stock (page 257),
   plus more for finishing, hot

200 grams unsalted butter, plus more for
   finishing, cut into chunks, cold

SERRANO HAM AND TRUFFLE SALAD

About sixty ¼-inch-thick batons black truffle

About thirty-six 2-by-¼-inch-thick batons
   serrano ham

About thirty-six 2-by-¼-inch-thick batons king
   trumpet mushrooms

About thirty-six 2-by-¼-inch-thick batons
   Veal Tongue (page 265)

Extra virgin olive oil

Sherry vinegar

Kosher salt

Small watercress leaves

This is an interpretation of a classic Escoffier preparation, veal *Zingara*, a rich meat braised with aromatics, served with a classical pommes puree, vegetables, truffles, and a veal-stock-based sauce. But it takes advantage of the extraordinary powers of sous vide to break down the connective tissue in the veal cheeks without overcooking the meat. The cheeks are cooked sous vide with stock and aromatic vegetables for eight hours, then finished in a pan on the stovetop and, finally, in the oven with additional stock to glaze them.

The potatoes, cooked in a pot of boiling water, are pureed and beaten vigorously with the butter so that the butter is virtually emulsified into the potatoes.

FOR THE VEAL CHEEKS—82.2°C (180°F); 8 HOURS

Trim the veal cheeks of any fat or visible silverskin (do not remove the silverskin that runs through the center of each cheek). Refrigerate the cheeks until cold.

Dry the cheeks with C-fold towels. Season on both sides with salt and pepper.

Heat a film of canola oil over medium-high heat in a pan large enough to hold the cheeks in one layer. Dust both sides of the meat with flour. Once the oil is hot, add the cheeks and brown on both sides, about 2 minutes. Transfer to a rack set over a sheet pan to drain and cool, then refrigerate until cold.

Meanwhile, reduce the heat under the pan to medium-low and add the leek greens, carrots, and onions. Sweat the vegetables for 8 to 10 minutes. Remove from the heat and let cool, then refrigerate until cold.

Make an herb sachet (see page 269) using the thyme sprigs, garlic cloves, and bay leaves. Place the cheeks in a large bag and add the vegetables, 335 grams of the stock, and the sachet. Vacuum-pack on medium.

Cook at 82.2°C (180°F) for 8 hours. Remove from the water and let the meat rest at room temperature for 5 to 10 minutes.

To complete: Drain the cheeks and transfer to a large sauté pan, along with the remaining 115 grams stock. Bring to a simmer, then baste the cheeks in the stock over medium-high heat for 1 to 2 minutes. Swirl in the butter and continue basting the cheeks for about 1 minute. Season as necessary with additional salt and pepper. Transfer to a 350°F oven to cook for 5 minutes, basting once halfway through the cooking.

FOR THE TRUFFLE SAUCE: Combine the veal sauce, truffles, and vinegar in a small saucepan; you shouldn't taste the vinegar—use it as you would use salt to enhance the other flavors. Simmer the sauce for 3 to 4 minutes, or until reduced enough to coat the back of a spoon. Remove from the heat.

To complete: Just before serving, reheat the sauce and season to taste with salt and pepper. Add a splash of Madeira, to taste.

MAKES ABOUT 175 GRAMS

FOR THE POTATO PUREE: Put the potatoes in a pot with enough water to cover them by at least 4 inches, bring to a boil, and boil gently until the potatoes are tender and offer no resistance when poked with a knife, 45 to 60 minutes, depending on their size. Drain the potatoes and return to the pot over medium heat for a minute to steam off the excess moisture. Peel the potatoes.

It is important to puree the potatoes while they are still hot. Pass the potatoes through a tamis into a pot. Stir in salt to taste and beat with a sturdy spoon over low heat to dry them out slightly. Add the 200 grams each of cream, stock, and butter a little at a time, alternating among them and beating vigorously without stopping, until very smooth. The puree should be sticking to the sides of the pot; it will be stiffer and more difficult to mix than traditional mashed potatoes. Remove from the heat. At this point the potatoes can be held in a bain-marie covered with buttered parchment paper for up to 4 hours.

To complete: Just before serving, set the potato puree over low heat and stir constantly to warm the potatoes. Stir in additional warm cream, stock, and butter until you have a smooth, rich puree, stirring and moving the pan on and off the heat to prevent the potatoes from scorching. Add additional salt to taste.

MAKES ABOUT 1.5 KILOGRAMS

FOR THE SALAD: Combine the truffles, ham, mushrooms, and tongue. Drizzle with a light coating of olive oil and a few drops of sherry vinegar, sprinkle lightly with salt, and toss gently.

AT SERVICE: Place a spoonful of the sauce on each plate and top with a veal cheek. Add a spoonful of potato puree to each, and top with the salad. Garnish with watercress leaves.

MAKES 12 SERVINGS

TRIPE OREGANATA, AMANDO MANNI EXTRA VIRGIN OLIVE OIL, AND HERBED BREAD CRUMBS

TRIPE

1 fresh honeycomb tripe (see Sources, page 282), about 4.5 kilograms

750 grams canola oil

500 grams coarsely chopped red onions

250 grams coarsely chopped carrots`

250 grams coarsely chopped fennel

Kosher salt and freshly ground black pepper

500 grams dry white wine, such as Sauvignon Blanc

25 grams basil leaves

10 grams sage leaves

5 grams bay leaves

25 grams rosemary sprigs

90 grams thyme sprigs

15 grams dried red chiles

500 grams White Veal Stock (page 255)

50 grams Roasted Garlic Puree (page 266)

One #10 can (100 grams) San Marzano tomatoes, with their liquid

CRUMB MIXTURE

150 grams fresh bread crumbs (see page 263)

10 grams Roasted Garlic Puree (page 266)

4 leaves *each* flat-leaf parsley, oregano, and sage, finely chopped

4 pinches thyme

Kosher salt

Amando Manni extra virgin olive oil (see Sources, page 282)

This dish combines two different techniques from two chefs, Anna Klinger and Marco Canora, with whom Jonathan Benno worked early in his career: blanching the tripe before cooking it and cooking it in a soffrito. Blanching cleans it, purging it of the organy flavors that can ruin a tripe dish. *Soffrito* is a carmelized vegetable preparation. You can take it to various depths of intensity and sweetness; ours is cooked to a golden brown.

We use only very fresh honeycomb tripe that we get from Four Story Hill Farm. The tripe can be braised traditionally in the soffrito in the oven (5 hours at 300°F) or cooked sous vide, as we do here. To finish it for service, we simply top it with brioche bread crumbs mixed with oregano and other herbs—the "oreganata"—and crisp them under a broiler. (With a poached egg on top, this makes an amazing breakfast dish.) We buy the whole tripe for this preparation, which is why the recipe serves so many.

FOR THE TRIPE—82°C (179.6°F); 8 HOURS

Cover the tripe with cold water and refrigerate for 12 hours, changing the water at least twice.

The following day, drain the tripe, transfer to a large rondeau, and cover with cold water. Bring the water to a boil. Drain the tripe and let cool.

Lay the tripe honeycomb side down on the work surface. There is a natural pocket of fat where the tripe folds over that should be cut away and discarded. Turn the tripe honeycomb side up. Trim the rough edges. Cut the tripe into strips about 3 inches long by ⅜ inch wide. Set aside.

Heat the oil in a large rondeau. Add the onions, carrots, and fennel and stir over medium-low to medium heat to combine. Season with salt and pepper and cook for 35 minutes. The vegetables should have a rich caramel color. Add the wine and simmer for about 10 minutes, or until it has evaporated.

To make an herb sachet, wrap the basil, sage, bay leaves, rosemary, thyme, and chiles in a large piece of cheesecloth and tie with kitchen twine. Add the veal stock, garlic puree, and sachet to the pot and bring to a boil.

Meanwhile, pour the liquid from the tomatoes into a container. Put the tomatoes in a colander and squeeze them to remove the seeds; discard the seeds. Crush the tomatoes in your hand and add to the tomato liquid.

When the stock comes to a boil, add the tomatoes and their liquid. Return to a simmer and cook for 45 minutes.

Stir in the tripe and simmer for another hour. Remove from the heat and cool to room temperature. Refrigerate until completely cold.

To complete: Discard the sachet and vacuum-pack all the ingredients on medium.

Cook at 82°C (179.6°F) for 8 hours.

FOR THE CRUMB MIXTURE: Put the bread crumbs and garlic puree in a food processor and pulse to combine. Add the herbs and salt to taste.

AT SERVICE: Place the tripe in heatproof serving bowls. Top with the bread crumb mixture and run under the salamander to brown the crumbs. Drizzle with olive oil. **MAKES 50 SERVINGS**

Opposite: Fricassée of Veal Kidney with Black Trumpet Mushrooms, Salsify, Brussels Sprouts, and Curry-Infused Veal Sauce (page 178)

FRICASSÉE OF VEAL KIDNEY WITH BLACK TRUMPET MUSHROOMS, SALSIFY, BRUSSELS SPROUTS, AND CURRY-INFUSED VEAL SAUCE

KIDNEY

1 whole veal kidney, with fat attached
   (about 455 grams)

Kosher salt and freshly ground black pepper

3 thyme sprigs

1 small rosemary sprig

1 bay leaf

All-purpose flour

Beaten egg

Finely ground panko

Clarified Butter (page 261)

30 grams unsalted butter

2 garlic cloves, cloves

Sel gris

SALSIFY

400 grams Vegetable Stock (page 260), cold

20 grams lemon juice

2 grams granulated sugar

1 bay leaf

1 thyme sprig

1 rosemary sprig

1 garlic clove, peeled

5 black peppercorns

Kosher salt

4 salsify roots (about 7 inches long)

Canola oil

Freshly ground black pepper

BRUSSELS SPROUTS

18 small Brussels sprouts

Kosher salt and freshly ground black pepper

Canola oil

10 grams unsalted butter

MUSHROOMS

18 black trumpet mushrooms

Canola oil

15 grams unsalted butter

Kosher salt and freshly ground black pepper

Quick Veal Sauce (page 260)

Curry Oil (page 267)

Sel gris

Freshly ground black pepper

Jonathan Benno *staged* at Auberge de Vieux Puits in the southwest corner of France, right on the border of Spain, where the chef would roast whole veal kidneys. He would wrap the kidney in foil and roast it, then hold it at the station to slice during service. Until then, Jonathan had seen kidney cooked only in lobes in a kind of fricassée. He liked this idea and wanted to take it to a higher level. So we render the abundant fat that surrounds the kidney, chill it, and then cut it in slabs to encase the kidney so that it is surrounded in fat as it cooks. Once it is medium-rare, it can be chilled and then, when ready to serve, the perfect slices are breaded with panko and sautéed until crisp. We love that it's served almost like a steak, but, if you prefer, the lobes can be separated and served in a fricassée style.

You need the best-quality kidney (nothing turns someone off kidney faster than kidney that hasn't been stored and cleaned well, no matter what the preparation). It should still be rosy in the center when done, and the flavor will have mellowed. **PHOTOGRAPH ON PAGE 177**

TO RENDER THE FAT—85°C (185°F); 1½ HOURS

Remove the fat from the kidney. There is a pocket of fat in the center of the kidney. Without cutting into the kidney, try to remove some of the fat with the artery that runs through the center.

The fat must be cold. Grind the fat in a grinder with a small die. Place in a bag and vacuum-pack on high.

Cook at 85°C (185°F). The fat should be rendered after about 1½ hours (see Rendered Fat, page 270).

Line a quarter sheet pan with food-safe plastic wrap. Pour in the rendered fat. Refrigerate or freeze until solidified.

TO COOK THE KIDNEY—82°C (179.6°F); 1 HOUR

Cut a slab of fat large enough to enclose the kidney, about 8 by 5 inches. Season the kidney with salt and pepper. Working quickly, place the kidney in the center of the fat. Lay 1 thyme sprig, the rosemary sprig, and the bay leaf over the top and use the plastic wrap to enclose the kidney in the fat. Leave the plastic wrap around the kidney, and refrigerate until it is completely cold and the fat is solidified around it.

Lay a piece of cheesecloth about 12 inches wide and 24 inches long on the work surface with a short end toward you. Unroll the kidney onto the cheesecloth, centering it on the bottom end, and discard the plastic wrap. Rolling it away from you, roll the kidney up in the cheesecloth into a tight log, twisting the ends as you roll to form it into a compact log.

Loop a length of string around your index finger. With the same hand, hold one end of the cheesecloth tightly and wind the string around the end of the kidney. Continue wrapping the string about ¼ inch into the kidney; this will help compress the kidney into a tight roll. Tie a knot around the cheesecloth. Repeat the procedure on the other end. Tie 3 pieces of string equally spaced around the log. Refrigerate for 30 minutes to set the fat.

Vacuum-pack on high. Remove to an ice bath to chill completely.

Cook the kidney at 82°C (179.6°F) for 1 hour.

Remove the kidney from the bag. With scissors, cut off the ends of the roll, then cut lengthwise through the cheesecloth and remove it. Dry the kidney on a C-fold towel.

Trim the ends of the kidney and cut crosswise into 6 slices about 1 inch thick, 50 grams. (Alternatively, to serve the kidney in a "fricassée" style, you could cut apart the nodes to make individual pieces, about 5 per person.)

Sprinkle both sides of the slices with salt and pepper. Dredge each slice in flour, coating the edges as well as both sides, pat off the excess, and then dip in the egg and, finally, the panko crumbs.

To complete: Heat a film of clarified butter in a sauté pan. Add the slices of kidney and sauté for 45 seconds to 1 minute, until the crumbs are golden brown. Turn the slices and cook for another minute, or until golden brown. Add the butter, the remaining 2 thyme sprigs, and the garlic and continue to cook, tilting the pan and basting the kidney with the butter, and turning the kidney as necessary for even cooking, for another 1½ minutes or so. Drain the slices on C-fold towels.

FOR THE SALSIFY—85°C (185°F); 1 HOUR

Whisk together the stock, lemon juice, sugar, bay leaf, thyme, rosemary, garlic, peppercorns, and a sprinkling of salt in a medium bowl. Peel the salsify, dropping each piece into the liquid as you finish it.

Transfer the salsify and all of the liquid to a large bag and vacuum-pack on medium. Chill until cold.

Cook at 85°C (185°F) for 1 hour. Remove the bag from the water and let rest for 10 minutes, then submerge in an ice bath to chill.

Remove the salsify from the bag, drain, and cut on the diagonal into 2½-inch sections.

To complete: Heat a film of canola oil in a sauté pan over medium-high heat. Add the salsify and sauté to caramelize. Season with salt and pepper.

FOR THE BRUSSELS SPROUTS: Trim the bottoms of the Brussels sprouts and discard any bruised outer leaves. Blanch the sprouts (see Big-Pot Blanching, page 268). Transfer to an ice bath to chill, then drain and dry on C-fold towels.

To complete: Cut the Brussels sprouts in half through the root end and season with salt and pepper. Heat a film of canola oil in a sauté pan. Add the sprouts cut side down and cook to caramelize them. Add the butter, tossing to coat.

FOR THE MUSHROOMS: Trim and clean the mushrooms. Heat a film of canola oil in a sauté pan and sauté the mushrooms for 3 to 5 minutes, or until cooked through. Swirl in the butter to coat and season with salt and pepper. Drain on C-fold towels.

AT SERVICE: Spoon some sauce and curry oil around each plate. Arrange the kidneys, Brussels sprouts, salsify, and mushrooms on the plates and sprinkle with sel gris and pepper. **MAKES 6 SERVINGS**

CORNED BEEF TONGUE *PAIN PERDU*, WATERCRESS LEAVES, HORSERADISH MOUSSE, AND OVEN-ROASTED TOMATOES

TONGUE AND BRINE

1 beef tongue (about 1.33 kilograms)

25 grams light brown sugar

5 grams Hobbs' Curing Salt

   (see Sources, page 282)

160 grams kosher salt

1.2 grams powdered ginger

2.2 kilograms water, cold

20 grams garlic cloves, crushed and peeled

1 bay leaf

5 grams black peppercorns

0.3 gram chile flakes

6 cloves

10 allspice berries

0.3 gram celery seeds

4 grams yellow mustard seeds

5 grams coriander seeds

PAIN PERDU

250 grams whole milk

250 grams heavy cream

30 grams Rendered Beef Fat (page 270)

3 large eggs

5 grams kosher salt

½ recipe Brioche (page 262), crusts removed

HORSERADISH MOUSSE

150 grams crème fraîche

15 grams grated fresh horseradish

   (grated on a rasp grater)

Kosher salt

Rendered Beef Fat (page 270)

40 watercress leaves

Extra virgin olive oil

Champagne vinegar

Kosher salt

40 Roasted Cherry Tomatoes (page 266)

This recipe has been evolving almost since the opening of The French Laundry. It began in the form of the "Tongue in Cheek" salad, which combined braised beef cheeks and veal tongue with greens, tomato confit, and a horseradish cream. It's transformed here into an upscale version of a deli sandwich—the slow-cooked beef is pickled and served with a savory bread pudding, roasted tomatoes, and a horseradish mousse. These are exquisite flavor pairings that work just as well in haute cuisine as they do at the Carnegie Deli.

The beef is pickled in a straightforward brine for 4 weeks. The recipe is based on one from Hilary Ziebold, mother of Eric, former French Laundry chef de cuisine and currently chef at CityZen in Washington, D. C.

FOR THE TONGUE—70°C (158°F); 24 HOURS

Trim off any large pieces of fat from the tongue; at this point, you do not need to trim off all of the fat. After trimming, the tongue will weigh about 1 kilogram. Reserve the trimmed fat to render for the pain perdu and the finishing of the dish.

For the brine: Combine the brown sugar, curing salt, kosher salt, and ginger in a container large enough to hold the tongue and brine. Bring about 500 grams of the water to a boil, pour the water into the container, and stir to dissolve the sugar and salt. Stir in the remaining water, and then stir in the remaining brine ingredients. Chill completely.

Add the tongue to the brine and store at 55°F (12.8°C) for 28 days.

To cook: First chill the tongue in the brine to 40°F (4.4°C) before transferring to the bag.

Transfer the tongue to a bag. Strain the brine. Add 500 grams to the tongue, and vacuum-pack on high. (Discard the remaining brine.)

Cook at 70°C (158°F) for 24 hours. Let rest for 10 minutes, then submerge in an ice bath to chill. The tongue can be stored in the brine for up to 2 weeks.

To complete: Drain the tongue and pat dry. Cut away the skin and membrane. Cut the tongue into 2 pieces, cutting on the diagonal at the point where the tongue begins to narrow.

Slice the wide part of the tongue crosswise on a meat slicer into ¹⁄₃₂-inch-thick slices. You will need 48 slices for the pain perdu.

Slice the narrow part of the tongue lengthwise on the slicer. You will need 30 of these pieces.

FOR THE PAIN PERDU: Spray an 8-inch square baking pan with non-stick spray. Line with parchment paper and spray the paper.

Combine the milk, cream, and the 30 grams fat in a saucepan and bring to a simmer. Put the eggs and salt in a Vita-Prep. With the machine running, pour in the hot liquid, blending until well combined. Strain through a chinois or fine-mesh conical strainer.

Cut enough brioche for two layers. Slice lengthwise into pieces about ⁵⁄₁₆ inch thick. As a test, line the bottom of the pan with enough slices to make a solid layer of brioche, trimming them as necessary to fit. Remove from the pan.

Coat the bottom of the pan with some custard base and then reinsert one layer of brioche slices to cover; do not overlap the slices. Begin to add additional custard to the pan, coating the bread as evenly as possible; use your fingers to move the bread and allow the custard to soak in. You will use slightly less than half the custard. Make a layer of tongue over the bread, using half the wide slices of tongue: arrange them side by side, overlapping them by about 1 inch. Spoon a light coating of custard on top, then make a layer of the remaining tongue over the top, with the slices running across the first slices to give the dish structure. Coat with

another layer of custard. Add another layer of bread, running at right angles to the first layer. Soak the bread with as much of the custard as it will absorb. You may have some custard remaining.

Bake the pain perdu at 300°F for 40 minutes. Stick the tip of a knife into the center of the pain perdu: it should come out clean. Refrigerate until cold.

To complete: Unmold the pain perdu onto a cutting board. Using a 4-inch round cutter, cut a half round from one edge, then move the cutter up and cut again, to form a fleuron, or crescent, about 3 inches long and ¾ inch wide. Continue cutting fleurons from the pain perdu; you will need 10 fleurons.

Heat a very thin film of beef fat in a nonstick sauté pan over medium-low heat. Add the pieces of pain perdu and sauté until golden brown on each side (if they seem too delicate to turn, sauté on the bottom side only).

Transfer to a tray and heat in a 350°F oven for about 5 minutes, or until hot. Blot off any fat with C-fold towels.

FOR THE MOUSSE: Whisk the crème fraîche, horseradish, and salt in a bowl over an ice bath. The crème fraîche will seem thin at first but will then thicken. Refrigerate until serving.   MAKES 165 GRAMS

AT SERVICE: Heat about 1 inch of beef fat in a saucepan to 49°C (120.2°F). Add the slices of tongue and heat for a minute or so to soften them.

Toss the watercress with a light drizzle of olive oil, a few drops of vinegar, and a sprinkling of salt.

Arrange the pain perdu, slices of tongue, and tomatoes on the plates. Scatter the watercress around. Garnish with the horseradish mousse.

MAKES 10 SERVINGS

CONFIT OF CALF'S HEART, TOASTED PECANS, BABY TURNIPS, BING CHERRIES, AND CHERRY-WOOD-AGED BALSAMIC VINEGAR

BRINE

180 grams kosher salt

60 grams Hobbs' Curing Salt

   (see Sources, page 282)

105 grams granulated sugar

3 kilograms water, cold

CALF'S HEART

1 calf's heart, about 850 grams

500 grams Rendered Duck Fat (page 270), cold

TURNIPS

8 baby turnips

15 grams Rendered Duck Fat (page 270), cold

Kosher salt

Granulated sugar

30 grams Chicken Stock (page 257)

PECANS

24 raw pecan halves

50 grams unsalted butter

Kosher salt

POACHED CHERRIES

500 grams dry red wine,

   such as Cabernet Sauvignon

12 black peppercorns

4 allspice berries

250 grams granulated sugar

250 grams water, hot

18 Bing cherries, pitted and stems trimmed to

   about ½ inch

Cherry-wood-aged balsamic vinegar

   (see Sources, page 282)

Baby mâche

Extra virgin olive oil

Champagne vinegar

Sel gris

Freshly ground black pepper

Calf's heart is very mild, as offal goes, a tough muscle that with thorough but gentle cooking becomes tender without getting mealy. We brine it, then cook it sous vide, and chill it; we slice it very thin and rewarm it in fat to serve. As with so many tough cuts of meat, sous vide is the perfect cooking method.

We began serving this in the summer when we had abundant cherries, which we soak in a spiced red wine mixture to offset the rich meat with a sweet-acidic component. We garnish it with glazed baby turnips, pecans, and mâche. **PHOTOGRAPH ON PAGE 185**

FOR THE BRINE: Combine the salt, curing salt, and sugar in a container large enough to hold the heart and brine. Bring about 750 grams of the water to a boil; pour the water into the container, stirring to dissolve the salt and sugar. Add the remaining water and chill completely.

FOR THE HEART—79.4°C (174.9°F); 24 HOURS

Add the heart to the cold brine and refrigerate for 24 hours. Dry the heart and place it in a bag with the duck fat. Vacuum-pack on high.

Cook at 79.4°C (174.9°F) for 24 hours.

To complete: Remove the heart from the bag and drain on C-fold towels. Pour the fat into a saucepan and heat the fat to 82°C (about 180°F).

Meanwhile, trim off the excess fat from the heart. Trim away any sections on the surface of the heart that may have discolored. Slice the heart as thin as possible, either by hand or on a meat slicer: cut the meat from the sides, working around the center of the heart; as you near the center of the heart, turn it to continue to cut solid slices. You want about 4 or 5 slices per person.

Add the slices to the fat to warm. Drain on a C-fold towel.

FOR THE TURNIPS—85°C (185°F); 30 MINUTES

Trim away the tops and cut each turnip into 4 wedges. With a paring knife, peel the wedges, then trim to round the sharp edges. Put them in a bowl and stir in the duck fat and a pinch each of salt and sugar.

Place the turnips in a bag in a single layer and vacuum-pack at medium-high. Refrigerate until cold.

Cook at 85°C (185°F) for about 30 minutes, until tender.

To complete: Transfer the turnips and liquid to a saucepan and add the chicken stock. Season with salt and glaze the turnips, moving them in the pan so they glaze evenly.

FOR THE PECANS: Put the pecans in a small saucepan, cover with cold water, and bring to a simmer. Drain and dry on C-fold towels.

Melt the butter in a small sauté pan over medium heat and let cook to a very pale golden brown. Add the pecans and stir with a spoon. The butter will continue to brown as the pecans do. Move the pan on and off the heat as necessary to toast the pecans evenly without scorching; this should take about 2 minutes. Remove the pecans from the heat and pour off the butter.

Sprinkle the pecans with salt to taste, tossing to coat evenly. Drain on C-fold towels.

FOR THE CHERRIES: Pour the red wine into a saucepan and set over the heat. Tie the peppercorns and allspice in a piece of cheesecloth to make a sachet and add to the pan. Bring to a boil, then flambé to burn off the alcohol. Remove from the heat and add the sugar and water, stirring to dissolve the sugar. Remove the sachet from the pan and discard.

Put the cherries in a container that holds them in a single layer. Pour the warm wine over the cherries. Let cool to room temperature.

AT SERVICE: Drizzle some balsamic vinegar onto each plate. Arrange the slices of heart, cherries, turnip, and pecans on the plates. Toss the mâche with a drizzle of oil and vinegar and mound on the plate. Sprinkle the heart with sel gris and pepper. **MAKES 6 SERVINGS**

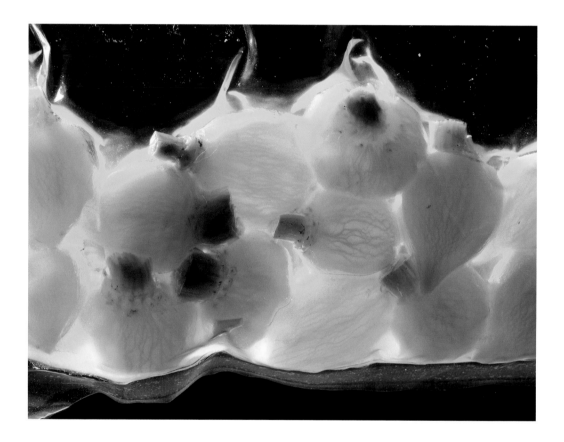

Above: turnips; opposite: Confit of Calf's Heart, Toasted Pecans, Baby Turnips, Bing Cherries, and Cherry-Wood-Aged Balsamic Vinegar (page 182)

MILK-POACHED CALF'S LIVER, CARAWAY-GLAZED CIPOLLINI, GRANNY SMITH APPLE, DIJON MUSTARD, AND *SAUCE LAURIER*

LIVER

1 piece center-cut calf's liver (1 kilogram), cold

3 to 4 kilograms plus 480 grams milk, cold

14 grams extra virgin olive oil

65 grams 2-inch pieces celery

50 grams 2-inch pieces peeled carrot

150 grams 2-inch pieces leek
(white and light parts only)

80 grams large shallots, peeled and
cut into thick slices

200 grams heavy cream

6 grams flat-leaf parsley stems

15 grams thyme sprigs

¼ fresh bay leaf

10 black peppercorns

10 grams kosher salt

2.5 grams chopped chives

APPLES

20 grams water

40 grams granulated sugar

Kosher salt

425 grams Granny Smith apples
(about 2), cold

CIPOLLINI

8 cipollini, peeled, cold

0.5 gram caraway seeds

Kosher salt

Granulated sugar

27 grams unsalted butter, cold

SAUCE

25 grams Dijon mustard

10 grams Banyuls vinegar

15 grams extra virgin olive oil

130 grams Quick Veal Sauce (page 260)

1 small bay leaf

Extra virgin olive oil

Sel gris

Freshly ground black pepper

Minced chives

Baby red mustard greens

Mustard flowers

Traditional pairings of liver and onion, and liver and mustard, are made special here by the soft texture and pure deep flavor of liver cooked sous vide. Because there's no sweetness or roasted flavors from searing, it's all liver. And the texture of the liver, cooked in milk and aromatics, becomes almost creamy.

We start with about 30 percent more liver than we will need to compensate for the trimming.

TO SOAK THE LIVER: Cut away all the skin, sinew, and membrane from the liver. Square off the edges. Put in a container and add enough cold milk (3 to 4 kilograms) to cover. Refrigerate overnight.

TO COOK THE LIVER — 65.5°C (149.9°F); 1 HOUR

Heat the olive oil in a pot. Add the vegetables and cook gently until softened, without browning, about 5 minutes. Remove from the heat and add the 480 grams milk, cream, parsley, thyme, bay leaf, peppercorns, and salt. Let steep for about 20 minutes, then chill until cold.

Drain the liver and discard the milk. Put the liver in a large bag with the cold cuisson. Lay the bag in the vacuum packer and let the liver sit flat against the surface to maintain its shape. Vacuum-pack on medium. Fold over and tape any excess bag.

Cook at 65.5°C (149.9°F) for 1 hour. Remove the liver from the bag, dry on C-fold towels, and let rest for a few minutes.

FOR THE APPLES: Combine the water, sugar, and a pinch of salt in a small saucepan and heat, stirring to dissolve the sugar and salt. Chill over an ice bath until cold.

Slice off the tops and bottoms of the apples, leaving them about 2 inches tall. Cut each apple into 6 wedges. Peel each wedge with a paring knife, cut out the core, and trim the sharp edges to smooth them.

Toss the apples with the syrup and place in a bag. Vacuum-pack on high. Refrigerate for 2 hours.

FOR THE CIPOLLINI—85°C (185°F); 1 HOUR TO 1 HOUR 10 MINUTES
Toss the onions with the caraway seeds, and a pinch each of salt and sugar. Add 25 grams of the butter.

Vacuum-pack on high.

Cook at 85°C (185°F) for 1 hour to 1 hour and 10 minutes, or until the onions are tender when squeezed through the bag.

To complete: Transfer the onions and their cooking liquid to a small sauté pan. Bring to a simmer, add the remaining 2 grams butter, and simmer to reduce the liquid and glaze the onions.

FOR THE SAUCE: Whisk the mustard and vinegar together, then whisk in the oil to emulsify.

To complete: Heat the veal sauce with the bay leaf. When it comes to a simmer, remove from the heat and keep warm to infuse the sauce with the flavor of the bay leaf. Taste as it sits until it achieves the desired strength, then remove the bay leaf. MAKES 50 GRAMS

AT SERVICE: Cut the liver crosswise into 4 slices, each about ¾-inch thick. Rub each one with olive oil and sprinkle with sel gris and pepper.

Spoon some mustard sauce onto each plate, arrange the liver, and garnish with the chives. Arrange the apple slices and cipollini on the plates. Add a spoonful of the sauce to each, and garnish with the mustard greens and flowers. MAKES 4 SERVINGS

FRIED PIG'S TAILS, FRENCH-CUT ROMANO BEANS, DEVILED QUAIL EGG, AND *SAUCE RAVIGOTE*

PIG'S TAILS

1 thyme sprig

1 bay leaf

1 gram black peppercorns

1 gram coriander seeds

1 garlic clove, peeled

4 pig's tails (500 grams total), cold

250 grams Chicken Stock (page 257), cold

1 carrot, cut into 1-inch dice

1 celery stalk, cut into 1-inch dice

¼ yellow onion, cut into 1-inch dice

Kosher salt and freshly ground black pepper

All-purpose flour

Beaten eggs

Finely ground panko crumbs
    (ground in a food processor)

Canola oil for deep-frying

SAUCE

26 grams Dijon mustard

10 grams minced shallot

30 grams champagne vinegar

5 grams granulated sugar

5 grams kosher salt, or to taste

90 grams extra virgin olive oil

90 grams canola oil

QUAIL EGGS

4 quail eggs

6 grams crème fraîche

Kosher salt and freshly ground white pepper

Spicy paprika

ROMANO BEANS

4 green romano beans

4 yellow romano beans

Extra virgin olive oil

Minced shallot

Kosher salt and freshly ground black pepper

FRISÉE SALAD

Frisée leaves

Extra virgin olive oil

Champagne vinegar

Minced chives

Kosher salt and freshly ground black pepper

Sel gris

The pig's tail is rarely used, and to transform it into an elegant and satisfying dish is the kind of cooking that is very exciting for us. Whole pig's tails are cooked sous vide with chicken stock and aromatics until the abundant collagen has melted and the tails are very tender. They're cooled, butterflied to remove the bones and cartilage, then rerolled back into shape, wrapped in plastic, and chilled. The abundant gelatin from the skin solidifies the tails, which are then breaded and fried—resulting in a crispy exterior and melting rich interior.

The tails are served with a sharp ravigote sauce, a mustard-shallot vinaigrette, romano beans, and frisée salad. **PHOTOGRAPH ON PAGE 191**

FOR THE PIG'S TAILS—82.2°C (180°F); 8 HOURS

Make an herb sachet (see page 269) with the thyme, bay leaf, peppercorns, coriander seeds, and garlic clove.

Arrange the tails in a single layer in a large bag and add the chicken stock, herb sachet, carrot, celery, and onion. Vacuum-pack on medium.

Cook at 82.2°C (180°F) for 8 hours. Let the pig's tails rest at room temperature just until they have cooled enough to handle. It is important to work with the tails while they are still warm; if they cool down too much and seize up, place them, with their liquid, in a saucepan and rewarm.

Remove the tails from the braising liquid; reserve the liquid. Place a tail on the work surface. Make a cut down the length and, using a knife and your hands, pull back the skin and meat to expose the bones, cutting against the bones to leave as much meat as possible attached to the skin. Remove the bones. Run your fingers over the meat to find any small pieces of cartilage, and remove them. Trim any rough edges. Bone and trim the remaining tails.

Dampen the work surface slightly with your hand. Place a piece of 18-inch-wide food-safe plastic wrap long enough to enclose a tail on the surface. Lay an opened tail across the bottom of the plastic. Season with salt and pepper. Moisten the top of the meat with about 5 grams of the braising liquid. (The liquid is so gelatinous that it will help to hold the tail together.) Roll the tail in the plastic to return it to its original shape—do not roll into a pinwheel; be careful to maintain the shape of the tail without crushing it or bending it. Tie the ends of the plastic. Repeat with the remaining tails. Refrigerate overnight, or chill in an ice bath.

Put the flour, beaten eggs, and panko crumbs in three separate shallow dishes. Season the tails with salt and pepper. Dip the tails into the flour, patting off any excess, then into the egg, and then into the panko crumbs. Dip into the egg and panko a second time. Refrigerate to chill and set the coating.

To complete: Heat the canola oil to 176°C (about 350°F). Be careful as you cook the tails: occasionally one may split or spit oil. Lower the tails 2 at a time into the oil and cook for 2 to 3 minutes, turning as necessary for even color. Drain on C-fold towels, and arrange on a sheet pan.

Transfer to a 350°F oven to heat for 3 minutes, or until hot throughout.

FOR THE SAUCE: Whisk together the mustard, shallot, vinegar, sugar, and salt in a medium bowl. Whisking constantly, drizzle in the olive oil and canola oil to emulsify. Season to taste with additional salt if necessary.

FOR THE QUAIL EGGS: Bring a medium pan of water to a boil. Add the eggs and simmer for 5 minutes. Transfer to an ice bath to chill.

Peel the eggs and cut them lengthwise in half. Remove the yolks and pass them through a fine-mesh sieve or tamis into a bowl. Stir in the crème fraîche. Season with salt and pepper to taste. Scrape into a small pastry bag fitted with a small star tip. Pipe the yolks into the egg whites and sprinkle with paprika. Refrigerate.

FOR THE BEANS: Blanch the beans (see Big-Pot Blanching, page 268). Chill in an ice bath. Cut off the ends of the beans and slice the beans ⅛ inch thick on a severe diagonal.

To complete: Toss the beans with a light coating of olive oil, minced shallot, and salt and pepper to taste.

FOR THE SALAD: Toss the frisée with a light coating of olive oil, a few drops of vinegar, chives, and salt and pepper to taste.

AT SERVICE: Spread a spoonful of ravigote sauce on each serving plate. Top with a pig's tail and a small stack of the romano beans. Sprinkle the pig's tails with sel gris. Mound the frisée on the tails. Add an egg to each plate. **MAKES 4 SERVINGS**

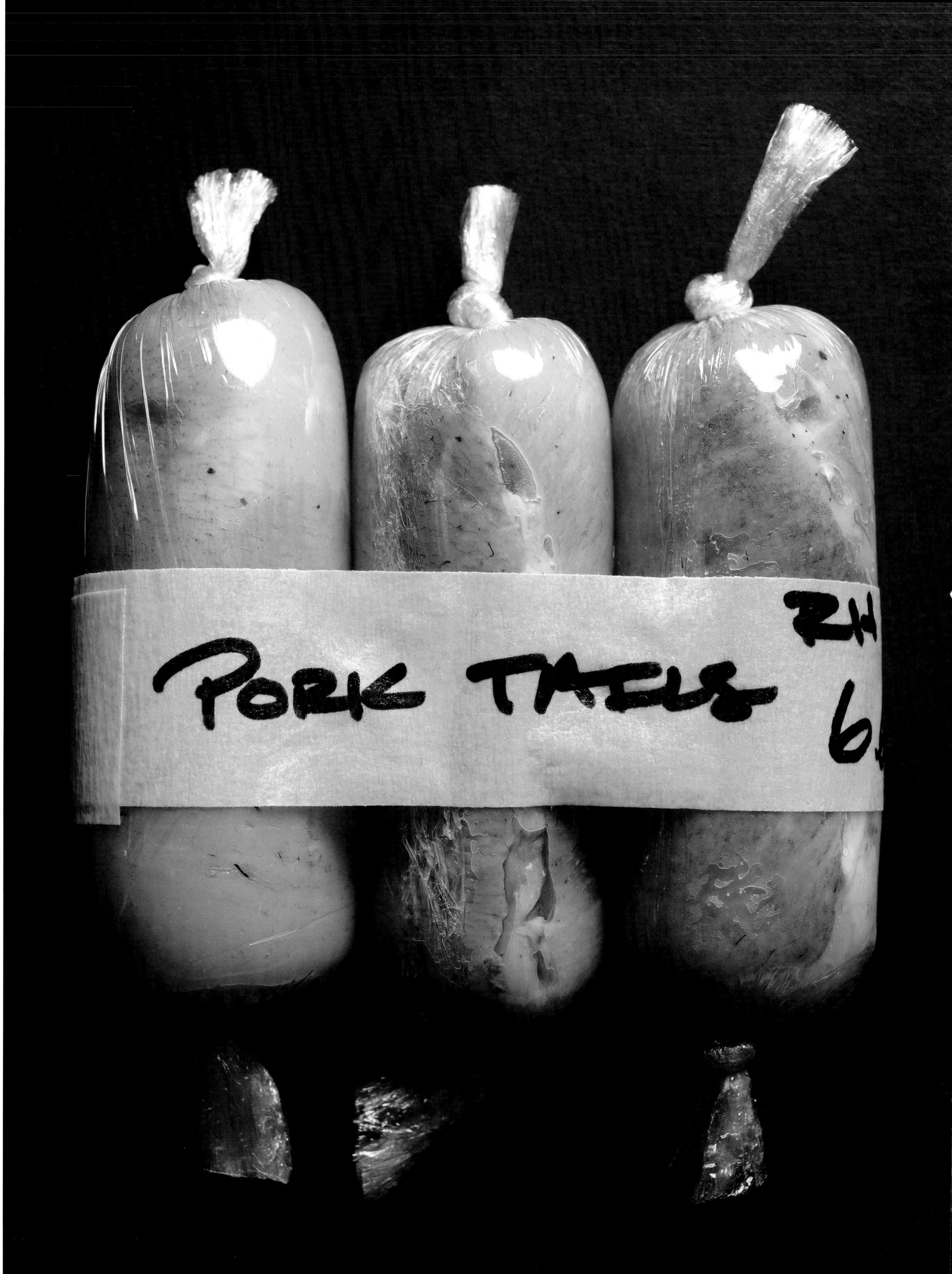
RH
PORK TAILS
6

Fried Pig's Tails, French-Cut Romano Beans, Deviled Quail Egg, and *Sauce Ravigote* (page 188)

CONFIT OF MOULARD DUCK FOIE GRAS
WITH VEGETABLES *À LA GRECQUE*

FOIE GRAS

1 piece center-cut Grade A foie gras (400 grams), large lobe only, cold

Kosher salt

400 grams Rendered Foie Gras Fat (page 270), cold

PEARL ONIONS

8 white pearl onions, peeled

Granulated sugar

Kosher salt

Extra virgin olive oil

RADISHES

3 to 4 large red French breakfast radishes

Lemon juice

Extra virgin olive oil

Kosher salt

CORIANDER SEEDS

16 coriander seeds

0.2 gram crushed coriander seeds

67 grams lemon juice

Granulated sugar

0.2 gram xanthan gum (see Sources, page 282)

VEGETABLES

4 baby fennel bulbs (about 3 to 4 inches long)

8 Thumbelina carrots

32 small chanterelles

13 grams extra virgin olive oil

13 grams Rendered Foie Gras Fat (page 270)

Kosher salt

Cilantro shoots

Sel gris

With sous vide, fat-rich duck liver can be cooked through without overcooking or rendering too much of its fat, resulting in pure foie gras flavor unencumbered by the sweet and roasted flavors you get when you use high heat. The foie gras is first cured for 6 hours in salt, then poached whole, sliced *à la minute,* and served with a cooked vegetable garnish, rewarmed in foie gras fat. A sharp lemon-coriander vinaigrette finishes the dish. The rendered foie gras fat used to reheat the vegetables in effect completes the vinaigrette on the plate.

Standard confit technique is to cure the meat in salt, poach it in its own fat, and cool it in the fat, then reheat it. In the same way that it's all but impossible to keep yourself from picking juicy bits off confit when it comes out of the oven after hours of gentle poaching, we find this foie gras confit impossible to resist as soon as it's done, warm and molten, straight out of the bag. So that's how we serve it.

FOR THE FOIE GRAS—64°C (147.2°F); 28 MINUTES

Score the top of the foie gras in a ¼-inch crosshatch pattern. Pack it in salt to cover. Refrigerate for 6 hours.

Remove the foie gras from the salt, rinse under cold water, and dry with a C-fold towel. Refrigerate until cold.

To complete: Put the foie gras and fat in a bag and vacuum-pack on medium.

Cook at 64°C (147°.2F) for 28 minutes. Drain the foie gras on a C-fold towel. Cut crosswise into 4 equal servings. Remove any visible veins.

FOR THE PEARL ONIONS—85°C (185°F); 30 MINUTES

Cut an X in the bottom of each pearl onion. Toss with a pinch each of sugar and salt and a drizzle of olive oil. Place in a bag in a single layer.

Vacuum-pack on high.

Cook at 85°C (185°F) for 30 minutes. Remove the onions from the bag and squeeze them to remove the outer layer of each onion.

FOR THE RADISHES—85°C (185°F); 6 MINUTES

Cut 1 radish into thin rounds on a Japanese mandoline and place in ice water. Cut the remaining radishes into balls using a #12 parisienne baller; you need 20 balls. Toss the balls with a few drops of lemon juice, a splash of olive oil, and a sprinkling of salt. Refrigerate until cold.

Place the radish balls in a bag in a single layer. Vacuum-pack on high. Cook at 85°C (185°F) for 6 minutes. Chill in an ice bath.

FOR THE CORIANDER: Bring a small saucepan of water to a boil. Add the coriander seeds and cook until soft, about 5 minutes. Drain and reserve for the garnish.

Meanwhile, combine the crushed coriander and lemon juice in a small saucepan, bring to a boil over medium heat, and reduce by half. Strain and stir in the sugar and xanthan gum.

FOR THE VEGETABLES: Trim the root ends of the fennel. Remove the outer layers and tops of the fennel. Trim the carrot greens, leaving about ¼ inch. Using a paring knife, trim the carrots from top to bottom, giving them a "turned" shape.

Blanch the fennel (see Big-Pot Blanching, page 268); chill in an ice bath. Blanch the carrots; chill in an ice bath.

To complete: Heat the olive oil, foie gras fat, and the lemon-coriander mixture in a sauté pan large enough to hold all of the vegetables in one layer. Add the mushrooms, followed by the pearl onions, fennel, carrot, and radish balls; season with salt and heat through.

AT SERVICE: Arrange the vegetables on the plates and garnish with the cilantro shoots and radish rounds. Place the foie gras slices alongside the vegetables and sprinkle with sel gris. Scatter a few coriander seeds over each serving.   **MAKES 4 SERVINGS**

POACHED MOULARD DUCK FOIE GRAS, CONCORD GRAPES, CELERY, SALTED VIRGINIA PEANUT NOUGATINE, BANANA PUREE, AND PEDRO XIMENEZ SHERRY VINEGAR

FOIE GRAS

1 piece center-cut Grade A foie gras (400 grams),
  large lobe only, cold

Kosher salt and freshly ground black pepper

250 grams Duck Consommé (page 259), cold

PEANUTS

20 grams roasted unsalted Virginia peanuts

5 grams pearl sugar

1 gram fleur de sel

PICKLED GRAPES

60 grams champagne vinegar

50 grams granulated sugar

100 kilograms ice water

12 large Concord grapes

BANANA PUREE

3 ripe bananas (about 600 grams)

150 grams water

150 grams granulated sugar

3 grams ascorbic acid

CELERY

4 celery stalks

12 light green celery leaves

Micro celery leaves

Beurre Monté (page 261)

Extra virgin olive oil

Champagne vinegar

Fleur de sel

100 grams Pedro Ximenez sherry vinegar
  (see Sources, page 282)

Another dish that shows how well liver responds to the gentle heat of sous vide. In this case, a generous slice from the large lobe of a foie gras is cooked in a rich duck bouillon, and the result is deeply flavored liver with a texture that's slightly more dense than foie gras poached in fat.

The accompaniments are sweet, tart, and nutty. Aged sherry vinegar is reduced and used sparingly as a sauce. Bananas cooked sous vide in a banana syrup are pureed to make a second sauce. Grapes are peeled and pickled. And toasted ground peanuts tossed with sugar and salt add textural contrast as well as flavor.

FOR THE FOIE GRAS — 68°C (154.4°F); 22 MINUTES

Score the top of the foie gras lobe in a ½-inch crosshatch pattern. Season on all sides with salt and pepper.

Place in a bag with the duck consommé. Vacuum-pack on medium-high.

Cook at 68°C (154.4°F) for 22 minutes. Let rest at room temperature for 5 to 10 minutes.

FOR THE PEANUTS: Grind the peanuts in a food processor, pulsing to finely chop them. Transfer the nuts to a coarse strainer set in a chinois or fine-mesh conical strainer, and tap the strainers to allow the very finely ground peanuts to fall through both. Spread the ground peanuts that remain in the fine-mesh strainer on a tray. The pieces that remain in the coarse strainer can be processed and sifted again, then added to the tray.

Toast the peanuts in a 350°F oven for 10 minutes, or until golden brown. Combine the sugar and fleur de sel in a bowl, add the peanuts, and toss.

FOR THE GRAPES: Combine the vinegar and sugar in a saucepan and bring to a simmer, stirring to dissolve the sugar. Remove from the heat and stir in the ice water. Transfer to a bowl.

Peel the grapes and add them to the pickling liquid. Refrigerate for at least 3 hours. Use the grapes within a few hours of pickling, or they may discolor.

To complete: Cut the grapes lengthwise in half.

FOR THE BANANA PUREE—85°C (185°F); 10 MINUTES
Slice one-third of the bananas and place in a saucepan with the water and sugar and bring to a simmer, stirring to dissolve the sugar. Let the bananas cool to room temperature in the liquid, then set the pan over an ice bath to chill completely.

Slice the remaining 2 bananas and place in a bag. Discard the cooked banana, and strain the cooking liquid into the bag. Vacuum-pack on high.

To complete: Cook at 85°C (185°F) for 10 minutes. Remove the bag and drain the bananas, reserving the liquid. Transfer the bananas to a Vita-Prep and puree. Add the ascorbic acid and just enough liquid to make a completely smooth puree. Pass through a chinois or fine-mesh conical strainer. MAKES ABOUT 150 GRAMS

FOR THE CELERY: Peel the celery stalks. Stand each one on the cutting surface and trim off about ¼ inch from each long edge to make a flatter piece of celery with only a very slight curve. Cut two 2½-inch pieces of celery from 1 stalk. Using a Japanese mandoline, slice lengthwise into ¼-inch-thick ribbons. Put the ribbons in a bowl of ice water. Add the 12 celery leaves.

Cut twelve 2½-inch diagonal slices from the remaining celery. Chill in ice water, then drain and blanch (see Big-Pot Blanching, page 268) until tender. Transfer to an ice bath.

To complete: Drain and dry the celery ribbons, leaves, and slices. Heat just the celery slices in enough beurre monté to warm and glaze them.

Combine the celery ribbons, celery leaves, and micro celery. Lightly dress with oil, vinegar, and a sprinkle of fleur de sel.

AT SERVICE: Boil the sherry vinegar in a small saucepan to reduce by half, to a light glaze. Dry the foie gras on C-fold towels and cut crosswise into slices.

Place a spoonful of banana puree on each plate and drizzle the plates with the vinegar. Place a slice of foie gras on each plate and garnish with the celery slices, the celery salad, and the grape halves. Sprinkle with the peanuts. MAKES 4 SERVINGS

SAUTERNES-POACHED MOULARD DUCK FOIE GRAS, TAHITIAN VANILLA BEANS, BRAISED RADISHES, AND PURSLANE

RADISHES

4 icicle radishes

4 Flambeau radishes

4 large red French breakfast radishes

3 strips ginger (about 1 inch long by ½ inch wide by ⅜ inch thick)

3 bay leaves

30 grams extra virgin olive oil

30 grams champagne vinegar

Kosher salt and freshly ground black pepper

FOIE GRAS

50 grams sauternes

½ Tahitian vanilla bean, split

1 piece center-cut Grade A foie gras (400 grams), large lobe only, cold

Kosher salt and freshly ground black pepper

20 grams Quick Duck Sauce (page 260)

Sel gris

Freshly ground black pepper

Purslane sprigs

Vanilla powder (see Note)

We began poaching foie gras in wine (Gewürztraminer) before we really began using sous vide. Here we use Sauternes, a traditional pairing with foie gras, flavor it with vanilla, and cook off some of the alcohol. The foie is scored, seasoned, added to the bag with the Sauternes, and cooked gently for about twenty minutes, really just to soften it all the way through. It is very rich and almost pudding-like in texture. This should be prepared *à la minute*, because the wine will begin to break down the foie if it is left in it too long.

The three different kinds of radish are also cooked sous vide—they really pick up the flavor of the aromatics added to the bag, so you don't want to overdo it. These keep well for several days refrigerated, so make extra if you wish.

The poached foie is sliced and heated in the oven—it will not be hot enough after the gentle sous vide cooking. It is simply served with the radishes, which have a solid texture and a peppery flavor, and a sauce made from the foie gras poaching liquid and duck sauce, with a little of the radish cooking liquid.

FOR THE RADISHES—85°C (185°F); 30 MINUTES

Put the radishes in a medium bowl, cover with cold water, and brush them to remove any dirt. Trim off the top and bottom of each icicle radish, and then, with a paring knife, peel and trim them into ovals. Cut off the tops and bottoms from the Flambeau and red radishes.

Place each type of radish into a small bag. Add 1 piece of the ginger, 1 bay leaf, 10 grams olive oil, 10 grams vinegar, a sprinkling of salt, and a grind of pepper to each bag. Vacuum-pack on medium.

Cook at 85°C (185°F) for about 30 minutes. The radishes should feel tender when you feel them through the bags. The red radishes may take about 10 minutes longer than the Flambeau and icicle radishes. Remove the bags and let cool to room temperature, then chill completely in an ice bath.

Transfer each type of radish, with its cooking liquid, to a container; discard the bay leaves and ginger.

To complete: Cut the larger red radishes into quarters and the Flambeau radishes in half; leave the icicle radishes whole. Put each type of radish in a small saucepan with the reserved liquid and simmer until the liquid reduces and glazes the radishes.

FOR THE FOIE GRAS—68°C (154.4°F); 25 MINUTES

Put the Sauternes in a small saucepan. Scrape the seeds from the vanilla pod and add both seeds and pod to the pan. Bring to a boil, then remove from the heat and cool to room temperature to let the flavors infuse. Refrigerate until cold.

Place the foie gras bottom side down on a cutting surface and trim the sides to create a neatly trimmed block. Reserve the trimmings for another

use. Score both sides of the foie gras in a shallow ½-inch crosshatch pattern, for even seasoning and cooking. Refrigerate the foie gras to chill completely, at least 30 minutes.

Season the foie on all sides with salt and pepper. Place in a medium bag with the Sauternes; discard the vanilla pod. Vacuum-pack on high.

Cook at 68°C (154.4°F) for 25 minutes. The foie gras will still be soft. Remove the foie gras from the bag and drain on paper towels. Strain the liquid into a small saucepan, add the duck sauce, and bring to a simmer. Add a small spoonful of the radish cooking liquid, to taste.

Cut the foie gras crosswise into 4 equal servings, remove any visible veins, and place on an ovenproof tray.

To complete: Place the tray of foie gras in a 350°F oven for about 2 minutes, to heat through.

AT SERVICE: Spoon some sauce around each plate. Arrange the foie on the plates and sprinkle with sel gris and pepper. Garnish with radishes and sprigs of purslane and sprinkle a small amount of vanilla powder over each plate.

MAKES 4 SERVINGS

NOTE TO MAKE VANILLA POWDER

Save the pods of vanilla beans when using the seeds for another purpose. Dry the pods in a dehydrator or in a warm spot over the stove, then transfer to a grinder and grind to a powder. Strain through a chinois or fine-mesh conical strainer and store in an airtight container at room temperature.

SALADE GOURMANDE

FOIE GRAS

1 piece center-cut Grade A foie gras (400 grams),
   large lobe only, cold

2 liters whole milk, cold

About 1 kilogram kosher salt

400 grams Rendered Foie Gras Fat (page 270),
   cold

CONFIT OF DUCK GIZZARDS

8 duck gizzards

Kosher salt

50 grams Rendered Duck Fat (page 270), cold

1 thyme sprig

1 bay leaf

1 garlic clove, peeled

HAZELNUT PUREE

100 grams peeled raw hazelnuts

250 to 350 grams whole milk

250 grams heavy cream

CANDIED HAZELNUTS

100 grams water

100 grams granulated sugar

100 grams peeled raw hazelnuts

Canola oil for deep-frying

Fleur de sel

12 haricots verts, trimmed and blanched
   (see Big-Pot Blanching, page 268)

White truffle oil

Extra virgin olive oil

Sherry vinegar

Fleur de sel

Thin 1-inch rounds of black truffle

Sprigs of pissenlit

Sel gris

This is a real cook's salad, with components such as foie gras, confited gizzards, hazelnuts, and truffles, but in proportions that are perfect for people who taste plenty of rich foods. Gizzards are one of the toughest muscles you can find, so cooking them sous vide, surrounded by fat and aromatics, works well. After the long time at a low temperature, they're very tender yet not overcooked. We like to shave the foie gras, but it can also be served in large solid portions. And we add haricots verts to balance out these luxurious ingredients, along with dandelion greens, called *pissenlit* in France. **PHOTOGRAPH ON PAGE 200**

FOR THE FOIE GRAS—64°C (147.2°F); 28 MINUTES

Put the foie gras in a container and cover with about three-quarters of the milk. Lay a clean kitchen towel over the foie gras (the towel will keep the foie gras submerged) and pour the remaining milk over the top. Let sit at room temperature for about 4 hours, to bring the foie gras to about 20°C (68°F).

Drain the foie gras, rinse with cold water, and pat dry. Remove any membranes from the outside of the foie gras. Locate the start of the primary vein at one end of the underside of the lobe and slice through the lobe to the vein, following its path and pulling the foie gras apart so you can see the vein clearly. Holding your knife at a 45-degree angle, make an outward cut on each side of the vein to butterfly the foie gras—cut far enough to open the folds and expose the interior of the liver. Use your fingers and knife to remove the primary vein. Remove any small veins that are easy to get at. Return the foie gras to its original shape.

Pack the foie gras in salt to cover. Refrigerate for 6 hours to cure.

Remove the foie gras from the cure, rinse under cold water, and dry with a C-fold towel. Wrap snugly in a long single layer of cheesecloth; do not compress; maintain its shape. Tie the ends of the cheesecloth with kitchen twine. Trim off the excess cheesecloth.

Place the foie gras and fat in a bag and vacuum-pack on medium-high.

Cook at 64°C (147.2°F) for 28 minutes. The foie gras will still feel very soft. Transfer it to a container and strain the fat over the top. Refrigerate.

To complete: Remove the cheesecloth, remove the foie gras from the fat, and scrape off the fat clinging to it. If you will be slicing the foie gras on a meat slicer, place it in the freezer until hard enough to slice evenly; or refrigerate until serving. (The fat can be strained, refrigerated, and reused up to 3 times.)

FOR THE DUCK GIZZARDS —82.2°C (180°F); 8 HOURS

Cut away the silverskin surrounding the gizzards. Pack the gizzards in salt to cover and refrigerate for 1 hour.

Rinse the gizzards under cold water and pat dry. Refrigerate for 30 minutes.

Place the cold gizzards in a bag and add the duck fat, thyme, bay leaf, and garlic. Vacuum-pack on medium.

Cook at 82.2°C (180°F) for 8 hours. Remove from the water and let the gizzards rest for 10 minutes at room temperature. Chill the bag in an ice bath, then refrigerate.

To complete: Remove the gizzards from the bag, wipe off any fat, and slice crosswise into thin slices. Discard the ends.

FOR THE HAZELNUT PUREE: Toast the hazelnuts in a 350°F oven until they are a rich golden brown, about 15 minutes.

Transfer the nuts to a saucepan and cover with 250 grams milk and the cream. Bring to a simmer and simmer gently for about 1½ hours, to soften the nuts enough to puree them in a Vita-Prep. If the liquid reduces too much, add up to 100 grams more milk to keep the nuts covered.

Drain the hazelnuts, reserving the liquid. Transfer the nuts to the Vita-Prep and, with the machine running, begin adding enough of the liquid to allow the nuts to spin. Continue adding liquid until you have a silky-smooth puree. Pass through a chinois or fine-mesh conical strainer. Refrigerate.   MAKES ABOUT 250 GRAMS

FOR THE CANDIED HAZELNUTS: Combine the water and sugar in a saucepan and bring to a boil over medium-high heat, stirring to dissolve the sugar. Add the hazelnuts to the syrup and reduce the heat to medium. (When you candy nuts, the simple syrup should just cover them.) Simmer very gently, adjusting the heat as necessary, for 45 to 55 minutes, until the syrup reduces and the nuts are glazed. As the syrup reduces, move the hazelnuts in the pan from time to time. Pour out onto a rack set over a sheet pan and separate any nuts that stick together.

To complete: Heat the canola oil in a sauté pan to 163°C (325°F). Add about half the nuts—do not overcrowd them—and cook until they are a rich brown, about 4 to 5 minutes. Remove to a parchment-lined sheet pan. Sprinkle with fleur de sel. Cook the remaining nuts.

AT SERVICE: Toss the beans and gizzard slices with a few drops each of truffle oil, olive oil, and sherry vinegar and a sprinkling of fleur de sel.

Spoon the hazelnut puree onto serving plates. Arrange the beans, gizzard slices, candied hazelnuts, and rounds of black truffle on the plates. If shaving the foie gras with a meat slicer, use the thinnest setting possible and arrange the shavings on the plates. If serving the foie gras in slabs, cut into ½-inch slices and score the tops with a ¼-inch crosshatch pattern; arrange over the salads. Garnish with pissenlit. Sprinkle the foie gras with sel gris.   MAKES 12 SERVINGS

Opposite: *Salade Gourmande* (page 198); above: *Chaud-Froid* of Moulard Duck Fois Gras, Musquée de Provence, Pomegranate Seeds, Mizuna Leaves, and Gingerbread Puree (page 202)

CHAUD-FROID OF MOULARD DUCK FOIE GRAS, MUSQUÉE DE PROVENCE, POMEGRANATE SEEDS, MIZUNA LEAVES, AND GINGERBREAD PUREE

FOIE GRAS

1 whole Grade A foie gras (1 kilogram),
    at room temperature

280 grams Foie Gras Cure (page 267)

500 grams Rendered Duck Fat (page 270), cold

GINGERBREAD CRUMBS AND PUREE

115 grams all-purpose flour

3 grams powdered ginger

1.5 grams ground allspice

2 grams baking soda

2 grams baking powder

2 grams kosher salt

60 grams unsalted butter, at room temperature

60 grams light brown sugar

1 large egg

115 grams molasses

About 115 grams water, hot

STREUSEL

35 grams almond flour

35 grams granulated sugar

40 grams all-purpose flour

35 grams unsalted butter

PUMPKIN

96 batons musquée de Provence
    (about 1½ inches by ¼ inch)

Extra virgin olive oil

Kosher salt

Granulated sugar

60 "buttons" musquée de Provence
    (about ¾ wide and ¼ inch thick)

POMEGRANATE REDUCTION

250 grams pomegranate juice

50 grams granulated sugar

20 grams Rendered Foie Gras Fat (page 270)

1 or 2 white or red pomegranates

Extra virgin olive oil

Micro mizuna greens

For this *chaud-froid* preparation, a slice of cold foie gras terrine is run under the salamander so that it's partly warm and crispy and partly cool and creamy. It also describes a method of making a foie gras terrine that is very easy thanks to sous vide techniques.

The whole foie gras is cleaned and packed in a salt cure for 24 hours. Then it's cooked sous vide with duck fat (the density of the added fat reduces the amount of fat that cooks out of the foie gras) and placed in a terrine mold, which will shape it as it cools. That's all there is to it. Once it's chilled, it's ready to slice. The slices are coated with a gingerbread-streusel mixture and then browned under the salamander. They are served with a puree made from the sauce of gingerbread crumbs, along with musquée de Provence, an aromatic sweet pumpkin, and a garnish of pomegranate seeds and mizuna.

PHOTOGRAPH ON PAGE 201

FOR THE FOIE GRAS—68°C (154.4°F); 20 MINUTES

Remove any membranes from the outside of the foie gras. Locate the start of the primary vein at one end of the underside of the lobe and slice through the lobe to the vein, following its path and pulling the foie gras apart so you can see the vein clearly. Holding your knife at a 45-degree angle, make an outward cut on each side of the vein to butterfly the foie gras—cut far enough to open the folds and expose the interior of the liver. Use your fingers and knife to remove the primary vein. Remove any small veins that are easy to get at. Return the foie gras to its original shape.

Pour about one-third of the foie gras cure into a container. Top with the foie gras and pack in the remaining cure. Refrigerate for 24 hours.

Rinse the foie gras and pat dry (discard the cure). Place the foie gras in a bag with the duck fat and vacuum-pack on medium.

Cook at 68°C (154.4°F) for 20 minutes.

Line a 6-by-3½-by-3-inch-high terrine mold with food-safe plastic wrap, leaving an overhang on the two long sides. Remove the hot foie gras from the bag and place it in the terrine. Cut a piece of cardboard that will rest on the foie gras, wrap it in plastic, and set on the foie gras. Place a weight or weights on the cardboard, and refrigerate overnight.

To complete: Remove the foie gras from the refrigerator. Remove the weight and cardboard. Run a hot knife around the edges of the terrine, and unmold it. Trim the sides of the terrine to even the edges and cut into thin slices.

FOR THE GINGERBREAD CRUMBS: Mix the dry ingredients. Cream the butter and brown sugar with a sturdy spoon or in the bowl of a stand mixer fitted with a paddle. Beat in the egg. Add the molasses. Sift in the dry ingredients and incorporate.

Line a half sheet pan with a Silpat. Spread the batter in an even layer about ⅛ inch thick, almost filling the pan. Bake in a 350°F oven for about 15 minutes, until golden, rotating the pan once or twice. Cool to room temperature.

Break up the sheet of gingerbread and process to fine crumbs in a food processor.   MAKES ABOUT 325 GRAMS

FOR THE STREUSEL: Combine the dry ingredients in a bowl. Add the butter and work it in with your fingertips to distribute it and form a crumbly mixture. The streusel will weigh 145 grams. Add an equal amount of gingerbread crumbs to the streusel.

Spread the mixture on a Silpat-lined sheet pan and bake at 350°F for 16 to 18 minutes, stirring halfway through to brown the crumbs evenly. Let cool.   MAKES ABOUT 275 GRAMS

FOR THE GINGERBREAD PUREE: Put the remaining gingerbread crumbs in a blender and slowly add enough hot water to form a puree. Pass through a chinois or fine-mesh conical strainer.

MAKES ABOUT 270 GRAMS

FOR THE PUMPKIN—85°C (185°F); 5 TO 6 MINUTES
Toss the batons with a drizzle of olive oil and a light sprinkling of salt and sugar. Line them up in a single layer in a bag and vacuum-pack on high. Repeat with the pumpkin buttons.

Cook at 85°C (185°F) for 5 to 6 minutes, until tender.

FOR THE POMEGRANATE REDUCTION: Combine the pomegranate juice and sugar in a saucepan and bring to a simmer, stirring to dissolve the sugar. Continue to simmer, to reduce to about 120 grams. Add the foie gras fat, remove from the heat; let cool to room temperature.

MAKES ABOUT 140 GRAMS

AT SERVICE: Break the pomegranates into small clusters and then into individual seeds. Toss with a drizzle of olive oil.

Spread a spoonful of gingerbread puree onto each serving plate and drizzle the plates with the pomegranate reduction.

Cut 12 slices of foie gras, each about 4 inches long by ¾ inch wide and ½ inch thick. Hold each piece on a palette knife over a plate and sprinkle with the streusel mixture, then transfer to an ovenproof tray. Briefly brown the tops under the salamander, and place a slice of foie gras on each plate. Garnish with the pomegranate seeds, pumpkin, and mizuna.

MAKES 12 SERVINGS

CHEESE & DESSERTS

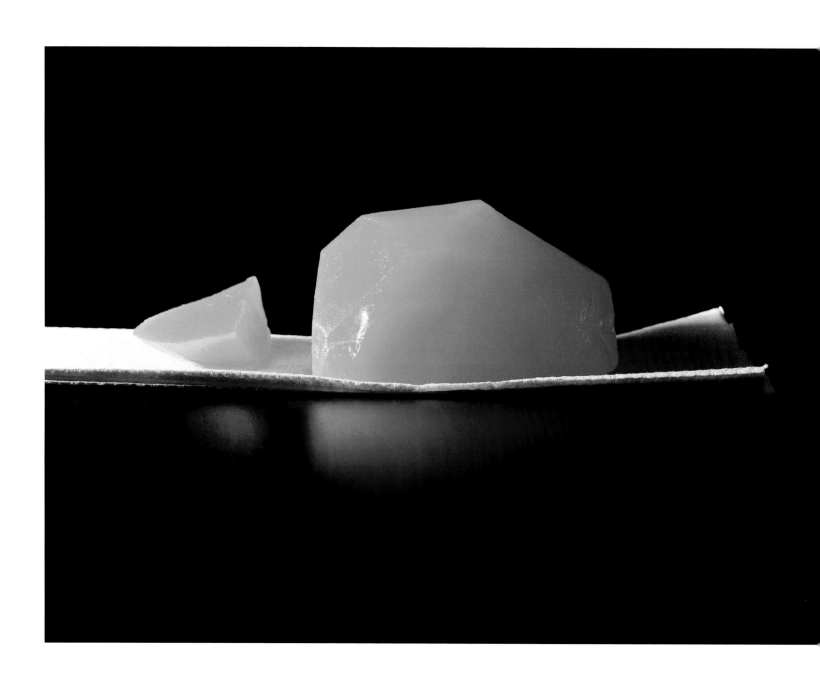

Overleaf and above: cantaloupe, before and after compression

THE SOUS VIDE APPLICATIONS FOR CHEESES AND DESSERTS FALL INTO THREE CATEGORIES:

preparing bases, compressing fruit, and cooking fruits and vegetables.

Custards, one such base preparation, are great to do sous vide because of convenience and shelf life. The process pasteurizes the mixture so that it stays very fresh for as much as 1 week in the bag. The custard is always consistent and, stored flat in its bags, it takes up less room than in a cooler.

Compressing fruit was a revelation discovered by Mark Hopper, chef de cuisine at Bouchon in Las Vegas. When he first showed us a piece of watermelon that looked like a slice of raw tuna, we were amazed. You can achieve such effects only with vacuum-packers.

And the fruits and vegetables that may be either garnish or the featured item on a dessert plate—apples and pears, endive—are often best cooked in the gentle airless environment of the sous vide bag. Some fruits, such as plums, become vividly translucent and so make a striking visual presentation.

ANDANTE DAIRY ACAPELLA, COMPRESSED SILVERADO TRAIL STRAWBERRIES, AND SICILIAN PISTACHIO SABLÉ

PISTACHIO SABLÉ

25 grams ground (see Note) raw green Sicilian
　　pistachios (see Sources, page 282)

50 grams unsalted butter, cut into pieces,
　　at room temperature

20 grams confectioners' sugar

3.5 grams egg yolk (beat the whole yolk
　　to break it up)

43 grams all-purpose flour, plus more for the
　　work surface

Pinch of kosher salt

STRAWBERRIES

8 medium strawberries, stemmed

100 grams water

100 grams granulated sugar

50 grams red wine vinegar

1 gelatin sheet (2 grams),
　　soaked in cold water to soften

CHEESE

1 wheel (150 grams) ripe Acapella cheese
　　(see Sources, page 282), at room temperature

80 grams crème fraîche

This dish was inspired by the Wimbledon tradition of Champagne and strawberries with scones and clotted cream. Goat cheese serves as the cream and buttery sablés, flavored with fresh Sicilian pistachios, become the scones. The goat cheese is made by Soyoung Scanlan at her Andante Dairy; Soyoung's collaboration, creating new products for us, is invaluable. Her Acapella becomes piquant and peppery when it's very mature, overripe. The strength of its flavor allows us to whip in crème fraîche that balances the flavor without overwhelming it and gives it a luxurious texture similar to clotted cream.

The Silverado Trail strawberries, practically from our backyard, are sealed sous vide with a sweet-sour syrup that infuses the berries, sweetening them and, in turn, pulling out juices that will flavor the syrup. The syrup is jelled and used to coat diced strawberries in the finished dish.

At our restaurants, we use a plate with a shallow well in the center to hold the strawberry gelatin. Alternatively, it can be served in very small shallow bowls. Note that, despite our suggesting this serves eight people, the size of your plate will affect serving size, so the yield can vary.

There may be extra cookies and there may be extra strawberry gelatin, again depending on the size of your plates.

FOR THE SABLÉ: Combine all the ingredients in a large bowl and work gently with your hands to form a dough. Wrap the dough and chill until it is firm enough to roll.

Sprinkle the work surface with flour and roll the dough into a 6-inch square that is about ¼ inch thick.

Place the sheet of dough on a Silpat-lined sheet tray. Bake at 350°F for 11 minutes. Remove from the oven and cut the sablé into 1⅛-inch rounds, or rounds slightly smaller than the individual strawberry gelatins will be. Bake for another 7 to 8 minutes, or until golden. Cool on a rack.

MAKES ABOUT TWENTY-FOUR 1 1/8-INCH COOKIES

FOR THE STRAWBERRIES: Cut 4 of the strawberries lengthwise in half. Cut the remaining 4 strawberries into ¼-inch dice.

Combine the water and sugar in a saucepan and heat, stirring to dissolve the sugar. Remove from the heat and add the red wine vinegar. Whisk over an ice bath or refrigerate until cold.

Combine the strawberry halves and the dice with the cold syrup in a medium bag. Vacuum-pack on high. Let stand at room temperature for about 2 hours.

Remove the strawberries from the bag and dry on C-fold towels. Separate the sliced berries from the diced. Set the sliced berries aside. Strain 125 grams of the liquid into a small saucepan (the extra liquid can be reserved for another purpose). Heat the liquid until hot, remove from the heat, and stir in the soaked gelatin to dissolve. Stir over an ice bath to cool to just above body temperature; you do not want the gelatin to begin to set.

Place a small spoonful of the diced strawberries in the depression in each serving dish (see headnote) or in small bowls. Spoon the strawberry liquid over to cover the berries. Refrigerate to set the gelatin.

FOR THE CHEESE: Cut off all the rind and put the cheese in a bowl. Stir in the crème fraîche. Pass the cheese through a chinois or fine-mesh conical strainer into another bowl. MAKES ABOUT 125 GRAMS

AT SERVICE: Top each strawberry gelatin with a sablé, a spoonful of cheese, and a half strawberry. **MAKES 8 SERVINGS**

NOTE

To grind the pistachios, pulse them in a food processor to finely chop them. Put the nuts in a fine-mesh basket strainer and tap to allow the finely ground pistachios to fall through. The larger pieces in the strainer can be reprocessed and strained again.

Above: sesame oil sablé (see page 247); opposite: wedge-cut Anjou pears (see page 216)

FOURME D'AMBERT, PAN-ROASTED CAULIFLOWER, ANJOU PEAR PUREE, AND TELLICHERRY PEPPER MELBA TOAST

CAULIFLOWER

Twelve ¾-inch cauliflower florets

Kosher salt and freshly ground Tellicherry pepper

70 grams unsalted butter

Clarified Butter (page 261)

Extra virgin olive oil

Champagne vinegar

PEAR GARNISH AND PUREE

145 grams water

145 grams granulated sugar

5 grams ascorbic acid

500 grams Anjou pears (2 to 3 pears)

Kosher salt and freshly ground Tellicherry pepper

MELBA TOAST

Clarified Butter (page 261)

Kosher salt and freshly ground Tellicherry pepper

Four 4-by-1-by-1/16-inch-thick strips Brioche
(page 262)

About 120 grams Fourme d'Ambert,
at room temperature

Micro arugula greens

Extra virgin olive oil

Kosher salt and freshly ground Tellicherry pepper

Fourme d'Ambert is a mild French blue cheese. Here it's paired with cauliflower and two pear preparations. Both the pears and the cauliflower are cooked sous vide. The vacuum pressure used to seal the cauliflower florets helps to preserve their shape as they cook, and there's no loss of flavor to the cooking environment. The same goes for the wedges of pear, a delicate fruit that can become too soft when poached. For the pear puree, we combine the pears with ascorbic acid, which helps keep them very bright. Just before serving, we caramelize the cauliflower in a sauté pan to give it color and more flavor.

FOR THE CAULIFLOWER—85°C (185°F); 15 MINUTES

Toss the cauliflower florets with a pinch each of salt and pepper and place in a bag with the butter. Vacuum-pack on medium-high.

Cook at 85°C (185°F) for 15 minutes, or until tender but not mushy. Chill in an ice bath.

To complete: Melt enough clarified butter to come about one-quarter of the way up the cauliflower in a small sauté pan. Add the cauliflower, stem end up, and sauté over medium-high heat to caramelize. Drain on a paper towel and rub the tops of the florets with a little olive oil and a couple of drops of vinegar.

FOR THE PEAR GARNISH AND PURÉE—83°C (181.4°F); 25 MINUTES/45 TO 60 MINUTES

Combine the water, sugar, and ascorbic acid in a saucepan and bring to a simmer, stirring to dissolve the sugar. Set the pan over an ice bath to cool the syrup completely.

For the garnish: Fill a bowl with acidulated water (see page 269). Cut both ends from 1 pear, then cut the pear lengthwise in half. Cut each half into 6 wedges and remove the cores. With a paring knife, peel each wedge and trim into an oval football shape. As you finish each wedge, drop it into the acidulated water. Use some of a second pear if necessary.

When you have 200 grams of pear wedges, remove them from the ice bath, transfer to a bag, and add 85 grams of the syrup. Vacuum-pack on medium-high.

For the puree: Peel the remaining pear(s) and cut into wedges the same size as those for the garnish—you will need a total of 12. Remove the cores and drop into the acidulated water as they are cut. Place the pears and the remaining syrup in a bag and vacuum-pack on high.

To cook: Cook both bags at 83°C (181.4°F). Cook the pear garnish for 25 minutes. The pears for the puree should be completely soft and will take 45 to 60 minutes.

To complete: Drain the pears for the puree and puree them in a blender, scraping down the sides of the container as necessary. Season with salt and pepper.   MAKES ABOUT 200 GRAMS PUREE

FOR THE MELBA TOAST: Line a sheet pan with a Silpat and brush with clarified butter. Sprinkle lightly with salt and pepper. Put the brioche slices on the Silpat and sprinkle lightly with salt and pepper. Brush a second Silpat with butter and place it butter side down over the brioche.

Bake at 300°F for 13 to 15 minutes, or until golden brown. Let cool.

AT SERVICE: Cut the cheese into 4 pieces and place a piece on each serving plate. Garnish with the pear puree, wedges of pear, cauliflower florets, and Melba toast.

Toss the arugula with a drizzle of olive oil and salt and pepper to taste. Arrange over the pears and cauliflower and add a grinding of black pepper to the plate.   **MAKES 4 SERVINGS**

JASPER HILLS WINNEMERE CROQUANTE, CONFIT POTATO, PAN-ROASTED SAVOY CABBAGE, AND BLIS MAPLE SYRUP

CHEESE

150 grams Jasper Hills Winnemere cheese
   (see Sources, page 282), trimmed of rind,
   at room temperature

50 grams mascarpone

Six 4-by-4-by-⅛-inch slices Brioche (page 262),
   crusts removed

Beaten eggs (2 large)

65 grams organic cornflakes,
   crushed into fine crumbs

Clarified Butter (page 261)

POTATOES

1 large Yukon Gold potato (150 grams), cold

Extra virgin olive oil

Kosher salt and freshly ground white pepper

CABBAGE

1 small head savoy cabbage

Clarified Butter (page 261)

Blis maple syrup (see Sources, page 282)

The inspiration for this was simple: the grilled cheese sandwich, a staple of our childhood. Winnemere, a delicate raw cow's-milk cheese washed with lambic-style beer, is available November through April. We whip it with mascarpone, pipe it onto thin slices of bread, and shape them into roulades. We freeze them to make them easier to work with. We coat the roulades with crushed cornflakes and sauté them in clarified butter. It's important to take care in coating the bread so that the cheese doesn't leak out when you heat it. The result is a golden crisp exterior and warm melting cheese within.

The confit potatoes are cooked sous vide with a little olive oil—that's it. The plate also includes glazed cabbage and, for sweetness, a little maple syrup.

FOR THE CHEESE: With a sturdy spoon, mix the Winnemere cheese and mascarpone together in a bowl until well combined. Transfer to a pastry bag fitted with a large (#8) plain tip.

Lay a piece of food-safe plastic wrap about 12 inches long on the work surface. Place a slice of bread in the center of the plastic. (Keep the remaining slices of bread covered as you work; if they dry out, they will not roll properly.) Pipe a strip of cheese across the bottom of the bread. Use the plastic wrap to help roll up the bread and cheese into a cylinder, and twist the ends of the plastic wrap to compress and shape the log. Knot the ends of the wrap and cut off any excess plastic. Repeat to make 5 more logs.

Freeze the logs for several hours, until completely frozen.

To complete: Unwrap the logs. Dip the frozen logs in the beaten egg and then into the cornflakes to coat completely.

Heat about ½ inch clarified butter in a medium sauté pan over medium to medium-high heat. Add the logs and roll in the butter to brown evenly on all sides and heat the cheese, about 2 to 3 minutes. Drain on C-fold towels.

FOR THE POTATOES—85°C (185°F); 1 HOUR
Trim the potato to a rectangle, then cut 6 thick matchsticks of potato about 2 inches by ¾ inch by ½ inch. (Reserve the remaining potato for another use.)

Toss the potatoes with a drizzle of olive oil and a sprinkling of salt and white pepper. Place in a bag in a single layer and vacuum-pack on high.

Cook at 85°C (185°F) for 1 hour, or until the potatoes are tender.

FOR THE CABBAGE: Core the cabbage and remove the outer leaves. Remove 3 or 4 unblemished leaves. (Reserve the remaining cabbage for another use.) Cut out and discard the ribs from the leaves, then cut the leaves into 2-inch triangles or diamonds. Blanch (see Big-Pot Blanching, page 268) just until tender. Chill in an ice bath.

To complete: Heat a film of clarified butter in a sauté pan. Add the cabbage and sauté for 3 to 4 minutes, until hot, tossing it several times. Remove the pan from the heat, drain off the clarified butter.

AT SERVICE: Place a small spoonful of maple syrup in the center of each plate. Place a strip of potato and some cabbage on each plate, and put the cheese logs on the potatoes. **MAKES 6 SERVINGS**

SALAD OF HEIRLOOM BEETS, ANJOU PEAR, MÂCHE, CANDIED WALNUTS, AND BLUE APRON GOAT CHEESE COULIS

BEETS

4 small red beets

4 small pink beets

4 small yellow beets

75 grams canola oil

15 black peppercorns

3 garlic cloves, crushed and peeled

9 thyme sprigs

30 grams kosher salt, plus more to taste

45 grams extra virgin olive oil

60 grams sherry vinegar

CANDIED WALNUTS

150 grams water

150 grams granulated sugar

100 grams raw walnuts

Canola oil for deep-frying

GOAT CHEESE COULIS

40 grams buttermilk

40 grams crème fraîche

25 grams canola oil

150 grams fresh goat cheese

2 grams champagne vinegar

Kosher salt

BEET REDUCTION

465 grams beet juice

5 grams granulated sugar

Red wine vinegar

Kosher salt

PEAR

1 kilogram cold water

3.3 grams ascorbic acid

1 Anjou or Asian pear

Extra virgin olive oil

Kosher salt

Baby mâche

Extra virgin olive oil

Champagne vinegar

Fleur de sel

Beet Powder (page 263)

We serve this traditional flavor pairing—beets, goat cheese, and walnuts—as a cheese course, but it could just as easily be an appetizer. The beets are not cooked sous vide, because in this dish we like the complex flavors that develop through roasting, but we do marinate the cooked and cooled beets in oil and sherry vinegar sous vide to give them even more flavor.

Blue Apron goat cheese is made specially for us, but any fresh goat cheese, such as Coach Farm, would work in this recipe. We blend the goat cheese with buttermilk and canola oil to make the coulis, then pass it through a strainer for a very smooth texture. The walnuts are first cooked in a simple syrup, then deep-fried until very crispy. The dish is finished with beet powder and a beet reduction, and a delicate salad of baby mâche. PHOTOGRAPH ON PAGE 217

FOR THE BEETS: Wash the beets and trim the stems to about 1 inch. Put each type of beet on a piece of aluminum foil. Divide the canola oil, peppercorns, garlic, thyme, and salt among the beets, wrap up in the foil, and place on a sheet tray. Roast at 400°F for 25 minutes, or until there is no resistance when the beets are pierced with a sharp knife. Cool slightly.

When they are cool enough to handle, rub each warm beet with a C-fold towel to remove the skin. Trim away the stems and roots.

Place each type of beet in its own bag and season each with 15 grams of the olive oil, 20 grams of the sherry vinegar, and salt to taste. Vacuum-pack on high. Refrigerate for 8 to 12 hours.

FOR THE CANDIED WALNUTS: Combine the water and sugar in a saucepan and bring to a boil over medium-high heat, stirring to dissolve the sugar. (When you candy nuts, the simple syrup should just cover them.) Stir in the walnuts and reduce the heat to medium. Simmer very gently, adjusting the heat as necessary, for 45 to 55 minutes, or until the liquid reduces and the nuts are glazed. As the syrup reduces, stir the nuts from time to time to cook them evenly. Pour out onto a rack set over a sheet pan. Separate any nuts that have stuck together.

To complete: Heat the canola oil to about 163°C (325°F). Add about half the nuts—do not crowd them—and fry, moving them around from time to time, until they are a rich brown, 4 to 5 minutes. Remove to a parchment-lined sheet pan. Repeat with the remaining nuts. Once cooled, the walnuts can be cut into smaller pieces as desired.

FOR THE GOAT CHEESE COULIS: Combine the buttermilk, crème fraîche, and oil in a Vita-Prep and blend well. Add the cheese and blend until smooth, scraping down the sides as necessary. Strain through a chinois or fine-mesh conical strainer into a bowl. Stir in the vinegar and season to taste with salt.   MAKES ABOUT 250 GRAMS

FOR THE BEET REDUCTION: Bring the beet juice to a boil in a saucepan over medium heat and boil to reduce. Each time you can see a ring around the side of the pan, strain the juice into a clean pan. Reduce until the juice has reduced by three-quarters. Add the sugar and stir until the sugar dissolves and the reduction is at the desired viscosity. Add a few drops of red wine vinegar and salt to taste.   MAKES ABOUT 110 GRAMS

FOR THE PEAR: Combine the water and ascorbic acid in a bowl, stirring to dissolve the ascorbic acid. Peel the pear. Working quickly, since the pear can discolor, cut into $\frac{1}{2}$-inch wedges: to cut perfect wedges, leave the pear whole and cut the wedges away from it, stopping short of the core (see photograph, page 211). As you cut, drop the wedges into the acidulated water.

Drain the wedges and toss with a light coating of olive oil and a sprinkling of salt. Place in a single layer in a bag and vacuum-pack on high.

AT SERVICE: With a spoon, sweep some goat cheese coulis across the top half of each plate. Brush a band of beet reduction over the bottom. Lightly dress the mâche leaves with olive oil, champagne vinegar, and fleur de sel. Arrange the beets on the plates, garnish with the mâche and walnut pieces, and sprinkle the plates with beet powder and fleur de sel.

MAKES 4 SERVINGS

Salad of Heirloom Beets, Anjou Pear, Mâche, Candied Walnuts, and Blue Apron Goat Cheese Coulis (page 215)

SWEET GARDEN CARROT CAKE, CREAM CHEESE ICING, CANDIED WALNUT CRUNCH, BLACK RAISIN COULIS, CARROT BUTTONS, INDONESIAN CINNAMON ICE CREAM, AND *GELÉE DE CAROTTE ET SA POUDRE*

CAKE

185 grams all-purpose flour

2.5 grams Indonesian cinnamon powder
   (see Sources, page 282)

3.5 grams baking soda

1.5 grams baking powder

205 grams granulated sugar

145 grams canola oil

75 grams lightly beaten eggs (1 to 2 large)

3 grams kosher salt

240 grams shredded carrots (8 to 9 medium)

CREAM CHEESE FROSTING

115 grams 83% unsalted butter,
   at room temperature

225 grams confectioners' sugar

4 grams vanilla extract

1 Madagascar vanilla bean

170 grams Philadelphia cream cheese, cold

CARROT BUTTONS

6 to 8 medium carrots, peeled

1.2 kilograms orange juice, cold

500 grams granulated sugar

CANDIED WALNUTS

115 grams water

210 grams granulated sugar

Kosher salt

100 grams walnut halves

CARROT GELÉE AND POWDER

About 500 grams carrots

75 grams Simple Syrup (page 267)

2 grams agar-agar (see Sources, page 282)

RAISIN COULIS

600 grams Poaching Liquid (page 267)

200 grams dark raisins

CINNAMON ICE CREAM

5 large egg yolks

90 grams granulated sugar

1.5 grams Indonesian cinnamon powder
   (see Sources, page 282)

38 grams dry milk powder

240 grams whole milk, cold

240 grams heavy cream, cold

2 cinnamon sticks

80 grams Sweet Base Syrup (page 268)

Small chervil sprigs

The first carrot cake Sebastien saw made an impression on him. He was sixteen years old, working in a restaurant, and saw a Japanese chef working with carrots and then suddenly there was a cake, made with carrots! It was new to him, and he loved the idea of using vegetables in desserts. In America, of course, carrot cake with a cream cheese icing is traditional—and that was the beginning of the dessert. These two components are pretty straightforward, traditional recipes, down to the Philadelphia cream cheese. The cinnamon ice cream is almost a joke on Sebastien, because the pastry chefs at per se know that he's always wondered why cinnamon is so predominant in America—everything has cinnamon in it, it seems. But here it pairs perfectly with the carrot. This is a rich dish, but because of the carrots, it feels light rather than heavy. PHOTOGRAPH ON PAGES 220-21

FOR THE CAKE: Line a quarter sheet pan with a Silpat and spray lightly with nonstick spray. Sift together the flour, cinnamon, baking soda, and baking powder.

Mix the sugar and oil together in a stand mixer fitted with the paddle attachment. Mix in half of the eggs, then mix in the remaining eggs. Add the salt.

Toss the shredded carrots with about 75 grams of the flour mixture. (Flouring the carrots will keep them from sticking together when they are added to the batter.) Add the remaining flour mixture to the batter in 2 additions. Mix in the carrots.

Spread the batter in the prepared pan and bake at 325°F for 18 minutes, or until the top is golden and a skewer or toothpick inserted into the center comes out clean. Cool briefly, then invert the cake onto a rack and let cool.

To complete: Cut the carrot cake into ¾-inch cubes.

FOR THE FROSTING: Cream the butter in a stand mixer fitted with the whisk attachment. Add the sugar and vanilla extract. Split the vanilla bean and scrape the seeds into the mixture. Mix well. Add the cream cheese and beat for 2 minutes, or until smooth and creamy.

MAKES 475 GRAMS

FOR THE CARROT BUTTONS—95°C (203°F); 3 HOURS
Scrape the exterior of the carrots gently with a peeler to remove any dirt. Slice about ⅛ inch thick; you need 100 buttons. Using a cutter, cut into rounds about ½ inch in diameter.

Place the carrots in five bags, 20 per bag. Add 240 grams of the orange juice and 100 grams of the sugar to each. Vacuum-pack on medium.

Cook at 95°C (203°F) for about 3 hours, or until the carrots are tender.

FOR THE WALNUTS: Combine the water, 105 grams of the sugar, and a pinch of salt in a saucepan and bring to a boil, stirring to dissolve the sugar. Add the walnuts and cook for 5 minutes.

Drain the walnuts, reserving the liquid, and pour the liquid into another pan. Add the remaining 105 grams sugar and bring to a boil, stirring to dissolve the sugar. Return the nuts to the syrup and cook for another 5 minutes.

Drain the nuts and spread them out in a single layer on a Silpat-lined half sheet pan. Bake at 300°F in a convection oven for 18 to 20 minutes, or until golden, turning and stirring the nuts every 5 minutes for even cooking and coloring.

Cool the nuts to room temperature. Process in a food processor until coarsely chopped. The nuts can be vacuum-packed and kept at room temperature for 1 month or in the freezer for several months.

MAKES 135 GRAMS

FOR THE CARROT GELÉE: Run the carrots through a juicer to yield 250 grams of carrot juice. Reserve some of the pulverized carrots for the carrot powder (see page 263).

Line a 9-inch square baking pan with food-safe plastic wrap, leaving an overhang on all sides. Bring the carrot juice and syrup to a boil in a saucepan. Once it boils, whisk in the agar-agar and simmer for 10 seconds. Strain through a chinois or fine-mesh conical strainer into the prepared pan. Let stand until the gelée is set, then refrigerate.

To complete: Cut the gelée into ⅜-inch squares.

FOR THE COULIS: Bring the poaching liquid to a simmer in a saucepan. Add the raisins and simmer for about 5 minutes, until plumped. Drain the raisins, reserving the liquid.

Transfer the raisins and 300 grams of the liquid to a Vita-Prep and process on high speed to a smooth paste. When there is a hole in the center of the mixture and you can see the bottom of the blender, the coulis is the correct consistency; add additional poaching liquid if necessary to reach the desired consistency.

Spoon the coulis onto a tamis set over a sheet pan. If the coulis is thinner than you would like, let the excess liquid drain, then discard it. Pass the coulis through the tamis. Keep refrigerated.

MAKES 210 GRAMS

FOR THE ICE CREAM—85° TO 82°C (185° TO 179.6°F); 20 MINUTES
In the bowl of a stand mixer, whisk the yolks and sugar to the ribbon stage, 5 to 7 minutes. Add the cinnamon, milk powder, whole milk, and cream and mix well. Strain the base into a bag and add the cinnamon sticks. Refrigerate until cold if necessary.

Vacuum-pack on medium: when the liquid begins to bubble, seal the bag.

Add the bag to 85°C (185°F) water and reduce the temperature to 82°C (179.6°F). Cook for 20 minutes.

The custard may look a bit broken when it comes out of the water. Lay the bag on a work surface and move the edges up and down so it recombines. Let sit at room temperature for 5 minutes, then put the bag in an ice bath. Refrigerate for a day to allow the flavors to develop.

Strain the base through a chinois or fine-mesh conical strainer into a bowl, and add the base syrup. Freeze in a PacoJet or ice cream machine.

MAKES ABOUT 500 GRAMS

AT SERVICE: Spoon some raisin coulis onto each serving plate. Arrange the cubes of cake, squares of gelée, and carrot buttons on the plates and garnish with the frosting. Sprinkle a bed of walnut crunch on each plate. Top with a scoop of ice cream. Garnish with a sprinkle of carrot powder and chervil sprigs.

MAKES 20 SERVINGS

Opposite: carrot rounds; above: Sweet Garden Carrot Cake, Cream Cheese Icing, Candied Walnut Crunch, Black Raisin Coulis, Carrot Buttons, Indonesian Cinnamon Ice Cream, and *Gelée de Carotte et Sa Poudre* (page 218)

PEANUT BUTTER MOUSSE WITH CARAMELIZED BANANAS, BANANA SHERBET, CHOCOLATE PUDDING, AND CACAO NIB COULIS

PEANUT BUTTER MOUSSE

167 grams eggs (3 to 4 large)

90 grams confectioners' sugar

240 grams heavy cream

3 gelatin sheets (2 grams each),
    soaked in cold water to soften

220 grams creamy peanut butter,
    at room temperature

PEANUT CRUNCH

52 grams milk chocolate

60 grams cocoa butter
    (see Sources, page 282)

235 grams creamy peanut butter

Kosher salt

75 grams Spanish peanuts, skinned and chopped

115 grams feuilletine (see Sources, page 282)

PEANUT GLAZE

125 grams heavy cream

375 grams neutral glaze
    (see Sources, page 282)

90 grams water

310 grams milk chocolate, melted

100 grams creamy peanut butter

BANANA TUILES

250 grams ripe bananas (2 to 3), peeled and cut
    into chunks

60 grams granulated sugar

50 grams all-purpose flour

50 grams whole milk

55 grams Valrhona 60% praline paste
    (see Sources, page 282)

60 grams unsalted butter, melted

BANANA MOUSSE

300 grams white chocolate, chopped

290 grams heavy cream

3 large egg yolks

125 grams Boiron banana puree
    (see Sources, page 282)

2½ gelatin sheets (2 grams each), soaked in cold
    water to soften

7 grams banana extract (see Sources, page 282)

BANANA SHERBET

225 grams granulated sugar

1 vanilla bean, split

1 kilogram orange juice

4 firm bananas (with pale green edges on the
    outside; 750 grams)

120 grams whole milk

325 grams Sweet Base Syrup (page 268)

PEANUT SABLÉ

100 grams roasted salted Spanish peanuts

60 grams 83% unsalted butter,
    at room temperature

40 grams granulated sugar

½ Madagascar vanilla bean, split

2 grams fleur de sel

55 grams all-purpose flour

CHOCOLATE PUDDING

110 grams Valrhona Manjari 64% chocolate
    (see Sources, page 282), coarsely chopped

162 grams heavy cream

½ Madagascar vanilla bean, split

1 large egg yolk

10 grams 83% unsalted butter,
    at room temperature

NIB COULIS

100 grams cacao nibs (see Sources, page 282)

300 to 325 grams Simple Syrup (page 267)

About 100 grams Cocoa Syrup
    (page 268; optional)

CARAMELIZED BANANAS

2 bananas, peeled and frozen

Granulated sugar

Everybody seems to love peanut butter in the United States. Sebastien didn't understand it when he first came to this country, but now that his daughters and wife eat it every day, he enjoys it as well, so he wanted to feature it in a dessert. He knew I would like it because I love Reese's Peanut Butter Cups. It was a natural idea for Sebastien to take a chocolate mousse and make it with peanut butter. Peanut butter can be difficult because it's so fatty and stiff. We like using Skippy Natural. We loosen it up in cream and milk and then more or less make a traditional sabayon with it. Peanut butter and bananas are a great combination, so we caramelize bananas and make a banana sherbet. For crunchy contrast, we add peanut butter and banana cookies.

To create the domed egg shapes, we use a Flexipan egg mold (see Sources, page 282) and a cutter that matches the size of the mold.

FOR THE PEANUT BUTTER MOUSSE: Beat the eggs and confectioners' sugar over a water bath until thickened, like a sabayon.

Meanwhile, bring the cream to a boil in a saucepan.

Remove the cream from the heat and add the gelatin to dissolve it.

Put the peanut butter in the bowl of a stand mixer fitted with the paddle. While beating, gradually pour the cream mixture into the peanut butter. Fold in the egg mixture.

Place the Flexipan egg mold (see headnote) on a sheet pan and pour the mixture into 20 of the cavities. Freeze until firm, about 1 hour.

FOR THE PEANUT CRUNCH: Melt the milk chocolate and cocoa butter together over a water bath.

Put the peanut butter in a stand mixer and beat with the paddle on low speed until smooth and creamy. Add a pinch of salt and the peanuts, then the chocolate mixture, and combine well. Add the feuilletine and mix for 30 seconds, being careful not to crush the feuilletine too much.

Place a piece of parchment paper on the back of a sheet pan. Pour the mixture onto the parchment and cover with a second piece of parchment. Roll out to a rectangle about 8 by 11 inches (use Plexiglas guides on each side if you have them). Refrigerate for about 1 hour, or until firm.

To complete: Cut 20 ovals of crunch with a cutter the same size as the bottoms of the peanut butter mousse. Unmold the mousse onto the peanut crunch ovals and return to the freezer.

FOR THE PEANUT GLAZE: Combine the cream, glaze, and water and bring to a boil.

Meanwhile, put the peanut butter in a container deep enough so you can use a hand blender. Pour the melted chocolate over the peanut butter and pour the boiling liquid over the top. Blend until the glaze emulsifies. Let cool to room temperature.   MAKES ABOUT 875 GRAMS

To glaze the mousse: Put the ovals of mousse on a rack over a parchment-lined sheet pan. Check the temperature of the glaze: 29° to 31°C (84.2° to 87.8°F) will give the best shine to the glaze. Using a funnel, a chinois à piston (see Sources, page 282), or a ladle, glaze the ovals, covering them completely.

Refrigerate for at least 1 hour to allow the glaze to set up and the mousse to defrost.

(To save the glaze on the parchment for another use, fold the parchment in half, hold it over the container of glaze with an open side down, fold the top over and squeeze downward to return the excess glaze to the container.)

FOR THE TUILES: Combine all the ingredients except the butter in a Vita-Prep and blend to a puree. With the machine running, carefully pour in the melted butter. Mix until combined.

Pass through a fine tamis, and transfer to a disposable piping bag. Cut off a very small opening in the end.

Pipe the batter in spaghetti-like strands down the length of a sheet pan lined with a Silpat or parchment paper. There will be some extra tuiles to allow for breakage.

Bake at 325°F in a convection oven for about 5 minutes, or until golden brown but still pliable. Remove the pan from the oven. Working quickly, while the tuiles are still hot, pick up one end of a strand, fold it in half, and fold in half again. Then slowly drop it onto the palm of your other hand, letting it harden into an irregular shape. Repeat with the remaining tuiles.   MAKES AT LEAST 20 TUILES

FOR THE BANANA MOUSSE: Melt the white chocolate. Meanwhile, whisk together 100 grams of the cream, the egg yolks, and banana puree in a saucepan and cook over medium heat, stirring with a silicone spatula, until the mixture coats the spatula and is 82°C (179.6°F). Stir in the softened gelatin.

Pour the cream mixture over the top of the chocolate and stir to combine, then strain the mixture through a chinois or fine-mesh conical strainer into a bowl. Chill to 25°C (77°F).

Whip the remaining 190 grams cream to soft peaks. Fold the whipped cream and the banana water into the chilled mixture. Pour into a container and refrigerate until set, at least 1 hour.   MAKES ABOUT 600 GRAMS

FOR THE BANANA SHERBET—85°C (185°F); 45 MINUTES
Put the sugar in a pan over medium heat and make a caramel, reducing the heat to low to medium-low as necessary. Scrape in the seeds from the vanilla bean, then add the vanilla pod. Begin adding the orange juice. The caramel will seize—let it dissolve, and add a bit more. Once it stops seiz-

ing, add the remaining orange juice and bring to a boil. Strain and cool over an ice bath. The syrup can be made ahead and refrigerated until ready to use.

Do not peel or cut the bananas until the syrup is cold and ready to be used or they will oxidize. Peel the bananas, put them in a bag, and cover with the cold syrup. Fold the bag around the bananas to keep the bananas submerged in the syrup as they cook, or they will blacken, then vacuum-pack on medium until the syrup bubbles, then seal. Fold over the end and tape it if needed to keep the bananas submerged in liquid.

Cook at 85°C (185°F) for 45 minutes, or until the bananas are mushy. They will keep their shape but should be completely soft. Strain the liquid into a container. If any sections of banana have darkened, cut the sections away.

Transfer the bananas to a Vita-Prep, add a bit of the syrup, and puree on the highest setting. The puree will be very thick. Add the milk, blending on high, so you don't need to add too much syrup. When there is a hole in the center of the puree and you can see the bottom of the blender, the puree is the correct consistency. If it seems too thick, add a bit more of the syrup.

Chill over an ice bath. Add the base syrup. Freeze in an ice cream machine.   MAKES ABOUT 950 GRAMS

FOR THE PEANUT SABLÉ: Remove the skins from the peanuts by rubbing the peanuts over a tamis. Process the peanuts in a food processor until coarsely ground; do not process to a paste.

Combine the butter and sugar in the bowl of a stand mixer. Scrape in the seeds from the vanilla bean and add the fleur de sel. Cream with the paddle attachment on medium speed for about 2 minutes, or until thoroughly blended; there should be no visible pieces of butter.

Mix the flour and peanuts together and add to the butter mixture, beating on low speed until well combined. Remove the dough from the mixer, shape it into a block, and wrap in plastic wrap. Refrigerate for 1 hour.

Roll the dough between two pieces of parchment paper until about ¼ inch thick. Place the dough, still between the parchment sheets, on a sheet pan and freeze until frozen hard, about 30 minutes.

Remove the top sheet of parchment. Bake at 325°F in a convection oven for 12 to 15 minutes, or until golden brown. Remove from the oven and let cool.

Process the sablé to fine crumbs in a food processor.

MAKES ABOUT 225 GRAMS

FOR THE PUDDING: Put the chocolate in a medium bowl.

Pour the cream into a saucepan, scrape in the seeds from the vanilla bean; then add the pod. Bring to a boil. Pour over the chocolate and stir to melt the chocolate and blend well. Stir in the yolk, followed by the butter. Refrigerate until cold.   MAKES 290 GRAMS

FOR THE COULIS: Combine the nibs and 300 grams syrup in a saucepan and boil until the syrup is cloudy and slightly thickened, about 3 to 5 minutes.

Pour the mixture into a Vita-Prep and process on high to a smooth paste. The coulis may separate somewhat, but it should not be at all chunky. When you have a hole in the center of the mixture and can see the bottom of the blender, the coulis is the correct consistency. Add additional simple syrup only as necessary.

To brighten the color of the coulis, stir in some of the cocoa syrup.

MAKES ABOUT 400 GRAMS

FOR THE CARAMELIZED BANANAS: Freezing the bananas means that the inside will remain white while the exterior caramelizes. Slice the frozen bananas into ⅛-inch slices. Cut each slice into a round with a round cutter or pastry tip to even the edges. Sprinkle the slices with granulated sugar and caramelize with a blowtorch.

AT SERVICE: Spoon one strip of coulis and another of pudding down each serving plate. (To make a broken line, place a small amount of the coulis on a teaspoon, hold the spoon vertically on the plate and run the spoon down the plate.) Place a mousse on each plate and garnish with slices of caramelized banana. Sprinkle the peanut crunch on top of the sherbet. Spoon some banana mousse and sherbet onto each plate and add a tuile.   MAKES 20 SERVINGS

NAPA VALLEY SUMMER BERRY CONSOMMÉ WITH CHAPUT ST. MAURÉ DU MANOIR SORBET AND WHITE BALSAMIC FOAM

CONSOMMÉ

455 grams strawberries, cold

295 grams blueberries, cold

365 grams raspberries, cold

170 grams blackberries, cold

1 mint sprig

125 grams dry red wine,

    such as Cabernet Sauvignon, cold

90 grams granulated sugar

GOAT CHEESE SORBET

1 log Chaput St. Mauré du Manoir goat cheese

    (about 300 grams; see Sources, page 282)

100 grams water

75 grams granulated sugar

50 grams atomized glucose

    (see Sources, page 282)

1.5 grams Cremodan 64 sorbet stabilizer

    (see Sources, page 282)

25 grams lemon juice

WHITE BALSAMIC FOAM

63 grams Simple Syrup (page 267)

4 gelatin sheets (2 grams each),

    soaked in cold water to soften

63 grams water

125 grams white balsamic vinegar

12 boysenberries

30 fraises des bois, halved

Micro mint leaves

This dessert evokes the Napa Valley, with its fresh berry flavor. It's uncomplicated, light and refreshing, perfect after a filling meal. A crystal-clear berry consommé is poured tableside to accompany the goat cheese sorbet, garnished with boysenberries and fraises des bois, and finished with white balsamic foam.

Sebastien prefers a goat cheese made in Canada, but traditional St. Mauré cheese from France's Loire Valley is fine.

FOR THE CONSOMMÉ—65°C (149°F); 45 MINUTES

Combine all the ingredients in a bag and vacuum-pack on medium. When the wine in the bag begins to bubble, seal the bag.

Cook at 65°C (149°F) for 45 minutes. Chill the bag in an ice bath, then lay the bag in the refrigerator to rest for 1 day.

Strain the liquid through a chinois or fine-mesh conical strainer into a bowl—let the liquid drain without pushing on the fruit; this will keep the consommé clear. Refrigerate the consommé (discard the fruit).

MAKES ABOUT 625 GRAMS

FOR THE SORBET: Remove the rind from the cheese. You will need 250 grams of cheese; reserve any remaining cheese for another use.

Heat the water to 35°C (95°F). Mix together the sugar, glucose, and stabilizer and add to the water. Bring the water up to 50°C (122°F). Add the lemon juice, bring to a boil, and boil for 1 minute. Cool over an ice bath until the liquid reaches about 4°C (39.2°F).

Transfer the liquid to a Vita-Prep, add the cheese, and puree until smooth. Strain through a chinois or fine-mesh conical strainer and let the base sit in the refrigerator for a day.

Freeze in a PacoJet or ice cream machine. MAKES ABOUT 400 GRAMS

FOR THE FOAM: Heat the simple syrup until it's warm enough to melt the gelatin. Squeeze the gelatin to remove excess water, add the gelatin, and stir to dissolve. Strain the syrup mixture into the water, then mix in the vinegar. Stir to combine well.

Just before serving, pour into a whipped cream dispenser (see Sources, page 282) or use a small hand-held milk frother (see Sources, page 282). If using a whipped cream dispenser, squirt the foam into a container rather than directly into the serving bowls so you have better control when plating.

AT SERVICE: Break some of the boysenberries into smaller pieces. Arrange the fraises des bois and boysenberries in serving bowls. Garnish with micro mint. Add the foam and garnish with the sorbet. At the table, pour the consommé around the fruit. MAKES 10 SERVINGS

GÉNOISE AUX POMMES, CANDIED APPLES, GINGER CUSTARD, MILK JAM, APPLE SORBET, AND APPLE CHIPS

GÉNOISE AUX POMMES

1 Fuji apple (about 250 grams), cold

300 grams granulated sugar

Citric acid (see Sources, page 282)

125 grams eggs (3 to 4 large), lightly beaten

115 grams cake flour, sifted

3 drops apple oil (optional; see Sources, page 282)

GINGER CUSTARD

650 grams 40% heavy cream

500 grams whole milk

100 grams peeled fresh ginger

5 grams powdered ginger

10 large egg yolks

125 grams granulated sugar

Kosher salt

2 gelatin sheets (2 grams each), soaked in cold water to soften

MILK JAM

500 grams whole milk

400 grams granulated sugar

1 Madagascar vanilla bean, split

100 grams liquid glucose

APPLE SORBET

4 Granny Smith apples (about 1 kilogram), stems removed, each cut into 8 wedges and juiced (with the skin)

16 baby spinach leaves

Citric acid

400 grams Sweet Base Syrup (page 268)

CANDIED APPLES

10 Golden Delicious apples

About 2 kilograms Poaching Liquid (page 267), cold

APPLE CHIPS

2 kilograms water

1 kilogram granulated sugar

1 to 2 Granny Smith apples

Chervil leaves

Apples are available in so many varieties, and each has its own story. We especially like the ones used here, as well as Pink Lady, Braeburn, Reinette, Pink Pearl, and Gravenstein. Apple and ginger is a good combination because ginger cuts the sweetness of the apple.

The cake, a traditional génoise, is made with apples that are cooked sous vide and then pureed, adding both flavor and moisture. We freeze this cake, like most of our cakes, to make unmolding and cutting it easy. If you can't get Fuji apples, use Golden Delicious in the cake too. The optional apple oil will increase the intensity of the flavor. PHOTOGRAPH ON PAGE 233

FOR THE GÉNOISE—85°C (185°F); 30 TO 40 MINUTES

Peel and core the apple and cut into 8 wedges. Toss with 20 grams of the sugar and a pinch of citric acid and place into a bag. Vacuum-pack on high.

Cook at 85°C (185°F) for 30 to 40 minutes, or until the apple is mushy. While the apple is still hot, transfer it to a Vita-Prep and puree until completely smooth. Cool the puree over an ice bath.

Line a quarter sheet pan with parchment paper and spray the paper with nonstick spray. Combine the eggs and the remaining 280 grams sugar in a stand mixer fitted with the whisk and whisk to the ribbon

stage, about 10 minutes. Fold in the cake flour, followed by the apple puree and apple oil, if using. Pour into the prepared pan.

Bake at 325°F in a convection oven for 22 to 25 minutes, or until the top is golden and a toothpick or skewer inserted into the center comes out clean. Remove from the oven and let cool to room temperature in the pan. Freeze in the pan.

To complete: Remove the cake from the freezer and unmold onto a piece of parchment paper. Cut into 2-inch rounds. Cover and bring to room temperature.

FOR THE CUSTARD—85° TO 82°C (185° TO 179.6°F); 20 MINUTES

Heat 500 grams of the cream and the milk in a saucepan until hot but not simmering. Smash the ginger and add to the liquid. Stir in the powdered ginger and remove from the heat. Cover the pan with food-safe plastic wrap and allow to infuse for 20 minutes.

Strain the liquid and discard the fresh ginger.

Whisk the yolks, sugar, and a pinch of salt to the ribbon stage in a stand mixer. On low speed, whisk in the milk/cream mixture. Strain through a chinois or fine-mesh conical strainer and chill over an ice bath.

Pour the liquid into a bag and vacuum-pack on medium until bubbles appear, then seal. If your machine has the option, double-seal the bag.

Add the bag to 85°C (185°F) water and reduce the temperature to 82°C (179.6°F). Cook for 20 minutes.

The custard may look a bit broken when it comes out of the water. Lay the bag flat on a work surface and move the edges up and down so it recombines. Let sit at room temperature for 5 minutes.

Squeeze the gelatin to remove excess water. Pour the custard into a bowl and stir in the softened gelatin to dissolve. Strain through a chinois or fine-mesh conical strainer into a bowl set over an ice bath and cool the custard to 25°C (77°F).

Whip the remaining 150 grams cream to soft peaks. Whisk one-third of the whipped cream into the custard, then fold in the remaining cream. Refrigerate for at least 1 hour, or until set, before serving.

MAKES ABOUT 630 GRAMS

FOR THE MILK JAM: Combine the milk and sugar in a saucepan. Scrape the seeds from the vanilla bean into the pan, then add the pod. Bring to a boil. Strain into another pan and discard the bean. Simmer over low heat, using a diffuser if needed, to reduce the milk for 2 to 2½ hours. As the water in the milk evaporates, the milk will begin to caramelize—be careful, because it can burn very easily.

When the consistency resembles sweetened condensed milk, add the liquid glucose and stir to dissolve. Strain through a chinois or fine-mesh conical strainer and cool over an ice bath.

Seal the jam in a bag and refrigerate. This can be used directly from the refrigerator, but if it becomes too thick, let it stand at room temperature or put in the microwave briefly before serving.   MAKES 250 GRAMS

FOR THE SORBET: Cut each apple into 8 wedges and remove the cores. (Leave the peel on; it will give color to the sorbet.) Place 2 wedges of apple in a juicer, then a spinach leaf to add color. Continue to alternate between the apple wedges and spinach. Once half the apples have been juiced, add a pinch of citric acid to retain the color. Continue alternating, adding another pinch of citric acid at the end.

Stir in the syrup and refrigerate until cold. Freeze in a PacoJet or ice cream machine.   MAKES ABOUT 800 GRAMS

FOR THE CANDIED APPLES—75°C (167°F); 3 HOURS
Peel the apples and scoop out balls with a #18 parisienne scooper (see Sources, page 282). You will need 7 to 8 apple balls per serving, 140 to 160 total.

Place 20 balls in each bag and add enough poaching liquid to cover the apples. Fold the bags over the apples to keep the balls submerged in the syrup, to prevent discoloring. Vacuum-pack on medium until the syrup bubbles, then seal. Fold over the end and tape it if needed to keep the apples submerged in the liquid. Refrigerate until cold.

Cook at 75°C (167°F) for about 3 hours. The apples should be candied throughout, without any areas in the center that look raw or under-cooked. Cool in an ice bath, then refrigerate until serving.

FOR THE APPLE CHIPS: Combine the water and sugar in a pot and bring to a boil, stirring to dissolve the sugar. Remove from the heat.

Slice the apples into very thin rounds with a Japanese mandoline. You will need 1 apple chip per serving, or 20 total. Using a round cutter that is just smaller than the apple slices, cut out rounds, discarding the skin. Remove any seeds.

Add the chips to the syrup. Put a C-fold towel on top to keep the chips submerged in the liquid. Set the pan on the side of a flattop, over a pilot light, or on a diffuser over the lowest possible heat, and cook at just a simmer for 1½ to 2 hours, until the chips are softened.

Drain the chips and place on a sheet pan lined with a Teflon sheet (see Sources, page 282). Cook in a 200°F convection oven until the slices are translucent and crisp, about 1 hour.

Using a small offset spatula, carefully transfer the chips to a rack to cool. The chips can be stored for a few days in an airtight container with a blue dessicant humidity absorber (see Sources, page 282). Put the dessicant in a resealable plastic bag, but leave the top of the bag open; the dessicant should not touch food.

AT SERVICE: Arrange 7 or 8 apple balls in a circle on each plate. Place a spoonful of ginger custard and a sweep of milk jam in front of them, and garnish the custard with a chervil leaf. Top the balls with a cake round, then top each cake round with sorbet. Garnish with the apple chips.

MAKES 20 SERVINGS

Dégustation des Pommes: Génoise aux Pommes, Candied Apples, Ginger Custard, Milk Jam, Apple Sorbet, and Apple Chips (page 230)

ENGLISH CUCUMBER SORBET WITH COMPRESSED MELONS, YOGURT CREAM, AND OLIVE OIL *BISCUIT*

MELON

1 small seedless watermelon, rind removed,
    cut into large rectangles about 1½ inches thick

½ honeydew melon, rind removed and seeded

½ cantaloupe, rind removed and seeded

Lemon oil (see Sources, page 282)

CUCUMBER SORBET

375 grams English cucumbers (2 to 3)

340 grams Sweet Base Syrup (page 268)

CAKE

150 grams cake flour

2 grams baking powder

188 grams lightly beaten eggs (6 to 7 large)

188 grams granulated sugar

125 grams low-fat yogurt

75 grams almond flour

150 grams Castello di Ama extra virgin olive oil
    (see Sources, page 282)

Grated zest of 1 lemon

YOGURT CREAM

125 grams low-fat yogurt

30 grams granulated sugar

1 gelatin sheet (2 grams),
    soaked in cold water to soften

50 grams crème fraîche, whipped to soft peaks

BALSAMIC REDUCTION

300 grams balsamic vinegar

20 grams glucose

Maldon sea salt

Lemon oil

Micro cilantro

Edible flowers

Adding a vegetable to a dessert provides a good way to move from the cheese course to the sweeter, richer desserts in a multicourse meal. The cucumber sorbet is refreshing, as is the melon, which is compressed to make it very vibrant—the color is extraordinary. When we write new recipes, I believe it's important that we not forget where we came from. The French Laundry is in the Napa Valley, where fresh vegetables and fruits are so abundant—so this is an appreciation of our terrain.

This dish is visually dynamic with the bright melon, pale sorbet, the nearly black balsamic reduction, and a garnish of micro greens. It's also dynamic from a technique standpoint, with a frozen sorbet, an olive oil cake, a reduction, and the compressed fruit. The ingredients are very simple but combined in a complex way. **PHOTOGRAPH ON PAGE 236**

FOR THE MELON: Place each melon in a separate bag and vacuum-pack on high. Refrigerate for at least 6 hours before using.

FOR THE SORBET: Run the cucumbers through a juicer. You need 750 grams of juice. Combine the juice and base syrup and refrigerate until cold.

Freeze in a PacoJet or ice cream machine.

FOR THE CAKE: Line a quarter sheet pan with a Silpat or parchment paper. Sift the cake flour and baking powder together.

Put the eggs in the bowl of a stand mixer fitted with a whisk. Beating on low speed, gradually add the sugar and whisk to the ribbon stage, 7 to 10 minutes. Whisk in the yogurt, followed by the almond flour. Add the flour mixture and incorporate it. With the mixer still running on low speed, drizzle in the oil. Add the lemon zest and mix to incorporate.

Spread in the prepared pan and smooth the top with an offset spatula. Bake in a 325°F convection oven for 18 minutes, or until the top is very light golden and a skewer or toothpick inserted into the center comes out clean.

Remove from the oven and let cool to room temperature. Freeze in the pan.

To complete: Unmold the cake onto a piece of parchment paper. Cut into desired shapes.

FOR THE YOGURT CREAM: Mix together the yogurt and sugar.

Squeeze the gelatin to remove excess water. Combine the softened gelatin in a bowl with about 2 tablespoons of the yogurt mixture. Put in the microwave to melt the gelatin.

Whisk the gelatin mixture into the yogurt mixture. Whisk in the crème fraîche.

Strain through a chinois or fine-mesh conical strainer into a bowl and refrigerate for about 1 hour, or until set. MAKES 390 GRAMS

FOR THE BALSAMIC REDUCTION: Pour the balsamic vinegar into a small saucepan set on a diffuser over very low heat and simmer gently until it has reduced to about 75 grams. Stir in the glucose.

MAKES ABOUT 95 GRAMS

AT SERVICE: Cut the melons into desired shapes and toss the pieces with a light coating of lemon oil.

Brush a sweep of balsamic syrup across each serving plate. Arrange the cake and melons on the plates. Add the sorbet. Garnish with salt, lemon oil, yogurt cream, cilantro, and flowers. **MAKES 20 SERVINGS**

English Cucumber Sorbet with Compressed Melons, Yogurt Cream, and Olive Oil *Biscuit* (page 234)

MADAGASCAR VANILLA BEAN CAKE, MORELLO CHERRY ICE CREAM, ITALIAN PISTACHIO COULIS, KIRSCH FOAM, AND CHERRY JAM

CAKE

50 grams all-purpose flour

105 grams confectioners' sugar

165 grams almond flour

275 grams egg whites (about 7 large)

120 grams granulated sugar

1 Madagascar vanilla bean, split

25 grams 40% heavy cream

17 grams vanilla extract

MORELLO CHERRY ICE CREAM

375 grams Boiron Bing cherry puree

   (see Sources, page 282)

375 grams Boiron Morello cherry puree

   (see Sources, page 282)

250 grams 40% heavy cream

250 grams whole milk

5 large egg yolks

31 grams granulated sugar

31 grams liquid glucose

131 grams Sweet Base Syrup (page 268)

PISTACHIO COULIS

100 grams Sicilian pistachios

   (see Sources, page 282)

200 grams Simple Syrup (page 267)

17 grams Sevarome pistachio paste

   (see Sources, page 282)

MACERATED CHERRIES

80 Rainier cherries

500 grams Poaching Liquid (page 267),

   cold

KIRSCH FOAM

50 grams Simple Syrup (page 267)

4 gelatin sheets (2 grams each),

   soaked in cold water to soften

100 grams water

50 grams kirsch

GELÉE DE CERISES

500 grams Boiron Bing cherry puree

   (see Sources, page 282)

90 grams granulated sugar

4.5 grams agar-agar (see Sources, page 282)

CHERRY JAM

200 grams Bing cherries, pitted, cold

75 grams granulated sugar

2 grams apple pectin

About 100 grams chopped raw Sicilian pistachios

   (see Sources, page 282)

Cherry and vanilla is a combination that's very popular in America, but in France, pistachio and cherry is a more common pairing. Sebastien uses both here, cherries with vanilla and pistachio cooked sous vide in white wine. The cherries, infused with the wine and syrup in the bag, become very vivid, almost translucent. And they will stay bright and fresh in the bag for a week. The ice cream base is also cooked sous vide.

The colors of this dish are very bright with the red and yellow cherries, the vivid green pistachio coulis. And the flavors, textures, and temperatures are diverse—cold ice cream, warm cake, soft, sweet, salty. We don't like desserts too sweet and always try to minimize sweetness in a dessert.

The cake is conventional—based on sweet meringue and flour—except that cream and unwhipped egg whites are stirred into the batter just before baking, which results in a cake that is soft even when frozen, so it's cake for serving chilled with ice cream.

FOR THE CAKE: Line a quarter sheet pan with a piece of parchment paper. Spray the paper with nonstick spray. Sift the all-purpose flour, confectioners' sugar, and almond flour together.

Whisk 200 grams of the egg whites in the bowl of a stand mixer, until soft peaks begin to form. Gradually add the granulated sugar and continue to whisk until stiff peaks form.

Scrape the seeds from the vanilla bean into the cream. Stir in the vanilla extract and add the remaining 75 grams egg whites.

Fold the dry ingredients into the meringue, then fold in the cream mixture.

Spread the batter evenly in the prepared pan. Bake at 325°F in a convection oven for 15 minutes, or until golden on top and a toothpick or skewer inserted in the center comes out clean. Remove from the oven and let cool to room temperature.

Freeze the cake in the pan.

To complete: Unmold the frozen cake onto a piece of parchment paper. Cut the cake into ½-inch cubes.

FOR THE ICE CREAM—85°/82°C (185°/179.6°F); 20 MINUTES
Combine the purees in a pot and simmer to reduce by half. Remove from the heat and add the cream and milk. Strain through a chinois or fine-mesh conical strainer.

Whisk the yolks, sugar, and glucose to the ribbon stage in a stand mixer, about 5 to 7 minutes. Add the cherry mixture and stir to combine. Strain through a chinois or fine-mesh conical strainer and refrigerate until cold.

Pour into a bag and vacuum-pack on medium until bubbles appear, then seal. If your machine has the option, double-seal the bag.

Add the bag to 85°C (185°F) water and reduce the temperature to 82°C (179.6°F). Cook for 20 minutes.

The custard may look a bit broken when it comes out of the water. Lay the bag on a work surface and move the edges up and down to allow it to recombine. Let sit at room temperature for 5 minutes, then chill in an ice bath.

Refrigerate the cold base for a day to allow the flavors to develop.

Strain the base through a chinois or fine-mesh conical strainer into a bowl and add the base syrup. Freeze in a PacoJet or ice cream machine.

MAKES ABOUT 800 GRAMS

FOR THE COULIS: Combine the pistachios and syrup in a saucepan, bring to a simmer, and cook until the syrup reduces by half.

Pour the mixture into a Vita-Prep and process on high, to avoid having to add too much water, to a smooth paste. Add a bit of cold water as necessary to allow the blade to turn. When you have a hole in the center of the mixture and can see the bottom of the blender, the coulis is the correct consistency. Add the pistachio paste and blend well.

Pass through a chinois or fine-mesh conical strainer. Cool over an ice bath to preserve the color, then refrigerate.

FOR THE MACERATED CHERRIES—65°C (149°F); 25 MINUTES
Cut the flesh of the cherries away from each side of the pit to create 2 halves with a flat surface. Place the cherries in a large bag and add the poaching liquid. Vacuum-pack on medium until the liquid begins to bubble, then seal.

Cook at 65°C (149°F) for 25 minutes. Chill in an ice bath. Refrigerate the cherries in the bag until ready to serve.

To complete: Remove the cherries from the bag and drain on C-fold towels.

FOR THE KIRSCH FOAM: Heat the simple syrup. Squeeze the gelatin to remove excess water, add the gelatin, and dissolve it in the warm syrup.

Pour the water into a bowl. Strain the syrup through a chinois or fine-mesh conical strainer into the water and stir in the kirsch. Let cool to room temperature. Do not refrigerate.

To complete: Just before serving, pour the mixture into a whipped cream dispenser (see Sources, page 282) or use a small hand-held milk frother (see Sources, page 282). If using a whipped cream dispenser, squirt the foam into a container rather than directly onto the serving plates for better control.

FOR THE GELÉE: Line a 9-inch baking pan with food-safe plastic wrap, leaving an overhang on all sides.

Pour the cherry puree into a saucepan and bring to a boil. Add the sugar, stirring to dissolve, and return to a boil. Add the agar-agar and boil for 1 minute. Strain through a chinois or fine-mesh conical strainer into the prepared baking dish. Let stand until the gelée is set, then refrigerate.

To complete: Cut the gelée into ⅜-inch cubes.

FOR THE CHERRY JAM—90°C (194°F); 45 MINUTES TO 1 HOUR

Cut the cherries in half. Place in a bag in a single layer and vacuum-pack on medium.

Cook at 90°C (194°F) for 45 minutes to 1 hour, or until completely softened; the exact cooking time will depend on the ripeness of the cherries.

Pour the cherries and their liquid into a Vita-Prep. Blend until smooth. Strain through a chinois or fine-mesh conical strainer into a saucepan.

Combine the sugar and pectin and add to the cherries. Bring to a boil to activate the pectin. Cool over an ice bath to preserve the color.

MAKES ABOUT 225 GRAMS

AT SERVICE: Spoon some pistachio coulis into each serving plate. Arrange the squares of cake and cherries on the plates. Add a spoonful of cherry jam. Mound some chopped pistachios on each plate to serve as a bed for the ice cream, and top with cherry ice cream. Garnish with the gelée and the foam.

MAKES 20 SERVINGS

SAUVIGNON-BLANC-BRAISED GOLDEN PINEAPPLE
WITH WHITE CHOCOLATE SNOWFLAKES, CILANTRO
COULIS, AND PASSION FRUIT GELÉE

WHITE CHOCOLATE SNOWFLAKES

80 grams white chocolate, chopped

50 grams cocoa butter (see Sources,
    page 282)

300 grams water

100 grams 40% heavy cream

30 grams granulated sugar

BRAISED PINEAPPLE

1 slightly underripe pineapple (about 1.5 kilograms)

250 grams granulated sugar

1 Madagascar vanilla bean, split

About 150 grams Poaching Liquid (page 267)

CILANTRO COULIS

2 bunches cilantro (about 225 grams)

30 to 75 grams Simple Syrup (page 267)

PASSION FRUIT GELÉE

187.5 grams granulated sugar

4.5 grams apple pectin

125 grams Boiron mango puree
    (see Sources, page 282)

37.5 grams Boiron passion fruit puree
    (see Sources, page 282)

56.2 grams glucose

2.5 grams citric acid (see Sources, page 282)

Micro cilantro sprigs

When Sebastien worked at The French Laundry, the meat station would always braise short ribs on Tuesdays. He was fascinated by the technique behind them and decided to braise something himself. He thought pineapple would be perfect. He liked its combination of intense sweetness and great acidity, and it's a sturdy, meaty fruit that he knew would work well with a high-heat technique.

The dry caramel, when it's melted, is very, very hot, a perfect medium for "searing" the pineapple (as one sears a short rib before braising it). We then add a white wine poaching liquid to the pan and simmer it to cook the pineapple (again, like a short rib) and create a flavorful cuisson that will glaze the fruit. Then the pineapple is chilled, vacuum-packed with the syrup, and cooked sous vide. The result is beautiful, vivid slices of pineapple that look almost like sashimi on the plate.

Cilantro and pineapple is an unusual, great flavor combination, and the coulis brings vibrant color to the dish. For the "snowflakes," we melt white chocolate and freeze it in a PacoJet. The rich chocolate mixture actually becomes flaky, and then the flakes melt when they hit your tongue. You can also freeze the white chocolate mixture like a granité, but it will not have the same texture achieved with the PacoJet. **PHOTOGRAPH ON PAGE 245**

FOR THE SNOWFLAKES: Melt the chocolate with the cocoa butter. Bring the water and cream to a boil in a saucepan. Add the sugar, stirring to dissolve, and pour over the cocoa butter mixture. Strain through a chinois or fine-mesh conical strainer.

Cool over an ice bath to 35°C (95°F). Pour into the canister of a PacoJet and freeze until solid.

To complete: Run the PacoJet. The snowflakes can be kept in the canister for up to 3 hours.   MAKES 495 GRAMS

FOR THE PINEAPPLE—75°C (167°F); 1 HOUR

Cut off both ends and peel the pineapple. Stand it on end and cut vertically through the pineapple, just to one side of the core. Cut away the flesh from the opposite side of the core. Trim the pieces of pineapple into rectangles, leaving them as large as possible.

Combine the sugar and vanilla bean in a sauté pan and cook to a caramel over medium heat, lowering the heat as necessary to avoid burning the caramel. When the caramel is medium amber, add about 50 grams of the poaching liquid and the pineapple. The caramel will seize, but the moisture of the pineapple will reliquefy it. Add enough additional poaching liquid to come about halfway up the sides of the pineapple. Cook for 3 to 5 minutes, or until the pineapple has taken on the rich color of the caramel glaze. Transfer the pineapple to a tray, cover with food-safe plastic wrap, and put in the freezer to chill completely. Strain the caramel syrup through a chinois or fine-mesh conical strainer into a bowl over an ice bath to cool, then refrigerate to chill completely.

Put each cold pineapple piece into a bag. Divide the caramel syrup among the bags (see photograph, page 244). Vacuum-pack on medium. When the liquid in each bag begins to boil, seal it.

Cook at 75°C (167°F) for 1 hour. Cool in an ice bath, then refrigerate.

To complete: Remove the pineapple from the bags and drain on C-fold towels.

FOR THE COULIS: Hold each bunch of cilantro and cut off and discard the large stems; small stems will work in the coulis. Blanch (see Big-Pot Blanching, page 268) for about 30 seconds, then transfer to an ice bath.

Squeeze the cilantro dry in a kitchen towel and transfer to a Vita-Prep. Turn the Vita-Prep on to the highest setting. Add just enough of the syrup to the center of the container to allow the cilantro to spin and form a puree; avoid adding too much syrup. Puree until a hole forms in the center and the coulis is emulsified and smooth. Strain through a chinois or fine-mesh conical strainer and cool over an ice bath.

FOR THE GELÉE: Line an 8-inch baking pan with plastic wrap, leaving an overhang on all sides.

Combine 4.5 grams of the sugar and the apple pectin and set aside.

Combine the purees in a medium saucepan and bring to a boil. Add the remaining 183 grams sugar, stirring to dissolve, and return to a boil. Add the glucose and return to a boil. Add the combined sugar and pectin and cook until the mixture reaches 108°C (226.4°F). To test the consistency, put a small amount of the mixture on a stainless steel work surface and let it cool and set up. If the mixture has not thickened enough, cook longer. Stir in the citric acid, and pour into the prepared dish.

Allow the gelée to stand until set; store at room temperature.

To complete: Cut into ½-inch cubes.

AT SERVICE: Cut the pineapple into desired shapes and place on serving plates. Place a piece of passion fruit gelée on each plate. Spoon some cilantro coulis on each plate and garnish with micro cilantro. Finish with the white chocolate snowflakes.   MAKES 12 SERVINGS

Opposite: pineapple in its caramel glaze (see page 243) ; above: Sauvignon-Blanc-Braised Golden Pineapple with White Chocolate Snowflakes, Cilantro Coulis, and Passion Fruit Gelée (page 242)

WHITE SESAME NOUGATINE WITH SESAME OIL SABLÉ, PLUMS, GOLDEN GOOSEBERRIES, AND JASMINE RICE SHERBET

SESAME NOUGATINE

17 grams whole milk

50 grams granulated sugar

17 grams light corn syrup

42 grams unsalted butter

7 grams all-purpose flour

50 grams white sesame seeds

SESAME OIL SABLÉ

76 grams all-purpose flour

44 grams almond flour

36 grams confectioners' sugar

44 grams cold unsalted butter, cut into small dice

30 grams white sesame oil

25 grams black sesame seeds

JASMINE RICE SHERBET

300 grams Jasmine rice, rinsed

1.05 kilograms whole milk

300 grams Sweet Base Syrup (page 268)

PLUMS

18 slightly underripe black plums, cold

2 Madagascar vanilla beans, split

700 grams Simple Syrup (page 267), cold

PLUM JAM

200 grams ripe black plums (about 3), cold

75 grams granulated sugar

2 grams apple pectin

Achva marble halvah (see Sources, page 282)

Silan date syrup (see Sources, page 282)

18 golden gooseberries

Citrus Powder (page 264)

Because we're always pushing ourselves to come up with new dishes, we often look to other culinary traditions for ideas and inspiration. The aroma of jasmine rice is so intriguing, we wanted to come up with a dessert that used it, and we thought of a sherbet. How to translate jasmine rice into a sherbet? The trick is to infuse the milk with the flavor of the rice without cooking the rice too much, so that it doesn't start releasing starch granules. Sous vide is the answer, allowing us to bring the rice and milk to a boil in the bag by lowering the pressure (rather than raising the heat), and then cooking it gently. The base is strained and sweetened with a simple syrup. The sherbet is paired with a sesame sablé, using a dough we sometimes make with olive oil but switching to sesame oil. The technique is to make a simple butter cookie first, then break it up and process it with the oil. It becomes like a shapeable dough, but it's been baked.

Plum is brilliant prepared sous vide—translucent and vivid (we leave the skin on for its color). The way the plum is sliced and put together on the plate with the sablé makes it look like a Buddha's hand, which is appropriate to the exotic theme of the dessert. **PHOTOGRAPH ON PAGE 249**

FOR THE NOUGATINE: Combine the milk, sugar, corn syrup, and butter in a saucepan, bring to a boil, and cook to 106°C (222.8°F). Off the heat, add the flour and sesame seeds and mix well. Pour the mixture onto a piece of parchment paper, cover with another piece, and roll out as thin as possible, to about 9 by 8 inches (the nougatine should be about the thickness of the sesame seeds). Transfer to a half sheet pan and freeze until firm.

Bake at 325°F in a convection oven until golden brown, about 10 minutes. The nougatine will be very sticky when it comes out of the oven. It needs to cool slightly, but not completely, before cutting. Cut into strips about 3 by ¾ inch. Cool on a rack. Store airtight at room temperature for 3 to 4 days.   **MAKES 18 PIECES**

FOR THE SABLÉ: Combine the flour, almond flour, sugar, and butter in a stand mixer fitted with the paddle and mix until sandy.

Spread the loose mixture on a parchment-lined half sheet pan. Bake at 325°F in a convection oven until golden brown, about 12 minutes. Cool on a rack, then place on a tray and freeze. The sablé can be kept in the freezer for a few weeks.

Break the sablé into pieces and blend to a powder in a food processor. With the machine running, drizzle in the sesame oil until a paste forms. Add the sesame seeds.

Roll the dough out between two pieces of parchment paper to a 14-by-10 inch rectangle about ⅛ inch thick. Transfer the dough, on the parchment, to a sheet tray and freeze until serving.

The dough becomes soft very quickly, so it must be cut still frozen. Use a knife or dough divider to cut it into pieces about 5 inches by 1 inch (see photograph, page 210).

MAKES 18 PIECES

FOR THE SHERBET—65.5°C (149.9°F); 30 MINUTES

Put the rice in a bag with the milk and vacuum-pack on medium. When the milk begins to bubble, seal the bag.

Cook at 65.5°C (149.9°F) for 30 minutes. Drain the rice, reserving the milk (see Note). Add the base syrup to the milk and chill until cold.

Freeze in an ice cream machine.

MAKES 1.175 KILOGRAMS

FOR THE PLUMS—75°C (167°F); 15 TO 20 MINUTES

Cut the flesh away from two opposite sides of each plum to create 2 halves with a flat surface. Using a paring knife, cut at a 45-degree angle in one direction and then the other to create "segments" (crescent moons) from the plums. You should get about 5 segments from each plum half. Divide the segments among four bags. Scrape the seeds from ½ vanilla bean into each bag and add the pod and 175 grams of the simple syrup.

Vacuum-pack on medium.

Cook at 75°C (167°F) for 15 to 20 minutes, or until the plums are tender; the cooking time may vary with the ripeness of the plums. Chill in an ice bath, then refrigerate for up to 2 days.

FOR THE PLUM JAM—90°C (194°F); 45 TO 60 MINUTES

Cut the flesh way from two opposite sides of each plum to create 2 halves with a flat surface. Put in a bag in a single layer. Vacuum-pack on medium.

Cook at 90°C (194°F) for 45 to 60 minutes, or until completely soft; the time will depend on the ripeness of the plums.

Transfer the plums to a Vita-Prep and puree. Strain through a chinois or fine-mesh conical strainer into a saucepan.

Combine the sugar and pectin and add to the pan. Bring to a boil to activate the pectin, stirring to dissolve the sugar. Cool over an ice bath to preserve the color.

MAKES ABOUT 200 GRAMS

FOR THE HALVAH: Cut the halvah into matchsticks that are about 2¼ inches by ¼ inch. You will need about 5 pieces per plate.

AT SERVICE: Swirl some Silan onto each serving plate. Drape a strip of sablé over each plate. Stack the matchsticks of halvah on the plates. Spoon some plum jam and sherbet onto each plate and garnish with the gooseberries, nougatine, and plums. Sprinkle the plates with citrus powder.

MAKES 18 SERVINGS

NOTE

The leftover rice can be used to make "rice crispies." Drain and dry the cooked rice on C-fold towels, then spread on a sheet pan to dry overnight. Coat the rice in flour, shaking off any excess, and deep-fry at 177°C (about 350°F).

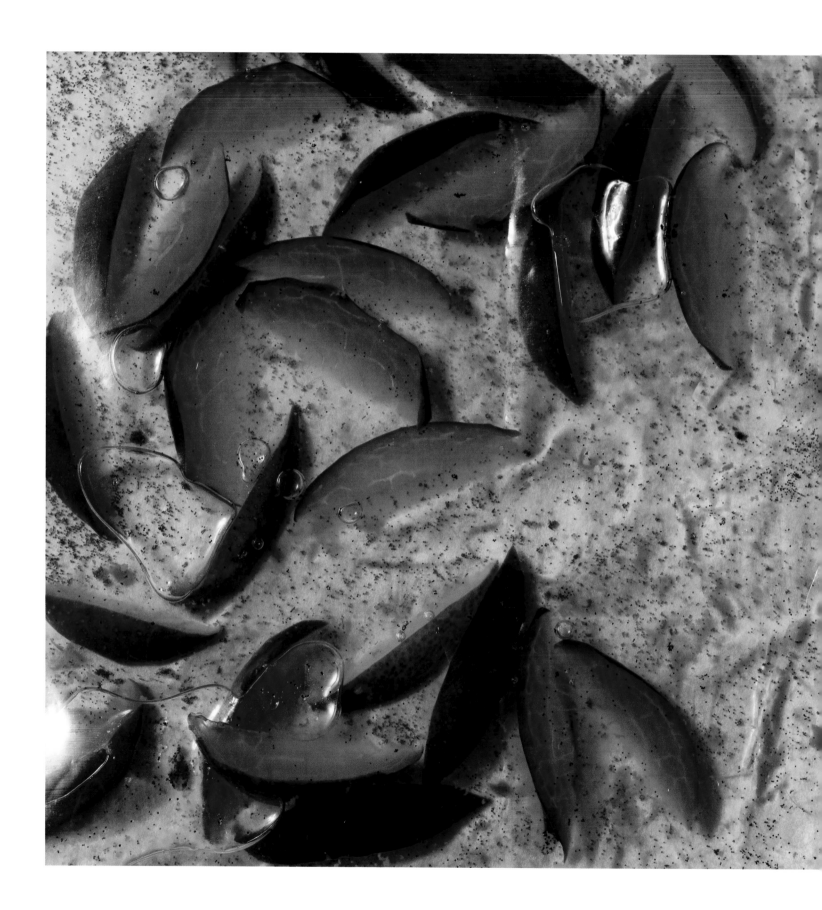

White Sesame Nougatine with Sesame Oil Sablé, Plums, Golden Gooseberries, and Jasmine Rice Sherbet (page 246)

"ICE CREAM SANDWICH"
VANILLA, CHOCOLATE, AND CASHEW ICE CREAM WITH BANANA ANGLAISE, CHOCOLATE *CRÉMEUX*, WAFFLE TUILE, AND *GASTRIQUE DE CEPA VIEJA*

VANILLA ICE CREAM

6 large egg yolks

90 grams granulated sugar

½ Madagascar vanilla bean, split

450 grams half-and-half

CHOCOLATE ICE CREAM

500 grams water

175 grams granulated sugar

5 large egg yolks

250 grams Valrhona cocoa powder
  (see Sources, page 282)

CASHEW ICE CREAM

250 grams raw unsalted cashews

Canola oil

5 large egg yolks

25 grams granulated sugar

125 grams 32% heavy cream

375 grams whole milk

25 grams atomized glucose
  (see Sources, page 282)

25 grams dry milk powder

93.5 grams Sweet Base Syrup (page 268)

CHOCOLATE VELVET

100 grams Valrhona 70% chocolate
  (see Sources, page 282)

30 grams Valrhona 100% cocoa paste
  (see Sources, page 282)

50 grams cocoa butter (see Sources, page 282)

About 125 grams Valrhona 70% chocolate, melted

BANANA ANGLAISE

6 large egg yolks

125 grams granulated sugar

Kosher salt

15 grams banana water (see Sources, page 282)

490 grams half-and-half

½ gelatin sheet (1 gram)

CHOCOLATE SABLÉ DUST

170 grams 83% unsalted butter,
  at room temperature

120 grams granulated sugar

194 grams all-purpose flour

66 grams Guittard Cocoa Rouge (see Sources,
  page 282), plus more for rolling the dough

1 gram baking soda

4 grams kosher salt

CHOCOLATE CRÉMEUX

235 grams Cacao Barry Alto el Sol 65% chocolate
  rounds (see Sources, page 282) or other high-
  quality chocolate, chopped

150 grams 40% heavy cream

2 gelatin sheets (2 grams each),
  soaked in cold water to soften

150 grams egg whites (4 to 5 large)

50 grams granulated sugar

GASTRIQUE DE CEPA VIEJA

100 grams granulated sugar

45 grams water

7 grams Cepa Vieja sherry vinegar
  (see Sources, page 282)

WAFFLE TUILES

1 large egg

148 grams granulated sugar

45 grams vanilla paste (see Sources, page 282)

303 grams all-purpose flour

9 grams baking powder

80 grams unsalted butter, melted

24 grams whole milk

85 grams egg whites (about 3 large)

The ice cream sandwich is a uniquely American invention, created during a hot New York summer. Sebastien, who loves to use his French sensibilities to reimagine American dishes, thought, "I've got to do an ice cream sandwich." But to do an ice cream sandwich in a four-star restaurant requires some thought and manipulation.

We use three different types of ice cream for the sandwich, each based on a slightly different technique. The vanilla is straightforward, but we use only half-and-half, which has less fat than a mixture of equal parts cream and milk. The chocolate has no milk or cream, just water, egg yolks, sugar, and cocoa

powder. The cashew ice cream is made with dry milk powder, which gives it its own unique feel on the palate, as well as whole milk. Then we make a chocolate sablé, using cocoa rouge, which gives us a very dark chocolate cookie, and pulverize it for garnish. The plate is finished with a banana anglaise and, for contrast, an acidic component in the form of a sherry vinegar *gastrique*.

To construct the ice cream sandwich and make perfectly even layers, we use twelve plastic strips that are about 16 inches long by 1 inch wide by ⅜ inch thick as guides (see Sources, page 282). **PHOTOGRAPH ON PAGE 253**

FOR THE VANILLA ICE CREAM—85°/82°C (185°/179.6°F); 20 MINUTES

Whisk the yolks and sugar to the ribbon stage in a stand mixer. Scrape the seeds from the vanilla bean into the mixture. Whisk in the half-and-half. Strain through a chinois or fine-mesh conical strainer and refrigerate until cold.

Pour the base into a bag and vacuum-pack on medium until bubbles appear, then seal. If your machine has the option, double-seal the bag.

Add the bag to 85°C (185°F) water and reduce the temperature to 82°C (179.6°F). Cook for 20 minutes.

The custard may look a bit broken when it comes out of the water. Lay the bag on the work surface and move the edges up and down to allow the mixture to recombine. Let sit at room temperature for 5 minutes, then chill in an ice bath. Refrigerate for a day to allow the flavors to develop. Freeze in an ice cream machine.   MAKES ABOUT 475 GRAMS

FOR THE CHOCOLATE ICE CREAM—82°/79°C (179.6°/174.2°F); 22 MINUTES

Combine the water and 75 grams of the sugar in a saucepan and bring to a simmer, stirring to dissolve the sugar.

Meanwhile, whisk the yolks and the remaining 100 grams sugar to the ribbon stage in a stand mixer.

Add the cocoa to the water mixture and stir to dissolve. With the mixer running on low, slowly whisk in the cocoa mixture. Strain through a chinois or fine-mesh conical strainer and refrigerate until cold.

Pour the base into a bag and vacuum-pack on medium until bubbles appear, then seal. If your machine has the option, double-seal the bag.

Add the bag to 82°C (179.6°F) water and reduce the temperature to 79°C (174.2°F). Cook for 22 minutes.

The custard may look a bit broken when it comes out of the water. Lay the bag on the work surface and move the edges up and down to allow the mixture to recombine. Let sit at room temperature for 5 minutes, then chill in an ice bath. Refrigerate for a day to allow the flavors to develop.

Freeze in an ice cream machine.   MAKES ABOUT 625 GRAMS

FOR THE CASHEW ICE CREAM—85°/82°C (185°/179.6°F); 20 MINUTES

Spread the cashews on a sheet pan and roast in a 300°F convection oven for about 4 minutes, to warm the nuts and release the oils. Transfer to a food processor and process to a paste. Add just enough canola oil to keep the nuts spinning until completely smooth. Strain through a chinois or fine-mesh conical strainer.

Whisk the yolks and sugar to the ribbon stage in a stand mixer.

Warm the cream and milk and add the glucose and dry milk powder, stirring to dissolve. Whisking on low speed, add the milk mixture to the yolks, mixing well. Strain through a chinois or fine-mesh conical strainer. Refrigerate until cold.

Pour the base into a bag and vacuum-pack on medium until bubbles appear, then seal. If your machine has the option, double-seal the bag.

Add the bag to 85°C (185°F) water and reduce the temperature to 82°C (179.6°F). Cook for 20 minutes.

The custard may look a bit broken when it comes out of the water. Lay the bag on the work surface and move the edges up and down to allow the mixture to recombine. Let sit at room temperature for 5 minutes.

Pour the warm base into a bowl and whisk in the cashew paste and base syrup. Chill over an ice bath, then refrigerate for a day to allow the flavors to develop.

Strain the base. Freeze in an ice cream machine.

MAKES ABOUT 550 GRAMS

FOR THE CHOCOLATE VELVET: Melt the chocolate with the cocoa paste and cocoa butter. Strain through a chinois or fine-mesh conical strainer set over a funnel into an airbrush canister (see Sources, page 282).

TO ASSEMBLE THE ICE CREAM SANDWICH: Lay a 16- to 18-inch square of acetate on a sheet tray. Position 4 of the plastic strips (see headnote) to create a square with a 14-inch opening. Use melted chocolate to secure the strips to the acetate.

Spread the thinnest-possible layer of chocolate in the opening of the square. Refrigerate or set aside until set.

Soften about 400 grams of the vanilla ice cream by stirring it in a small bowl with a wooden spoon. Spread over the melted chocolate, using the top of the strips as a guide for the top of the ice cream layer. Freeze until firm.

Place 4 more strips on top of the first strips, using melted chocolate to secure. Soften about 400 grams of the chocolate ice cream and spread it over the vanilla ice cream, using the top of the strips as a guide for the top of the chocolate ice cream layer. Freeze until firm.

Place 4 more strips on top of the other strips, using melted chocolate to secure. Soften about 400 grams of the cashew ice cream and spread it over the chocolate ice cream, using the top of the strip as a guide for the top of the cashew ice cream layer. Freeze until firm.

To finish: Spray the top of the sandwich with the chocolate velvet. Remove the plastic strips. Cut into 18 rectangles, each about 1¾ by 2⅓ inches. Return to the freezer.

FOR THE ANGLAISE—85°/82°C (185°/179.6°F); 20 MINUTES

Whisk the yolks and sugar to the ribbon stage in a stand mixer. Whisk in a pinch of salt, the banana water, and half-and-half. Strain through a chinois or fine-mesh conical strainer and refrigerate until cold.

Pour the base into a bag and vacuum-pack on medium until bubbles appear, then seal. If your machine has the option, double-seal the bag.

Add the bag to 85°C (185°F) water and reduce the temperature to 82°C (179.6°F). Cook for 20 minutes.

The custard may look a bit broken when it comes out of the water. Lay the bag on the work surface and move the edges up and down to allow the mixture to recombine. Let sit at room temperature for 5 minutes, then chill in an ice bath. Refrigerate for a day to allow the flavors to develop.

Pour about 55 grams of the anglaise into a microwave-safe container. Add the gelatin and let it soften, then microwave just to dissolve the gelatin. Stir the gelatin mixture into the remaining anglaise and refrigerate for at least 1 hour, or up to 2 days. MAKES ABOUT 600 GRAMS

FOR THE CHOCOLATE SABLÉ DUST: Cream the butter and sugar in a stand mixer fitted with the paddle. Sift the remaining ingredients together, add to the butter mixture, and mix until combined.

Shape the dough into a block, wrap in food-safe plastic wrap, and refrigerate for 1 hour.

Unwrap the dough and dust on both sides with cocoa powder. Roll out between 2 pieces of parchment paper to a rectangle about 15 by 12 inches and ⅛ inch thick, dusting with cocoa as necessary to keep the dough from sticking to the paper. Transfer to a sheet pan and refrigerate for 30 minutes.

Lift off the top sheet of parchment and bake in a 325°F convection oven for 15 minutes. Cool on a rack.

Break up the cookie, transfer to a food processor, and process to a fine powder. MAKES ABOUT 500 GRAMS

FOR THE CHOCOLATE CRÉMEUX: Put the chocolate in a bowl. Bring the cream to a boil. Remove from the heat, add the gelatin, and whisk to combine. Pour the cream over the chocolate.

Whisk the egg whites and sugar in the bowl of a stand mixer until soft peaks form. Fold one-third of the whites into the chocolate to lighten the mixture. Fold in the remaining whites. Refrigerate for 2 hours.

MAKES ABOUT 550 GRAMS

FOR THE GASTRIQUE: Caramelize the sugar in a pan over medium heat. When the caramel is golden amber, add the water and vinegar, stir to dissolve any lumps of caramel, and reduce to a glaze. (If making the *gastrique* ahead, rewarm before serving.) MAKES ABOUT 115 GRAMS

FOR THE TUILES: Whisk the egg and sugar to the ribbon stage in a stand mixer. Add the vanilla paste. Sift the flour and baking powder together and add to the egg mixture. Add the melted butter and milk.

Whip the egg whites to soft peaks, and fold into the batter. The batter will be very thick.

Using a small offset spatula, put a small dollop of batter on a Silpat-lined sheet pan and spread as thin as possible into desired shape. Repeat with the remaining batter, using additional sheet pans as necessary: you need 18 tuiles.

Bake in a 325°F convection oven for 4 to 6 minutes, or until lightly golden. Cool on a rack. MAKES ABOUT 700 GRAMS

AT SERVICE: Place an ice cream sandwich on each plate. Drizzle some banana anglaise and *gastrique* onto each plate. Sprinkle some of the crumbs over and next to each sandwich. Place a quenelle of *crémeux* on each sandwich and lean a tuile against it. **MAKES 18 SERVINGS**

"Ice Cream Sandwich": Vanilla, Chocolate, and Cashew Ice Cream with Banana Anglaise, Chocolate *Crémeux*, Waffle Tuile, and *Gastrique de Cepa Vieja* (page 250)

BASICS

VEAL STOCK

4.5 kilograms veal bones, necks, and backs

1 calf's foot, split

23 liters water, cold

450 grams tomato paste

340 grams carrots cut into 1-inch mirepoix

340 grams leeks cut into 1-inch mirepoix (white and light green parts only)

225 grams onions cut into 1-inch mirepoix

1 head garlic, halved horizontally, broken into pieces, root end and excess skin removed

42 grams flat-leaf parsley sprigs

14 grams thyme sprigs

2 bay leaves

455 grams tomatoes, cut into 1-inch chunks

Rinse the bones in cold water and put the bones and calf's foot in a stockpot with at least a 19-liter capacity. Fill the pot with cold water, adding twice as much water as you have bones. Slowly bring to a simmer; this coagulates the blood proteins and brings other impurities to the surface. Move the bones around from time to time as the water comes to a simmer, but do not stir, as this would disperse the impurities. Skim the scum that rises to the surface. As soon as the liquid comes to a simmer, remove the pot from the heat. (If the bones are blanched for longer than is necessary to coagulate the blood proteins and draw out other impurities, more of their flavor will be extracted into a liquid that you will end up discarding, rather than into the liquid that will become your stock.)

Drain the bones in a China cap and rinse to remove any scum. It is important that the bones be rinsed while they are hot; if they are allowed to cool first, the impurities will cling to the bones and go into your stock. Clean the stockpot.

For Veal #1: Return the bones to the stockpot, and add 11.5 liters of the cold water. Place the stockpot off to one side of the burner. This will cause any impurities that rise to gather at one side of the pot, making it easier to skim. Slowly bring the water to a simmer. Skim continually! (It is easier to skim before the aromatics are added, and the more you skim, the better your chances are for a clear stock.)

Once the liquid is at a simmer, skim and then stir in the tomato paste. Add all the aromatics and the tomatoes, bring back to a simmer, and simmer for 6 hours: skim, skim, skim.

Strain the liquid, first through a China cap, then through a chinois or fine-mesh conical strainer into a second container. Do not press on the solids in the strainer or force through any liquid that does not pass on its own; reserve the bones and aromatics. You should have 7.5 to 9.5 liters of liquid. Place in a saucepan and reduce over low heat as you cook Veal #2. It is not critical how much the stock reduces at this point.

For Veal #2—The *rémouillage*: Return the bones and aromatics to the clean stockpot. Add the remaining 11.5 liters cold water and slowly bring to a simmer, skimming often. Simmer for another 6 hours, skimming frequently.

Strain the liquid twice, as for Veal #1. You should have 7.5 to 9.5 liters of liquid.

For the "marriage" of Veal #1 and Veal #2: Clean the stockpot and combine Veal #1 and Veal #2. Slowly bring to a simmer until the stock reduces to approximately 1.75 liters. It should have a rich brown color and a sauce-like consistency. Cool over an ice bath or in a blast chiller. Refrigerate for up to 3 days, or freeze in several containers for longer storage. **MAKES ABOUT 1.75 LITERS**

WHITE VEAL STOCK

4.5 kilograms veal bones, necks, and backs

1 calf's foot, split

9.5 liters water, cold

450 grams leeks cut into 1-inch mirepoix (white and light green parts only)

450 grams onions cut into 1-inch mirepoix

1 head garlic, halved horizontally, broken into pieces, root end and excess skin removed

14 grams flat-leaf parsley sprigs

5 thyme sprigs

2 bay leaves

Rinse the bones in cold water and put the bones and calf's foot in a 15-liter stockpot. Fill the pot with cold water, adding at least twice as much water as you have bones. Slowly bring the water to a simmer; this coagulates the blood proteins and brings other impurities to the surface. This may take from 1 to 1½ hours. Move the bones around from time to time as the water comes to a simmer, but do not stir, as this would disperse the impurities. Skim the scum that rises to the surface. As soon as the liquid comes to a simmer, remove the pot from the heat. (If the bones are blanched for longer than is necessary to coagulate the blood proteins and draw out other impurities, more of their flavor will be extracted into a liquid that you will end up discarding rather than into the liquid that will become your stock.)

Drain the bones in a China cap and rinse to remove any scum. It is important that the bones be rinsed while they are still hot; if they are allowed to cool first, the impurities will cling to the bones and go into your stock.

Clean out the stockpot and return the bones to it. Add the cold water. Place the stockpot off to one side of the burner. This will cause any impurities that rise to gather at one side of the pot, making it easier to skim. Slowly bring to a simmer. Skim continually. (It is easier to skim before the aromatics are added, and the more you skim, the better your chances are for a clear stock.)

Once the liquid is at a simmer, add the aromatics. Bring back to a simmer, and simmer for 6 hours, skimming frequently. The stock will have a noticeable clarity.

Turn off the heat and allow the stock to stand for about 20 minutes; this allows any particles left in the stock to settle in the bottom of the pot.

Set a chinois or fine-mesh conical strainer over a large container. Carefully ladle the stock off the top, disturbing the bones as little as possible so that the impurities that have settled are not mixed into the stock. Once you reach the bones, tilt the pot to reach the stock. Once again, be extremely careful not to move the bones. Do not press on the solids in the strainer or force through any liquid that does not pass on its own. Discard any stock at the bottom of the pot that is cloudy with impurities.

Cover over an ice bath or in a blast chiller. Refrigerate the stock for up to 3 days, or freeze for longer storage.   **MAKES ABOUT 3 LITERS**

LAMB STOCK

4.5 kilograms lamb bones,
    chopped into 1-inch cubes
120 grams canola oil
1 calf's foot, split
9.5 liters water, cold
450 grams tomato paste
340 grams carrots cut into 1-inch mirepoix
450 grams leeks cut into 1-inch mirepoix
    (white and light green parts only)
225 grams onions cut into 1-inch mirepoix
1 head garlic, halved horizontally, broken into pieces,
    root end and excess skin removed
42 grams flat-leaf parsley sprigs
14 grams thyme sprigs
2 bay leaves
450 grams tomatoes cut into 1-inch chunks

Coat the lamb bones with oil and spread in a roasting pan that is large enough to hold them in one layer. (The calf's foot is not roasted, as that would reduce the extraction of gelatin.) Roast at 400°F for about 1½ hours, stirring occasionally to ensure even browning. Once the bones are a rich deep brown color, transfer them to a large stockpot.

Deglaze the roasting pan, adding just enough water to barely cover the bottom of the pan and scraping up the glaze and bits of meat on the bottom, then add this to the stockpot.

Add the calf's foot and the cold water to the pot. Place the stockpot off to one side of the burner. This will cause any impurities that rise to gather at one side of the pot, making it easier to skim. Bring slowly to a simmer, skimming continually. (It is easier to skim before the vegetables are added.) Once the liquid is at a simmer, skim and then stir in the tomato paste. Add all the aromatics and the tomatoes, bring back to a simmer, and simmer for 6 hours, skimming frequently.

Strain the liquid, first through a China cap, then through a chinois or fine-mesh conical strainer into a large container Do not press on the solids in the strainer or force through any liquid that does not passs on its own. Discard any stock at the bottom of the pot that is cloudy with impurities.

You should have about 2.75 liters of stock. (If necessary, return the strained stock to the heat and reduce to 2.75 liters. Strain through a chinois or fine-mesh conical strainer and cool over an ice bath or in a blast chiller.) Refrigerate for up to 3 days, or freeze in several containers for longer storage.

MAKES ABOUT 2.75 LITERS

CHICKEN STOCK

2.25 kilograms chicken bones,
    necks, and backs

450 grams chicken feet

3.75 liters cold water

2 liters ice cubes

225 grams carrots cut into 1-inch mirepoix

225 grams leeks cut into 1-inch mirepoix
    (white and light green parts only)

225 grams onions cut into 1-inch mirepoix

1 bay leaf

Rinse the bones and chicken feet thoroughly under cold water to remove all visible blood. Remove any organs still attached to the bones. (Rinsing the bones and removing any organs is an essential first step in the clarification of the stock, as any blood proteins would coagulate when heated and could cloud your stock.)

Put all the bones and the feet in a 15-liter stockpot. Cover with the cold water. Place the stockpot off to one side of the burner. This will cause any impurities that rise to gather at one side of the pot, making it easier to skim. Bring slowly to a simmer, skimming continually. (It is easier to skim before the vegetables are added.) Once the liquid is at a simmer, add the ice, which will cause the fat to coagulate, then remove the fat. Skim off as much of the impurities as possible

Add all the aromatics and slowly bring the liquid back to a simmer, skimming frequently. Simmer for another 30 to 40 minutes, skimming often. Turn off the heat and allow the stock to rest for about 20 minutes; this allows any particles left in the stock to settle at the bottom of the pot.

Set a chinois or fine-mesh conical strainer over a large container. Carefully ladle the stock off the top, disturbing the bones as little as possible so that the impurities that have settled are not mixed into the stock. Once you reach the bones, tilt the pot to reach the stock. Once again, be

extremely careful not to move the bones. Do not press on the solids in the strainer or force through any liquid that does not pass on its own. Discard any stock at the bottom of the pot that is cloudy with impurities.

Cool over an ice bath or in a blast chiller. Refrigerate the stock for up to 3 days, or freeze in several containers for longer storage.

MAKES ABOUT 5.5 LITERS

BEEF STOCK

2.25 kilograms meaty beef neck or leg bones, cut into 2- to 3-inch sections

25 grams canola oil

225 grams Spanish onions, peeled

About 5 liters water, cold

85 grams carrots cut into 1-inch mirepoix

85 grams leeks cut into 1-inch mirepoix (white and light green parts only)

1 large thyme sprig

1 large flat-leaf parsley sprig

3 bay leaves

0.5 gram black peppercorns

½ head garlic (halved horizontally), broken into pieces, root end and any
    excess skin removed

Toss the bones with half the oil. Put a large roasting pan in the oven to heat at 475°F for about 10 minutes.

Spread out the bones in a single layer. Roast for about 45 minutes, turning occasionally, until richly browned on all sides.

Meanwhile, cut 1 onion crosswise in half. Heat a small heavy sauté pan over medium-high heat until hot. Place 1 onion half cut side down to one side of the pan, so that it is not over direct heat, and let it brown and then char to a rich, dark brown, about 30 minutes. (This will add color to the stock.)

Remove the roasting pan from the oven and transfer the bones to a large colander set over a baking sheet to drain. Drain the fat from the roasting pan, add about 275 milliliters of water to the pan, and deglaze. Pour the resulting *fond* into a large stockpot.

Transfer the bones to the stockpot and add enough water to just cover them. Skim off any fat, then add the charred onion half. Place the stockpot off to one side of the burner. This will cause any impurities that rise to gather at one side of the pot, making it easier to skim. Bring to a simmer over medium heat, skimming continually, and simmer for 5 hours, skimming frequently. Add water if necessary to keep the bones covered.

Meanwhile, cut the remaining onions into quarters. Put the onions, carrots, and leeks in a roasting pan that will hold them in a single layer and toss with the remaining 10 grams canola oil. Roast in a 400°F oven for 20 minutes. Stir and roast for another 20 minutes, or until the vegetables are richly caramelized.

After the stock has simmered for 5 hours, add the vegetables, herbs, peppercorns, and garlic and simmer for 1 hour longer.

Strain the liquid, first through a China cap, then through a chinois or fine-mesh conical strainer into a large container. Do not press on the solids in the strainer or force through any liquid that does not pass on its own. Discard any stock at the bottom of the pot that is cloudy with impurities.

If necessary, reduce the stock to 3.25 liters. Strain through a chinois or fine-mesh conical strainer and cool over an ice bath or in a blast chiller. Refrigerate the stock for up to 3 days, or freeze in several containers for longer storage. **MAKES ABOUT 3.25 LITERS**

DUCK STOCK

2.25 kilograms duck bones, chopped into 2- to 3-inch pieces

120 grams canola oil

450 grams duck feet

5.5 liters water, cold

175 grams tomato paste

225 grams carrots cut into 1-inch mirepoix

225 grams leeks cut into 1-inch mirepoix
   (white and light green parts only)

225 grams onions cut into 1-inch mirepoix

28 grams flat-leaf parsley sprigs

450 grams tomatoes cut into 1-inch chunks

Rinse the duck bones well to remove any traces of blood. Using a towel, dry the bones well (wet bones would steam rather than roast). Coat the bones with oil. Put the bones in a roasting pan that is large enough to hold them in one layer. (The duck feet are not roasted, as that would reduce the extraction of gelatin.) Roast at 425°F for about 1½ hours, until

a rich, deep red-brown. As the bones roast, water and fat will leach from them; remove it as it accumulates, or you risk the bones steaming rather than roasting. Once the bones are roasted, transfer them to a 12-liter stockpot.

Set the roasting pan over medium heat to concentrate any remaining liquid, then deglaze the pan, adding just enough water to barely cover the bottom of the pan and scraping up the glaze and bits of meat. Add this to the stockpot.

Add the duck feet, if using, and the cold water to the pot. Place the stockpot off to one side of the burner. This will cause any impurities that rise to gather at one side of the pot, making it easier to skim. Bring slowly to a simmer, skimming continually. (It is easier to skim before the vegetables are added.)

Once the liquid is at a simmer, skim and then stir in the tomato paste. Add all the aromatics and the tomatoes, bring back to a simmer, and simmer for 4 hours, skimming frequently.

Strain the liquid, first through a China cap, then through a chinois or fine-mesh conical strainer into a large container. Do not press on the solids in the strainer or force through any liquid that does not pass on its own. Discard any stock at the bottom of the pot that is cloudy with impurities.

The stock should be a deep red-brown color, with a pronounced duck flavor. If it looks red and is watery, reduce it further as necessary. Strain and chill over an ice bath or in a blast chiller.

Refrigerate the stock for up to 3 days, or freeze in several containers for longer storage. **MAKES ABOUT 3 LITERS**

VARIATION: REDUCED DUCK STOCK. Slowly reduce the stock to 0.5 liter. Strain and chill over an ice bath. Refrigerate the stock for up to 3 days, or freeze in one or two containers for longer storage.

MAKES 0.5 LITER

DUCK CONSOMMÉ

25 grams chopped shallot

35 grams chopped carrot

35 grams chopped button mushrooms

75 grams egg whites

750 milliliters Duck Stock (page 258)

250 milliliters water

60 grams finely chopped lean duck meat

To make the raft, whisk the shallots, carrots, mushrooms, and egg whites together until the egg whites begin to froth.

Combine the stock and water in a small deep saucepan and heat until barely tepid. Stir in the duck meat. Whisk in the raft mixture to combine, then heat over high heat, stirring to prevent scorching, until the raft forms on top of the liquid.

Turn down the heat so the liquid simmers, and use a spoon or ladle to create a "breathing" hole in the raft. Simmer for about 45 minutes, until the consommé is clarified (you may still see some small particles circulating in the consommé).

Line a chinois or fine-mesh conical strainer with a towel or large coffee filter. Gently pour the consommé and raft into the strainer and let stand until all the consommé has drained through; do not press on the solids.

Return the consommé to the heat and bring to a simmer. Simmer to reduce to 0.5 liter. Cool over an ice bath.

Refrigerate the consommé for up to 3 days, or freeze for longer storage.   **MAKES 0.5 LITER**

MUSHROOM STOCK

450 grams coarsely chopped button mushrooms

135 grams coarsely chopped carrots

90 grams coarsely chopped leeks (white and light green parts only)

125 grams coarsely chopped onions

6 grams flat-leaf parsley sprigs

60 grams canola oil

1.5 grams curry powder

1 bay leaf

1 large thyme sprig

3.75 liters water

Finely grind the mushrooms, carrots, leeks, onions, and parsley separately in a grinder or food processor. If using a food processor, pulse and scrape down the sides as necessary.

Heat the oil in a stockpot. Add the vegetables, parsley, and curry powder and sweat for 2 minutes, stirring occasionally, then add the bay leaf, thyme, and 2 liters of the water. Bring to a simmer and simmer for 45 minutes.

Strain the stock through a chinois or fine-mesh conical strainer, pressing down on the solids, and return the vegetables to the stockpot. Set the stock aside. Add the remaining 1.75 liters water to the pot and return to a simmer. Simmer for another 45 minutes. Strain.

Combine the two batches of stock in a pot, bring to a boil, and reduce to 650 milliliters. Strain and cool over an ice bath. Refrigerate for up to 3 days, or freeze for longer storage.   **MAKES 650 MILLILITERS**

VEGETABLE STOCK

680 grams coarsely chopped leeks (white part only)

450 grams coarsely chopped peeled carrots

680 grams coarsely chopped Spanish onions

1 small fennel bulb, trimmed and coarsely chopped

56 grams flat-leaf parsley sprigs

60 grams canola oil

2 bay leaves

2 thyme sprigs

4 liters water

Finely grind the leeks, carrots, onions, fennel, and parsley separately in a grinder or a food processor. If using a food processor, pulse and scrape down the sides as necessary.

Heat the canola oil in a stockpot and sweat the vegetables over low heat for 5 to 8 minutes, or until softened. Add the bay leaves, thyme, parsley, and enough water to cover by 2 inches. Bring to a gentle simmer, skimming frequently, and simmer for 45 minutes.

Strain the stock through a chinois, pressing on the vegetables to extract the stock, then pass through a fine-mesh conical strainer. Cool over an ice bath.

Refrigerate for up to 2 days.   **MAKES 3 TO 3.75 LITERS**

QUICK SAUCES

120 grams canola oil

700 grams chicken, squab, duck, pork, rabbit, or veal bones, chopped into 1-inch pieces

750 milliliters water

750 milliliters Chicken Stock (page 257) or water

125 grams onions cut into ½-inch mirepoix

90 grams leeks cut into ½-inch mirepoix (white and light green parts only)

135 grams carrots cut into ½-inch mirepoix

60 grams tomatoes cut into ½-inch pieces

500 milliliters Veal Stock (page 255; or 250 millliliters Veal Stock plus 250 milliliters strained stock made with the same bones as above)

Heat the canola oil over high heat in a wide heavy pot large enough to hold the bones in one layer. When it just begins to smoke, add the bones and brown them, without stirring, for about 10 minutes. (They should be well browned before they are moved, or they will give off their juices and begin to steam rather than brown.) Turn the bones and cook for about 10 minutes longer, or until evenly colored.

For the first deglazing: Add 250 milliliters of the water to the pot. You will hear the water sizzling as it hits the hot pot; then, as it reduces, it will become quiet. Stirring with a wooden spoon, scrape up any glazed juices clinging to the bottom of the pot and cook until the liquid has evaporated and the pot is glazed and sizzling again. (Don't worry about the oil still in the pot; it will be removed later.)

For the second deglazing: Deglaze the pot with 250 milliliters of the chicken stock and cook as above. As the stock boils down this time, the color of the bones and liquid will become deeper and the natural gelatin in the stock will glaze the bones.

For the third deglazing: Add the onions, leeks, and carrots; the water content of the vegetables provides the liquid for this deglazing. Cook as above until the moisture has evaporated and the vegetables are lightly caramelized.

For the fourth deglazing: Add the tomatoes and cook until the moisture has evaporated.

For the fifth deglazing: Add the remaining 500 milliliters chicken stock, the veal stock, and the remaining 500 milliliters water. Deglaze the pot, then transfer the stock and bones to a taller, narrower pot so that it will be easier to skim. Bring to a simmer (with the pot set partially off the burner to force the impurities to one side) and ladle off the oil as it rises to the top. Simmer for 45 minutes, skimming often, until the stock has reduced to the level of the bones.

Strain the sauce through a China cap and then again through a chinois or fine-mesh conical strainer; do not force any of the solids through the strainer, or they will cloud your sauce. You should have about 450 milliliters of liquid. Pour the liquid into a small pot, reduce to about 200 milliliters, and strain again.

Refrigerate the sauce for up to 3 days, or freeze for longer storage.

MAKES ABOUT 200 MILLILITERS

VARIATION: LAMB SAUCE. Use lamb bones. During the fourth deglazing, add 7 grams thyme sprigs, and 2 medium garlic cloves, crushed, along with the tomatoes. Continue as in the main recipe.

MAKES ABOUT 200 MILLILITERS

MORNAY SAUCE

43 grams unsalted butter

65 grams ¼-inch dice Spanish onion

Kosher salt

26 grams all-purpose flour

500 grams whole milk

250 grams heavy cream

1 bay leaf

3 black peppercorns

3 cloves

Freshly ground white pepper

30 grams grated Comté or Emmenthaler

Melt the butter in a saucepan on a diffuser over medium heat. Add the onion and a pinch of salt and cook slowly until the onion is translucent. Sprinkle in the flour and cook, stirring constantly so the roux does not color, for about 3 minutes. Whisking constantly, add the milk and cream, whisking until fully incorporated. Bring to a simmer, then add the bay leaf, peppercorns, and cloves. Move the pan to one side of the diffuser, away from direct heat, to prevent scorching and simmer gently for 30 minutes.

Remove the sauce from the heat and season with salt and a pinch of pepper. Strain the sauce through a chinois or fine-mesh conical strainer, add the cheese, and whisk until melted and smooth.

MAKES ABOUT 0.75 LITER

BORDELAISE SAUCE

225 milliliters red wine, such as Cabernet Sauvignon

30 grams sliced shallot

60 grams sliced carrots

15 grams sliced mushrooms

15 grams sliced garlic

10 parsley sprigs

2 thyme sprigs

1 bay leaf

6 black peppercorns

225 milliliters Veal Stock (page 255)

In a saucepan, bring the wine, shallot, carrots, mushrooms, garlic, parsley, thyme, and bay leaf to a simmer, and simmer until almost all the liquid has evaporated. Add the peppercorns and the veal stock and simmer for 10 to 15 minutes, or until the stock is reduced to a sauce consistency. Strain the sauce through a chinois or fine-mesh conical strainer into a small saucepan.

MAKES ABOUT 110 MILLILITERS

CLARIFIED BUTTER

450 grams unsalted butter, cut into 1-inch cubes

Melt the butter in a small saucepan and over low heat. Do not stir. Once the butter has melted, skim off the foamy layer that has risen to the top and discard. Carefully pour off the clear yellow liquid, the clarified butter. Discard the white milky layer in the bottom of the pan.

MAKES ABOUT 350 GRAMS

BEURRE MANIÉ

30 grams all-purpose flour

30 grams unsalted butter, at room temperature

Mix the flour and butter together to create a smooth paste.

MAKES 60 GRAMS

BEURRE MONTÉ

Water

Unsalted butter, cut into 1-inch cubes

No matter what quantity of beurre monté you will be making, you need a thin layer of water at the bottom of a pot to start the emulsion process. Put the water in a saucepan or in a large rondeau and bring to a simmer. Reduce the heat to low and begin whisking in the butter, bit by bit, to emulsify. Once you have established the emulsion, continue to add pieces of butter until you have the quantity of beurre monté you need. It is important to keep the level of heat gentle and consistent in order to maintain the emulsification. Make the beurre monté close to the time it will be used, and keep it in a warm place.

Extra beurre monté should be clarified for additional use.

VARIATION: BEURRE MONTÉ BATH FOR LOBSTER. Select a container that will allow the lobster tails to be submerged with enough room for the beurre monté to circulate. Make Beurre Monté (we normally use about 5 kilograms of butter) and then whisk in 1 part water to every 3 parts beurre monté. Place in the container and heat to 59.5°C (139.1°F) for 15 minutes.

BRIOCHE

75 grams water, warm (43.3° to 46.1°C; 110° to 115° F)

1 package (about 7 grams) active dry yeast (not quick-rising)

297 grams cake flour

288 grams all-purpose flour

70 grams granulated sugar

8 grams kosher salt

6 large eggs, at room temperature

290 grams unsalted butter, cut into 1-inch cubes,
    at room temperature, plus butter for the pans

Combine the water and yeast in a small bowl. Let sit for 10 minutes, then stir until the yeast is completely dissolved. Set aside.

Sift together the flours, sugar, and salt into the bowl of a stand mixer fitted with the dough hook. Add the eggs and beat for 1 minute at low speed, scraping down the sides with a rubber spatula as needed. Slowly add the dissolved yeast and continue beating at low speed for 5 minutes. Stop the machine, scrape any dough off the dough hook, and beat for another 5 minutes. Add the butter cubes in batches, about one-quarter of them at a time, beating for about 1 minute after each addition. Once all the butter has been added, beat for 10 to 15 minutes more.

Transfer the dough to a large floured bowl and cover with food-safe plastic wrap. Set aside in a warm place until doubled in size, about 3 hours.

Turn the dough out onto a generously floured work surface and gently work out the air bubbles by folding the dough over several times while lightly pressing down on it. Return the dough to the bowl, cover with plastic wrap, and refrigerate overnight.

Generously butter two 8½-by-4½-by-3-inch loaf pans. Turn the dough out onto a floured work surface. With floured hands, divide the dough in half and shape it into two rectangles to fit the loaf pans. Place the dough in the pans and let rise uncovered in a warm place until it is about ½ inch above the top of the pans, about 3 hours.

Bake the brioche in a 350°F oven until the loaves are well browned on top and sound hollow when tapped on the bottom, 35 to 40 minutes. Immediately turn the brioche out onto a wire rack.

If using immediately, let the breads cool for 10 minutes, then slice and serve. If serving within a few hours, promptly wrap the hot bread in aluminum foil and store at room temperature until ready to use. If freezing, immediately wrap the hot bread in foil and freeze; when ready to use, reheat (without thawing, and still wrapped in foil) in a 250°F oven until heated through, 20 to 25 minutes. The bread can be kept frozen for up to 1 month. If using the brioche for croutons, let the loaf sit at room temperature, uncovered, to dry for 1 day.

MAKES TWO 8 1/2-BY-4 1/2-BY-3 INCH LOAVES

PASTA DOUGH FOR ROLLING

1 kilogram Tipo 00 pasta flour (see Sources, page 282) plus additional
    for kneading

2 large eggs

460 grams egg yolks

80 grams whole milk

32 grams extra virgin olive oil

Durum semolina flour

Mound the flour on a board or other surface and create a well in the center, pushing the flour to all sides to make a ring with sides about 1 inch wide. Add the eggs, egg yolks, milk, and oil to the well. Use your fingers to break up the eggs and stir the eggs in a circular motion. This allows the eggs to gradually pull in the flour from the sides of the well; it is important that the flour not be incorporated too rapidly, or the dough will be lumpy. Use a pastry scraper to occasionally push the flour toward the eggs. The mixture will eventually thicken too much to continue stirring with your fingers. Continue incorporating the remaining flour with the pastry scraper, cutting it into the dough.

Bring the dough together with the palms of your hands and form it into a ball. Knead the dough in a forward motion with the heel of your hand. Form the dough into a ball again and repeat several times. The dough should feel moist but not sticky. Let it rest for a few minutes.

Clean the work surface, dust with flour, and knead the dough until it is silky smooth, about 10 to 15 minutes.

Double-wrap the dough in food-safe plastic wrap and let it rest for at least 30 minutes, and up to 1 hour, before rolling it through a pasta machine. The dough can be made a day ahead, wrapped, and refrigerated; bring to room temperature before rolling. **MAKES ABOUT 1.65 KILOGRAMS**

PASTA DOUGH FOR EXTRUDING

900 grams semolina flour
300 milliliters water

Line a sheet pan with parchment paper.

Place the flour into a pasta extruder fitted with the candele die. Drizzle in the water. Allow the machine to knead the dough until it forms pellets the size of coffee beans. Extrude the dough and cut every 12 inches.

Place the pasta on the parchment-lined pan to dry for a day, then cook as directed in the recipe. **MAKES ABOUT 1 KILOGRAM**

BREAD CRUMBS

25 grams Brioche (page 262), crusts removed

Place the brioche in a food processor and pulse to crumbs.

For dried bread crumbs, spread the crumbs in a baking pan and toast in a 350°F oven for about 3 minutes. Toss the crumbs, bake for another 3 minutes, and toss again. Continue to bake until evenly golden brown, about another 3 minutes. Let cool.

MAKES ABOUT 25 GRAMS FRESH (LESS IF DRIED)

PEPPER CONFETTI

Red, yellow, and/or green "fancy" bell peppers

Cut off the tops and bottoms of the peppers, then cut the peppers into sections following the natural lines in the skin. Trim away the ribs and seeds. Peel off the skin, using a vegetable peeler. Cut the peppers into 1/16-inch julienne strips.

Lay the strips on a dehydrator tray and dry completely .

Line up the dried strips side by side and cut them into small dice. Store in an airtight container at room temperature.

CARROT POWDER

About 55 grams very finely chopped carrots (chopped in a food processor; or use the pulp left from juicing carrots in a juicer)

Squeeze the carrots in a towel or blot on C-fold towels to remove excess moisture. Spread in a thin even layer on a dehydrator tray and dry completely. Let cool to room temperature.

Grind the carrots to a powder in a coffee or spice grinder. Store in a tightly covered container or jar. **MAKES ABOUT 10 GRAMS**

BEET POWDER

About 55 grams finely chopped beets (chopped in a food processor; or use the pulp left after juicing beets in a juicer)

Blot the beets with C-fold towels to extract excess moisture. Spread in a thin even layer on a dehydrator tray and dry completely. Let cool to room temperature.

Grind the beets to a powder in a coffee or spice grinder. Store in a tightly covered container or jar. **MAKES ABOUT 10 GRAMS**

TOMATO POWDER

About 55 grams finely chopped tomato pulp (from a peeled and seeded tomato)

Squeeze the tomato pulp in a towel to extract excess moisture. Spread in a thin even layer on a dehydrator tray and dry completely. Let cool to room temperature.

Grind the tomato as finely as possible in a coffee or spice grinder. There may be some pieces that will not break up, so when you feel the powder is as fine as it will get, sift it through a chinois or fine-mesh conical strainer, stirring with a spoon. Use the fine powder that falls through the strainer. The tomatoes left in the strainer can be used as a more coarse powder, or ground again if desired. Store in a tightly covered container or jar. **MAKES ABOUT 10 GRAMS**

CITRUS POWDER

30 grams julienned orange zest

30 grams julienned lime zest

30 grams julienned lemon zest

Use a zester to remove the zests of the fruits in a fine julienne.

Place each type of zest in a separate small pan, cover with cold water, and bring to a boil. Drain the zests and return to the pans. Repeat the blanching process 2 more times. Dry the zests on C-fold towels.

Spread the zests in an even layer on a dehydrator tray and dry completely. If one type of zest dries before the others, remove it. Let cool to room temperature.

Grind all the zests together in a coffee or spice grinder until as fine as possible. Sift the powdered zests through a chinois or fine-mesh conical strainer, stirring with a spoon. Use the fine powder that falls through the strainer. The zest left in the strainer can be used as a more coarse powder, or ground again if desired. Store in a tightly covered container or jar.

MAKES ABOUT 12 GRAMS

PRESERVED LEMONS

6 lemons or Meyer lemons, washed and dried

Kosher salt

Granulated sugar

Extra virgin olive oil

Stand each lemon on end and cut into quarters from the top to close to the bottom, leaving the bottom end intact. Mix equal parts of salt and sugar. Spread a thin layer in the bottom of a container. Stand the lemons in the container and pack the remaining mixture all around them; the lemons should be totally encased in the mixture.

Let cure in a cool, dry spot or refrigerate for 2 months. The preserved lemons can be frozen indefinitely.

QUICK METHOD: Cut the ends off each lemon so that it can stand without tipping. Slice each lemon crosswise into paper-thin slices, keeping the slices together, because the lemons will be re-formed. Remove

any seeds. Re-form each lemon: Lay the bottom slice on a work surface and sprinkle with a light dusting of salt. Top with the next slice of lemon and a light dusting of sugar. Continue alternating the slices with layers of salt and sugar.

When all the lemons are re-formed, stand them in a snug-fitting container. Refrigerate for 24 hours.

Pour enough olive oil into the container to cover the lemons and return to the refrigerator for 3 days before using. The lemons still in the oil can be used for 3 weeks. Then drain the oil and reserve for other uses. At this point the lemons can also be frozen for longer storage.

MAKES 6 PRESERVED LEMONS

CHORIZO

1 kilogram pork trimmings, cold

40 grams kosher salt

4 grams Hobbs' Curing Salt (see Sources, page 282)

12 grams ground cumin

10 grams Aleppo pepper (see Sources, page 282)

8 grams sweet pimentón (see Sources, page 282)

10 grams piment d'Espelette (see Sources, page 282)

25 grams garlic cloves, peeled

550 grams fatback, cold

60 grams dry milk powder

Hog casings, soaked in cold water

Keep all the ingredients as cold as possible while you work with them. Cut the pork into 1-inch pieces. Mix with the salts, spices, and garlic and grind once through the large die of a meat grinder. Transfer to a bowl set over an ice bath.

Cut the fatback into 1-inch pieces. Be sure it is very cold and grind it once through the small die of the grinder.

Add the fat to the ground pork mixture, add the milk powder, and mix by hand until the fat is emulsified with the meat. Using a sausage stuffer, stuff the mixture into the hog casings, making 6-inch links.

Hang the sausage in a controlled-temperature room (15.6°C/60°F, and 60 percent humidity) for 5 to 6 weeks, or until firm.

MAKES ABOUT 1.6 KILOGRAMS

VEAL TONGUE

1 veal tongue (170 to 225 grams)

35 grams ½-inch dice onion

28 grams ½-inch dice carrot

28 grams ½-inch pieces leek (white and light green parts only)

1 garlic clove, peeled

1 thyme sprig

1.5 grams kosher salt

400 milliliters White Veal Stock (page 255),
    Chicken Stock (page 257), or water

16 grams champagne vinegar

Combine the tongue and the remaining ingredients in a pot. Add a little water if necessary so that the tongue just floats, and bring the liquid to a simmer (the tongue will swell as it heats; add more water if necessary). Cover with a parchment lid (see page 270). Transfer to a 300°F oven, and braise for about 4 hours, until the tongue is very tender and the skin can be peeled off easily.

Remove the tongue and peel it while still hot. Strain the stock through a chinois or fine-mesh conical strainer into a container and add the tongue. Refrigerate in the liquid until needed.

DUCK TONGUE

225 grams duck tongues (see Sources, page 282)

Kosher salt

½ small garlic clove, crushed

1 thyme sprig

2 black peppercorns

½ small bay leaf

100 grams Rendered Duck Fat (page 270)

70°C (158°F); 8 HOURS

Soak the duck tongues in cold water, changing the water often, for 2 hours, or until the water stays clear.

Drain and dry the duck tongues. Cover them with salt and let sit at room temperature for 2 hours to confit.

Rinse and dry the duck tongues and refrigerate until cold.

Make an herb sachet (see page 269) with the garlic, thyme, peppercorns, and bay leaf. Place the tongues in a bag with the sachet and fat and vacuum-pack on medium.

Cook at 70°C (158°F) for 8 hours. Remove from the water and let rest at room temperature for 10 minutes.

Remove the duck tongues from the bag (reserve the fat), drain, and let sit at room temperature until cool enough to handle. Pull out and remove the piece of cartilage from the center of each tongue, pulling from the wide end of the tongue. Put the tongues in a container, strain the fat over them, and refrigerate. **MAKES ABOUT 175 GRAMS**

PORK BELLY

BRINE

60 grams kosher salt

20 grams Hobbs' Curing Salt (see Sources, page 282)

35 grams granulated sugar

1 liter water

2 black peppercorns

1 small bay leaf

1 thyme sprig

½ medium carrot, cut into 1-inch pieces

½ small leek (white and light green parts only), cut into 1-inch pieces

½ small onion, cut into 1-inch pieces

700 grams pork belly (in one piece)

If brining a baby pork belly (see page 156), adjust the brine ingredients proportionately.

To make the brine, mix the salt, curing salt, and sugar in a large container. Heat about one-quarter of the water and add to the dry mixture, stirring to dissolve the salts and sugar. Add the remaining water and remaining brine ingredients. Chill the brine.

Add the pork belly to the brine and refrigerate overnight.

Remove the pork from the brine (discard the brine) and brush off any seasonings adhering to it.

ROASTED GARLIC PUREE

20 grams unsalted butter

3 large heads garlic (about 200 grams)

3 grams kosher salt

Put the butter on a double thickness of foil and smash it to make a base for the garlic. Top with the garlic and sprinkle with the salt. Fold over the edges to make a package and roast at 300°F for 1½ hours, or until the garlic is soft.

While it is still warm, scrape the softened garlic through a tamis or pass it through a food mill, leaving behind the skins. Use the puree the same day it is prepared. **MAKES ABOUT 90 GRAMS**

ROASTED CHERRY TOMATOES

80 grams cherry tomatoes (about 32), peeled

1 gram confectioners' sugar

Kosher salt and freshly ground black pepper

Toss the tomatoes in a bowl with the sugar and a sprinkling of salt and pepper.

Place the tomatoes on a rack set over a sheet pan and bake at 150°F for about 3 hours, or until they are half-dried; they should be shrunken but still moist. The tomatoes can be kept refrigerated for up to 3 days.

ARTICHOKES BARIGOULE

CUISSON

30 grams extra virgin olive oil

40 grams thinly sliced carrot

35 grams thinly sliced shallots

30 grams thinly sliced onion

Kosher salt

30 grams ¼-inch dice serrano ham

5 grams minced garlic

2 globe artichoke hearts (about 90 grams; see page 269),
    cut into ¾-inch pieces

70 milliliters dry white wine, such as Sauvignon Blanc

150 milliliters Chicken Stock (page 257)

150 milliliters White Veal Stock (page 255)

ARTICHOKES

8 medium (36 count) globe artichokes,
    trimmed (see page 269) and held in acidulated water (page 269)

FOR THE CUISSON: Heat the olive oil in a wide saucepan. Add the carrots and sweat for 2½ minutes. Add the shallots, onions, and a pinch of salt and cook another 1½ minutes. Stir in the ham and cook for about 1 minute, then add the garlic and cook for 1 minute. Add the artichokes and cook for 2 minutes. Add the white wine and turn the artichokes in the wine for about 1 minute, to help keep them from oxidizing.

Add the chicken and veal stock, bring to a simmer, and cook for 10 minutes to infuse the flavors. Strain the cuisson and chill until cold.

FOR THE ARTICHOKES—85°C (185°F); 45 MINUTES TO 1¼ HOURS
Place the artichokes in a single layer in a bag, add the cuisson, and vacuum-pack on high.

Cook at 85°C (185°F) for 45 minutes to 1¼ hours, or until tender.

GLAZED PEARL ONIONS

24 red pearl onions

24 white pearl onions

5 grams granulated sugar

3 grams kosher salt

90 milliliters water

30 grams unsalted butter

15 grams champagne vinegar

15 grams red wine vinegar

85°C (185°F); 35 MINUTES

Cut an X in the root end of each onion. Put the red and white onions in separate bowls and pour in boiling water to cover. When the onion skins have softened enough to be easily peeled, drain the onions. Peel them when they are cool enough to handle and trim the roots as necessary. Refrigerate until cold.

Place the red and white onions in separate bags. Add half of the sugar, salt, water, and butter to each bag. Vacuum-pack on medium.

Cook at 85°C (185°F) for 35 minutes, or until tender. Chill in an ice bath if not proceeding with the recipe.

To complete: Pour the onions, with their liquid, into separate small saucepans. Boil to reduce the liquid by about two-thirds. Add the champagne vinegar to the white onions and the red wine vinegar to the red onions and reduce the liquid, rolling the vegetables around in the glaze to coat them.

GLAZED CARROTS

Twenty-four ¾-inch-by-⅜-inch-thick carrot rounds,
    8 quartered Thumbelina carrots, or 16 turned carrots

2.5 grams granulated sugar

1.5 grams kosher salt

45 milliliters water

15 grams unsalted butter

85°C (185°F); 35 TO 40 MINUTES

With a paring knife, trim the sharp edges of the carrot disks to smooth them.

Place the carrots in a single layer in a medium bag and add the sugar, salt, water, and butter. Vacuum-pack on medium.

Cook at 85°C (185°F) for 35 to 40 minutes, or until tender. Chill in an ice bath if not proceeding with the recipe.

To complete: Pour the carrots, with their liquid, into a small saucepan. Boil to reduce the liquid, rolling the carrots around in the glaze to coat them.

CURRY OIL

28 grams curry powder

15 grams coriander seeds

One ½- to ¾-inch piece cinnamon stick

21 grams ground mace

3.5 grams cayenne pepper

240 grams canola oil

Toast the curry powder and coriander seeds in separate small sauté pans just until fragrant. Transfer to a coffee or spice grinder, add the cinnamon stick, mace, and cayenne, and grind to a powder.

Transfer to a small bowl and stir in enough of the oil to moisten the spices. Put the spices in the blender, add the remaining oil, and blend well. Pour into a container and let sit for a day.

Strain the oil through a cheesecloth-lined fine-mesh sieve. Store in an airtight container at room temperature.   **MAKES ABOUT 120 GRAMS**

FOIE GRAS CURE

8 parts kosher salt

3 parts Hobbs' Curing Salt (see Sources, page 282)

1 part granulated sugar

1 part freshly ground white pepper

Mix all the ingredients together.

POACHING LIQUID

500 milliliters dry white wine, such as Sauvignon Blanc

500 milliliters water

500 grams granulated sugar

Combine the wine, water, and sugar in a saucepan and bring to a boil, stirring to dissolve the sugar. Let cool, and store in the refrigerator.

   MAKES ABOUT 1.3 LITERS

SIMPLE SYRUP

500 grams granulated sugar

500 milliliters water

Bring the sugar and water to a boil in a heavy saucepan, stirring to dissolve the sugar. Let cool to room temperature, then refrigerate.

   MAKES ABOUT 700 MILLILITERS

COCOA SYRUP

100 milliliters water

20 grams heavy cream

60 grams superfine sugar

30 grams Valrhona cocoa powder (see Sources, page 282)

This syrup is used to brighten the color of the Cacao Nib Coulis (page 223). You can also use it to make hot chocolate, add it to any coffee drinks, or serve as a garnish for desserts.

Combine all of the ingredients in a saucepan, bring to a boil, stirring to dissolve the sugar, and boil for 1 minute. Strain into a bowl and chill over an ice bath. Store in the refrigerator. **MAKES ABOUT 145 MILLILITERS**

SWEET BASE SYRUP

700 grams granulated sugar

8 grams sorbet stabilizer (see Sources, page 282)

1 liter water

200 grams atomized glucose (see Sources, page 282)

Combine 8 grams of the sugar with the stabilizer.

Bring the water and the remaining 692 grams sugar to a boil in a large pot, stirring to dissolve the sugar. Add the glucose and return to a boil. Add the combined sugar and stabilizer, being very careful, because the syrup can boil over. Bring back to a boil, and boil for 30 seconds.

Let cool, and store in the refrigerator. **MAKES ABOUT 1.4 LITERS**

BIG-POT BLANCHING

Blanching green vegetables in a big pot with a lot of water and a lot of salt until they are thoroughly cooked is critical to the finished product. It's entirely a color and flavor issue. I want green vegetables to be bright, bright green so their color can launch the flavor and impact of the entire dish. The old saying "We taste first with our eyes" is true. The faster a vegetable is cooked, the greener it becomes.

Raw green vegetables appear dull because a layer of gas develops between the skin and pigment. Heat releases this gas, and the pigment floods to the surface. But this happens fast, and pretty soon, as the vegetable cooks, the acids and enzymes in the vegetable are released, dulling the green color. At the same time, pigment begins to leach out into the water. So the challenge is to fully cook a vegetable before you lose that color, which means cooking it as fast as possible. There are three key factors in achieving this. First, blanch the vegetables in a large quantity of water so you won't significantly lower the boiling temperature when you add the vegetables. (We chill the vegetables before blanching them to ensure a brighter color—this makes it even more important to use enough water.) If you lose the boil, not only do the vegetables cook more slowly, but the water becomes a perfect environment for the pigment-dulling enzymes to go to work (these enzymes are destroyed only at the boiling point). Furthermore, using a lot of water means the pigment-dulling acids released by the vegetables will be more diluted.

Second, use a lot of salt—about 190 grams of salt per 4 liters of water. The water should taste like the ocean. Salt helps prevent color from leaching into the water. A side benefit is that the vegetables will be uniformly seasoned when they are done.

Third, the final critical step: Stop the vegetables from cooking by plunging them into a large quantity of ice water. Leave them there just until they are chilled through, then drain and dry them. You can store them in a dry container for a day until ready to use.

The results of big-pot blanching are dramatic. It's not hard—you only have to decide to do it.

We don't give times for big-pot blanching in the recipes, because times vary according to the type, size, and quality of the vegetable. There is only one certain way to tell if a fava or a bean or pea is done: put it in your mouth and eat it.

HERB SACHETS

Herbs, spices, and garlic should not come in direct contact with food that is vacuum-packed and cooked sous vide, as the flavor will be stronger in areas where there is direct contact. To avoid this, we make sachets, which allows the flavors to infuse the other ingredients evenly.

Place a piece of food-safe plastic wrap large enough to roll up the herbs, spices, and garlic on the work surface. Lay the herbs on the wrap and nestle any garlic and spices in the herbs. Roll up the sachet, and cut off the ends of the roll. Add the sachet to the sous vide bag with the other ingredients; discard after cooking.

BRUNOISE

2 parts carrots, peeled and sliced lengthwise on a Japanese mandoline into
    $1/_{16}$-inch-thick strips
2 parts turnips, peeled and sliced lengthwise on a Japanese mandoline into
    $1/_{16}$-inch-thick strips
1 part leek (white and light green parts only), cut lengthwise into
    $1/_{16}$-inch-wide thick strips

Working with one vegetable at a time, cut into a very fine dice. Bring a saucepan of lightly salted water to a boil. Blanch the carrots and turnips for 30 seconds. Add the leeks for another 30 seconds. Drain and shock in an ice bath until cold. Dry on C-fold towels. Refrigerate for up to 1 day.

ACIDULATED WATER

3 liters water
10 grams ascorbic acid

Combine the water and ascorbic acid, stirring to dissolve the ascorbic acid.   **MAKES 3 LITERS**

TRIMMING ARTICHOKES

FOR 8 GLOBE ARTICHOKES OR 16 VIOLET ARTICHOKES
3 liters water
10 grams ascorbic acid
1 lemon, halved

Combine the water and ascorbic acid in a bowl, stirring to dissolve. Place the artichokes in the acidulated water as soon as they are prepped, so they will not oxidize.

For globe artichoke hearts (trimmed artichokes): Hold an artichoke with the stem end toward you and pull off the very small bottom leaves. Be careful to break them high enough in order not to penetrate the heart. Working your way around the artichoke, bend back the lower leaves until they snap and break, then pull them off. Continue removing the tough outer leaves until you reach the cone of yellow inner leaves. Repeat with the remaining artichokes.

Cut off the artichoke stems flush with the bottoms (unless the recipe instructs you to leave the stems attached). Rub a lemon half over the exposed surfaces as you work. Turn each artichoke on its side and cut off the top two-thirds of the leaves. Discard the trimmings.

Hold an artichoke heart in your hand stem end down and, using a sharp paring knife, trim away the tough dark green exterior all around the heart. Turn the heart stem end up and trim the bottom of the heart to remove the dark green exterior and expose the light green flesh; rub all the cut surfaces with lemon.

With a melon baller or sharp spoon, scrape out the fuzzy choke and discard. Drop the heart into the acidulated water and place a kitchen towel over it to keep it submerged. Repeat with the remaining artichokes.

For violet artichokes: Pull off the small bottom leaves from each artichoke, then, working your way around the artichoke, bend back the outer leaves and snap them off. Continue until you reach the pale, tender inner leaves. With a paring knife, trim the outside of the artichoke slightly, starting from the top of the heart downward, creating a smooth line. Cut off the bottom of the stem. Cut off the top of the artichoke at the point where the leaves begin to take on a pink hue, and put the artichoke in the acidulated water. Repeat with the remaining artichokes. Cut the trimmed hearts vertically in half.

PREPARING LOBSTERS

Put the lobsters in a heatproof container that holds them snugly. Cover with cold water, then drain off the water, measure it, and pour it into a large pot. Bring the water to a boil and add 110 grams white vinegar for every 7.5 liters of water. Pour the boiling liquid over the lobsters and let them steep for 2 minutes if using 450- to 680-gram lobsters, 3 minutes for 900-gram lobsters.

Remove the lobsters from the hot water, but do not discard the water. Twist off the tails. Twist and pull off the claws and return them to the hot water for 5 minutes; remove from the water. Reserve the bodies.

To remove the tail meat: Hold each tail flat and twist the tail fan to one side; pull off and discard. Use your fingers to gently push the meat through from the tail end and pull the meat out through the large opening at the other end. Discard the shell. With a pair of tweezers, pull out the vein that runs the length of each tail. Trim the edges.

To remove the knuckle and claw meat: Twist off each knuckle to remove it. Hold each claw in your hand and pull down to loosen the lower pincer. Push it to either side to crack it, and pull it straight out. Still holding the claw, crack the top of the shell with the heel of a knife, about ¼ inch from the joint where the knuckle was attached. Wiggle your knife to loosen and crack the shell. Shake the claw to remove the meat. Trim away the tip of the claw meat.

Cut off the top joint of each knuckle, the one that was attached to the lobster's body. Use scissors to cut through the shell along the smooth outside edge of the knuckle. Pry open the shell and remove the meat.

Cover all the lobster meat and refrigerate.

For the bodies: Pull back and discard the top shell of each lobster, including the head and antennae. Remove and discard the light green tomalley, the feathery lungs, and the sac behind the head. If the lobsters are female, remove the dark green roe (coral) and reserve for another use or discard. The bodies can be used for stock or sauce.

RENDERED FAT

For foie gras: Cut the foie gras (or trimmings) into ¼-inch pieces.

For beef marrow: Cut the fat into ¼-inch pieces.

For duck fat and skin: Grind through a grinder fitted with a medium die.

For beef fat and sinew: Grind through a grinder fitted with a medium die.

Vacuum-pack the fat in a bag on medium. Cook at 85°C (185°F). The foie gras fat should be rendered after about 45 minutes, the marrow after about 1 hour, and the duck and beef fat after about 1½ hours.

When fat is rendered on the stovetop, any water evaporates in the cooking process. Here it remains in the bag and so must be separated from the fat. Strain the rendered fat through a chinois or fine-mesh conical strainer into a deep, narrow container and refrigerate. The fat will rise to the top and solidify. Remove the fat and refrigerate, or freeze for longer storage. The remaining liquid, which may jell, can be discarded or used for another purpose, such as fortifying a stock or sauce.

85°C (185°F); 45 MINUTES TO 1½ HOURS

PARCHMENT LIDS

Cut or tear a square of parchment bigger than the pot to be covered. Fold two opposite corners together to form a triangle, then fold this triangle in half into a smaller triangle; it will have two short sides and one long side. Position the triangle so that one of the short sides faces you. Fold this bottom edge up, making a narrow triangle, and crease it, maintaining the point of the triangle, as if you were making a paper airplane. Fold this "wing" over again, maintaining the point, and continue folding in this manner until you get to the other side—about five or six folds in all. You should finish with a very slender triangle.

To gauge the size, place the tip over the center of the pot to be covered, mark the edge of the pot with your thumb, and cut off the end of the triangle at this point. Cut ¼ inch off the tip. Unfold the triangle. It will be a circle the size of your pot, with a steam hole in the center. Place the paper lid in the pot so that it rests gently on the food you're cooking.

ABOUT GELATIN

Commercial gelatin—a protein derived from animal connective tissue, commonly pig skin and beef bones, but also chicken and fish—is an important tool that helps us to achieve specific textures and consistencies in the sweet kitchen. It comes in two different forms, and even similar forms differ from brand to brand, so it's important to know the qualities of each form of gelatin.

Gelatin comes in brittle translucent sheets, called leaf gelatin, and as powder. Powdered gelatin, especially the brands common in grocery stores, is derived from beef bones and adds an unpleasant bone flavor to food; powdered gelatin can also be a little more gluey on the palate. If you must use powdered gelatin, use a brand derived from pork products instead of beef.

We prefer leaf gelatin. It has very little flavor of its own and results in a bind that's not sticky on the palate. Leaf gelatin comes in different strengths, labeled bronze, silver, and gold, with bronze being the thickest and strongest. We use silver. But even these strengths vary, so some manufacturers note what's called a gelatin's "bloom value" on the package; the number ranges from 50 to 300, weakest to strongest. Not all manufacturers apply a bloom value to their gelatin, however, so usually the best way to gauge the strength of a gelatin is by weight. It's best always to use the same brand and type so that all your recipes are consistent, but when the brand you usually use is not available, you should be able to use bloom values and weight as a guide.

To use leaf gelatin, soak or "bloom" it in water until it's completely pliable. Carefully wring all the water out (if you don't wring it out, you may dilute your recipe). Dissolve the gelatin in a small amount of the liquid you intend to gel, then add the warm dissolved gelatin to the rest of the liquid. (If you're adding gelatin to a liquid that is already warm, just squeeze it out, add it to the warm liquid, and allow it to dissolve completely.) Also keep in mind:

- Gelatin can be melted in a microwave oven.
- Gelatin incorporated into a food will melt at room temperature.
- Adding gelatin to a boiling liquid will diminish its strength.
- Kiwi, papaya, mango, and especially pineapple contain enzymes that break down proteins and thus can wreak havoc on your gelatin. To combine these fruits with gelatin successfully, either increase the amount of gelatin you use or steam the fruits beforehand.

Gelatin is not used solely for setting liquids. It can be used as a stabilizer, emulsifier, foaming agent, or thickener. It's also a tool for achieving body and texture (this is especially valuable in creating lower-fat preparations). Gelatin melts at body temperature, giving jelled foods that wonderful, melting quality that's so satisfying on the palate.

Gelatin is also an excellent clarifier. Add it to a fruit juice and freeze it. After it's frozen, put it in a cloth-lined strainer and allow to melt. The gelatin will trap the solid particles and the resulting liquid will be perfectly clear.

Remember that gelatin is an animal product, so when jelling food for vegetarian and vegan dishes, use alternatives such as agar-agar, natural gum, carrageenan, or pectin, sometimes called K-gelatin.

PRODUCT, TEMPERATURE, AND TIME

The following is a list of recipe components that utilize sous vide, along with their temperatures and cooking times.

ITEM	RECIPE	TEMPERATURE	TIME	PAGE
FRUIT				
APPLES, FOR SAUCE	Torchon of Monkfish Liver with Green Apple Jelly and Ossetra Caviar	85°C (185°F)	25 minutes	104
APPLES	Glazed Breast of Pork with Swiss Chard, White-Wine-Poached Granny Smith Apples, and Green Mustard Vinaigrette	85°C (185°F)	30 minutes	148
APPLES, FOR PUREE	*Dégustation des Pommes: Genoise aux Pommes,* Candied Apples, Ginger Custard, Milk Jam, Apple Sorbet, and Apple Chips	85°C (185°F)	30 to 40 minutes	230
APPLES, CANDIED	*Dégustation des Pommes: Genoise aux Pommes,* Candied Apples, Ginger Custard, Milk Jam, Apple Sorbet, and Apple Chips	75°C (167°F)	3 hours	230
BANANA	Poached Moulard Duck Foie Gras, Concord Grapes, Celery, Salted Virginia Peanut Nougatine, Banana Puree, and Pedro Ximinez Sherry Vinegar	85°C (185°F)	10 minutes	194
BANANAS, FOR SHERBET	Peanut Butter Mousse with Caramelized Bananas, Banana Sherbet, Chocolate Pudding, and Cacao Nib Coulis	85°C (185°F)	45 minutes	223
BERRIES, FOR CONSOMMÉ	Napa Valley Summer Berry Consommé with Chaput St. Mauré du Manoir Sorbet and White Balsamic Foam	65°C (149°F)	45 minutes	228
CHERRIES, MACERATED	"Cherry-Vanilla": Madagascar Vanilla Bean Cake, Morello Cherry Ice Cream, Italian Pistachio Coulis, Kirsch Foam, and Cherry Jam	65°C (149°F)	25 minutes	239
CHERRIES, FOR JAM	"Cherry-Vanilla": Madagascar Vanilla Bean Cake, Morello Cherry Ice Cream, Italian Pistachio Coulis, Kirsch Foam, and Cherry Jam	90°C (194°F)	45 minutes to 1 hour	239
PEARS	Fourme d'Ambert, Pan-Roasted Cauliflower, Anjou Pear Puree, and Tellicherry Pepper Melba Toast	83°C (181.4°F)	25 minutes	212

ITEM	RECIPE	TEMPERATURE	TIME	PAGE
PEARS, FOR PUREE	Fourme d' Ambert, Pan-Roasted Cauliflower, Anjou Pear Puree, and Tellicherry Pepper Melba Toast	83°C (181.4°F)	45 to 60 minutes	212
PINEAPPLE	Sauvignon-Blanc-Braised Golden Pineapple with White Chocolate Snowflakes, Cilantro Coulis, and Passion Fruit Gelée	75°C (167°F)	1 hour	242
PLUMS	White Sesame Nougatine with Sesame Oil Sablé, Plums, Golden Gooseberries, and Jasmine Rice Sherbet	75°C (167°F)	15 to 20 minutes	246
PLUMS FOR JAM	White Sesame Nougatine with Sesame Oil Sablé, Plums, Golden Gooseberries, and Jasmine Rice Sherbet	90°C (194°F)	45 to 60 minutes	246

VEGETABLES

ITEM	RECIPE	TEMPERATURE	TIME	PAGE
ARTICHOKES BARIGOULE	Artichokes Barigoule	85°C (185°F)	45 minutes to 1¼ hours	266
GLOBE ARTICHOKE HEARTS AND HALVES	Globe Artichokes *à la Barigoule,* Spring Garlic, Flat-Leaf Parsley, and Shaved Serrano Ham	85°C (185°F)	45 minutes to 1¼ hours	52
GLOBE ARTICHOKE HEARTS	*Artichauts en Vierge:* Globe Artichokes, Sunchokes, Crosnes, Meyer Lemon Suprêmes, Castelvetrano Olives, and Trappitu Extra Virgin Olive Oil	85°C (185°F)	45 minutes to 1¼ hours	56
GLOBE ARTICHOKE HEARTS, FOR PUREE	Globe Artichokes *à la Barigoule,* Spring Garlic, Flat-Leaf Parsley, and Shaved Serrano Ham	85°C (185°F)	1½ hours	52
VIOLET ARTICHOKES	*Artichauts en Vierge:* Globe Artichokes, Sunchokes, Crosnes, Meyer Lemon Suprêmes, Castelvetrano Olives, and Trappitu Extra Virgin Olive Oil	85°C (185°F)	40 minutes	56
ASPARAGUS, WHITE	White Asparagus with Field Rhubarb and Black Truffle Coulis	85°C (185°F)	30 minutes	66
ASPARAGUS, WHITE	St. Peter's Fish with Black Truffle Mousse, White Asparagus, and Mousseline	85°C (185°F)	30 minutes	66

ITEM	RECIPE	TEMPERATURE	TIME	PAGE
CARROTS	Globe Artichokes *à la Barigoule,* Spring Garlic, Flat-Leaf Parsley, and Shaved Serrano Ham	85°C (185°F)	35 to 40 minutes	52
CARROTS, GLAZED	Glazed Carrots	85°C (185°F)	35 to 40 minutes	267
CARROTS, ROUNDS	Sweet Garden Carrot Cake, Cream Cheese Icing, Candied Walnut Crunch, Black Raisin Coulis, Carrot Buttons, Indonesian Cinnamon Ice Cream, and *Gelée de Carotte et Sa Poudre*	95°C (203°F)	3 hours	218
CAULIFLOWER	Fourme d'Ambert, Pan-Roasted Cauliflower, Anjou Pear Puree, and Tellicherry Pepper Melba Toast	85°C (185°F)	15 minutes	212
CELERY ROOT, FOR PUREE	Chestnut-Stuffed Four Story Hills Farm Chicken with Celery and Honey-Poached Cranberries	85°C (185°F)	1½ hours	114
CORN	Sweet Corn Soup with Summer Succotash and Pork Belly Dumplings	85°C (185°F)	30 minutes	48
CORN	Sirloin of Devil's Gulch Ranch Rabbit Wrapped in Hobbs' Applewood Smoked Bacon with Summer Succotash and Corn "Pudding"	85°C (185°F)	1 hour	138
CROSNES	*Artichauts en Vierge:* Globe Artichokes, Sunchokes, Crosnes, Meyer Lemon Suprêmes, Castelvetrano Olives, and Trappitu Extra Virgin Olive Oil	85°C (185°F)	30 minutes	56
FENNEL	Squab with Piquillo Peppers, Marcona Almonds, Fennel, and Medjool Date Sauce	85°C (185°F)	40 minutes	124
FENNEL, BABY	Caramelized Fennel, Marcona Almonds, Navel Orange Confit, Caraway Seeds, and Fennel Puree	85°C (185°F)	40 minutes	64
FENNEL, FOR PUREE	Caramelized Fennel, Marcona Almonds, Navel Orange Confit, Caraway Seeds, and Fennel Puree	85°C (185°F)	45 minutes to 1 hour	64

ITEM	RECIPE	TEMPERATURE	TIME	PAGE
FENNEL, WEDGES	Caramelized Fennel, Marcona Almonds, Navel Orange Confit, Caraway Seeds, and Fennel Puree	85°C (185°F)	40 minutes	64
ONIONS, CIPOLLINI	Salad of New-Crop Onions, Pickled Ramps, and Sauce Soubise	85°C (185°F)	35 minutes	60
ONIONS, CIPOLLINI	Globe Artichokes *à la Barigoule,* Spring Garlic, Flat-Leaf Parsley, and Shaved Serrano Ham	85°C (185°F)	35 to 40 minutes	52
ONIONS, CIPOLLINI	Milk-Poached Calf's Liver, Caraway-Glazed Cipollini, Granny Smith Apple, Dijon Mustard, and *Sauce Laurier*	85°C (185°F)	1 hour to 1 hour 10 minutes	186
ONIONS, CIPOLLINI	"Quail in a Jar": Quail Stuffed with Moulard Duck Foie Gras, Cipollini, Figs, and Port Wine Glaze	85°C (185°F)	1 hour	130
ONIONS, PEARL	Glazed Pearl Onions	85°C (185°F)	35 to 40 minutes	266
ONIONS, PEARL	Salad of New-Crop Onions, Pickled Ramps, and Sauce Soubise	85°C (185°F)	35 minutes	60
ONIONS, PEARL	Globe Artichokes *à la Barigoule,* Spring Garlic, Flat-Leaf Parsley, and Shaved Serrano Ham	85°C (185°F)	35 to 40 minutes	52
ONIONS, PEARL	Confit of Moulard Duck Foie Gras with Vegetables *à la Grecque*	85°C (185°F)	30 minutes	192
ONIONS, SWEET	Salad of New-Crop Onions, Pickled Ramps, and Sauce Soubise	85°C (185°F)	25 minutes	60
ONIONS, WHITE, FOR SAUCE	Salad of New-Crop Onions, Pickled Ramps, and Sauce Soubise	85°C (185°F)	6 hours	60
POTATOES	Confit of Liberty Pekin Duck Leg, *Pommes Sarladaise,* Fried Hen Egg, and Frisée Salad	85°C (185°F)	20 to 25 minutes	122
POTATOES	Jasper Hills Winnemere Croquante, Confit Potato, Pan-Roasted Savoy Cabbage, and Blis Maple Syrup	85°C (185°F)	1 hour	214

ITEM	RECIPE	TEMPERATURE	TIME	PAGE
PUMPKIN	*Chaud-Froid* of Moulard Duck Foie Gras, Musquée de Provence, Pomegranate Seeds, Mizuna Leaves, and Gingerbread Puree	85°C (185°F)	5 to 6 minutes	202
PUMPKIN, MUSQUÉE DE PROVENCE	Musquée de Provence, Roasted Brussels Sprouts, King Trumpet Mushrooms, and Black Truffle Syrup	85°C (185°F)	20 minutes	62
RADISHES, BALLS	Confit of Moulard Duck Foie Gras with Vegetables *à la Grecque*	85°C (185°F)	6 minutes	192
RADISHES, PICKLED	Puree of Sunchoke Soup with Arugula Pudding and Pickled Radishes	85°C (185°F)	25 minutes	50
RADISHES	Sauternes-Poached Moulard Duck Foie Gras, Tahitian Vanilla Beans, Braised Radishes, and Purslane	85°C (185°F)	30 minutes	196
RHUBARB	White Asparagus with Field Rhubarb and Black Truffle Coulis	61°C (141.8°F)	15 minutes	66
RUTABAGA	*Dégustation de Porcelet,* Rutabaga Mostarda, Wilted Mustard Greens, and Potato "Mille-Feuille"	85°C (185°F)	2 hours	156
TURNIPS	Confit of Calf's Heart, Toasted Pecans, Baby Turnips, Bing Cherries, and Cherry-Wood-Aged Balsamic Vinegar	85°C (185°F)	30 minutes	182
SALSIFY	Gratin of Salsify, Black Trumpet Duxelles, and Preserved Meyer Lemon *Glaçage*	85°C (185°F)	1 hour	68
SALSIFY	Fricassée of Veal Kidney with Black Trumpet Mushrooms, Salsify, Brussels Sprouts, and Curry-Infused Veal Sauce	85°C (185°F)	1 hour	178
SUNCHOKES	*Artichauts en Vierge:* Globe Artichokes, Sunchokes, Crosnes, Meyer Lemon Suprêmes, Castelvetrano Olives, and Trappitu Extra Virgin Olive Oil	85°C (185°F)	40 to 60 minutes	56
SWISS CHARD, STEMS	Glazed Breast of Pork with Swiss Chard, White-Wine-Poached Granny Smith Apples, and Green Mustard Vinaigrette	85°C (185°F)	1¼ hours	148

ITEM	RECIPE	TEMPERATURE	TIME	PAGE
FISH AND SHELLFISH				
BASS, STRIPED	Double Chop of Striped Bass Belly *en Persillade,* Black-Eyed Peas, and Whole-Grain Mustard Sauce	62°C (143.6°F)	11 minutes	100
CUTTLEFISH	"Tagliatelle" of Cuttlefish and Hawaiian Heart of Peach Palm, White Nectarine, Sweet Pepper Confetti, and Vinaigrette *à l'Encre de Seiche*	64°C (147.2°F)	10 hours	74
EEL	*Anguille à la Japonaise*	59°C (138.2°F)	10 minutes	92
LOBSTER, TAILS	Butter-Poached Maine Lobster, Tomato *Pain Perdu,* Celery, and "Russian Dressing"	59.5°C (139.1°F)	15 minutes	80
LOBSTER, TAILS	*Homard au Vin:* Butter-Poached Maine Lobster Tail, Hen-of-the-Woods Mushrooms, Bone Marrow, Sweet Carrots, and Pearl Onions	59.5°C (139.1°F)	15 minutes	82
MACKEREL	Spanish Mackerel and Serrano Ham *en Brioche,* Capers, Piquillo Peppers, and Lemon Confit	61°C (141.8°F)	12 minutes	88
MONKFISH, LIVER	Torchon of Monkfish Liver with Green Apple Jelly and Ossetra Caviar	64°C (147.2°F)	3¼ hours	104
OCTOPUS, TENTACLES	Grilled Octopus Tentacles, Chorizo, Fingerling Potatoes, Green Almonds, and Salsa Verde	77°C (170.6°F)	5 hours	78
ST. PETER'S FISH	St. Peter's Fish with Black Truffle Mousse, White Asparagus, and Mousseline	60°C (140°F)	10 minutes	86
STURGEON	Columbia River Wild Sturgeon Confit à la Minute, Herb Spaetzle, Heirloom Beets, Dill "Mousse," and Borscht Sauce	61°C (141.8°F)	16 minutes	96
TUNA	Olive-Oil-Poached Bluefin Tuna, Jacobsen's Farm Tomatoes *en Vierge,* Toasted Pine Nuts, Niçoise Olives, and Basil Seeds	59.5°C (139.1°F)	13 minutes	106

ITEM	RECIPE	TEMPERATURE	TIME	PAGE
POULTRY AND MEATS				
BEEF, SIRLOIN	Sirloin of Prime Beef, Spring Garlic Cloves, Glazed Carrots, Cèpes, Bone Marrow, and Bordelaise Syrup	59.5°C (139.1°F)	45 minutes	164
CHICKEN, LEGS	Chestnut-Stuffed Four Story Hills Farm Chicken with Celery and Honey-Poached Cranberries	64°C (147.2°F)	1 hour	114
DUCK, BREAST	"Pastrami": Liberty Pekin Duck Breast, Coleslaw, Rye Melba Toast, and 1000 Island *Gastrique*	60.5°C (140.9°F)	25 minutes	120
DUCK, LEG	Confit of Liberty Pekin Duck Leg, *Pommes Sarladaise,* Fried Hen Egg, and Frisée Salad	82.2°C (180°F)	8 hours	122
EGG	Soft-Boiled Hen Egg with Green Asparagus, Crème Fraîche aux Fines Herbes, and Butter-Fried Croutons	62.5°C (144.5°F)	45 minutes to 1¼ hours	69
LAMB, SADDLE AND TENDERLOIN	Medallions of Elysian Fields Farm Lamb Saddle, Garden Vegetables, and Bagna Cauda Sauce	60.5°C (140.9°F)	35 minutes	160
PORK, BELLY	Glazed Breast of Pork with Swiss Chard, White-Wine-Poached Granny Smith Apples, and Green Mustard Vinaigrette	82.2°C (180°F)	12 hours	148
PORK, BABY, BELLY	*Dégustation de Porcelet,* Rutabaga Mostarda, Wilted Mustard Greens, and Potato "Mille-Feuille"	82.2°C (180°F)	12 hours	156
PORK, BABY, LEG AND SHOULDER	*Dégustation de Porcelet,* Rutabaga Mostarda, Wilted Mustard Greens, and Potato "Mille-Feuille"	80°C (176°F)	8 hours	156
PORK, BABY, RACKS AND LOINS	*Dégustation de Porcelet,* Rutabaga Mostarda, Wilted Mustard Greens, and Potato "Mille-Feuille"	60.5°C (140.9°F)	20 minutes	156
POULARDE	*Rouelle* of Four Story Hills Farm Poularde Wrapped in Swiss Chard with Hobbs' Applewood Smoked Bacon and *Pruneaux d'Agen*	62°C (143.6°F)	1½ hours	112

ITEM	RECIPE	TEMPERATURE	TIME	PAGE
QUAIL	"Quail in a Jar": Quail Stuffed with Moulard Duck Foie Gras, Cipollini, Figs, and Port Wine Glaze	64°C (147.2°F)	1 hour	130
RABBIT, FLANK	Rabbit and Bacon *Pressé*, Slow-Poached Royal Blenheim Apricots, Rabbit Liver Mousse, and Green Pistachios	74°C (165.2°F)	12 hours	134
RABBIT, LOIN	Sirloin of Devil's Gulch Ranch Rabbit Wrapped in Hobbs' Applewood Smoked Bacon with Summer Succotash and Corn "Pudding"	64°C (147.2°F)	12 minutes	138
SAUSAGE, GARLIC	*Saucisson à l'Áil,* Shaved Cornichons, Compressed White Peach, Pickled Pearl Onions, and Dijon Mustard	70°C (158°F)	2 hours	152
SQUAB, BREASTS	Squab with Piquillo Peppers, Marcona Almonds, Fennel, and Medjool Date Sauce	59.5°C (139.1°F)	30 minutes	124
SQUAB, BREASTS	*Pigeon aux Truffes Noires,* Candele Pasta Gratin, Brussels Sprouts, and *Sauce Périgourdine*	60.7°C (141.3°F)	20 minutes	128
SQUAB, LEGS	Squab with Piquillo Peppers, Marcona Almonds, Fennel, and Medjool Date Sauce	68°C (154.4°F)	2 hours	124
VEAL, CALOTTE	*Blanquette de Veau*	60.5°C (140.9°F)	15 minutes	142
VEAL, TENDERLOIN	Tenderloin of Nature-Fed Veal, Artichokes Barigoule, Caramelized Garlic, Picholine Olives, Tomato "Marmalade," and Barigoule Emulsion	61°C (141.8°F)	30 minutes	144

VARIETY MEATS

ITEM	RECIPE	TEMPERATURE	TIME	PAGE
BEEF FAT	Rendered Fat	85°C (185°F)	1½ hours	270
BEEF TONGUE	Corned Beef Tongue *Pain Perdu,* Watercress Leaves, Horseradish Mousse, and Oven-Roasted Tomatoes	70°C (158°F)	24 hours	180
CALF'S HEART	Confit of Calf's Heart, Toasted Pecans, Baby Turnips, Bing Cherries, and Cherry-Wood-Aged Balsamic Vinegar	79.4°C (174.9°F)	24 hours	182

ITEM	RECIPE	TEMPERATURE	TIME	PAGE
CALF'S LIVER	Milk-Poached Calf's Liver, Caraway-Glazed Cipollini, Granny Smith Apple, Dijon Mustard, and *Sauce Laurier*	63°C (145.4°F)	1 hour	186
DUCK FAT	Rendered Fat	85°C (185°F)	1½ hours	270
DUCK GIZZARDS	*Salade Gourmande*	82.2°C (180°F)	8 hours	198
DUCK TONGUE	Duck Tongue	70°C (158°F)	8 hours	265
FOIE GRAS	Confit of Moulard Duck Foie Gras with Vegetables *à la Grecque*	64°C (147.2°F)	28 minutes	192
FOIE GRAS	Sauternes-Poached Moulard Duck Foie Gras, Tahitian Vanilla Beans, Braised Radishes, and Purslane	68°C (154.4°F)	25 minutes	196
FOIE GRAS	Poached Moulard Duck Foie Gras, Concord Grapes, Celery, Salted Virginia Peanut Nougatine, Banana Puree, and Pedro Ximinez Sherry Vinegar	68°C (154.4°F)	25 minutes	194
FOIE GRAS	*Salade Gourmande*	64°C (147.2°F)	28 minutes	198
FOIE GRAS	*Chaud-Froid* of Moulard Duck Foie Gras, Musquée de Provence, Pomegranate Seeds, Mizuna Leaves, and Gingerbread Puree	68°C (154.4°F)	20 minutes	202
FOIE GRAS, FAT	Rendered Fat	85°C (185°F)	45 minutes	270
KIDNEY	Fricassée of Veal Kidney with Black Trumpet Mushrooms, Salsify, Brussels Sprouts, and Curry-Infused Veal Sauce	82°C (179.6°F)	1 hour	178
MARROW FAT	Rendered Fat	85°C (185°F)	1 hour	270
PIG'S TAILS	Fried Pigs' Tails, French-Cut Romano Beans, Deviled Quail Egg, and *Sauce Ravigote*	82.2°C (180°F)	8 hours	188
TRIPE	Tripe Oreganata, Amando Manni Extra Virgin Olive Oil, and Herbed Bread Crumbs	82.2°C (180°F)	8 hours	175

ITEM	RECIPE	TEMPERATURE	TIME	PAGE
VEAL CHEEKS	Veal Cheeks *Zingara:* Braised Veal Cheeks, Puree of Yukon Gold Potatoes, Serrano Ham, and Black Truffles	82.2°C (180°F)	8 hours	173

BASES FOR DESSERTS

ITEM	RECIPE	TEMPERATURE	TIME	PAGE
BANANA ANGLAISE	"Ice Cream Sandwich": Vanilla, Chocolate, and Cashew Ice Cream with Banana Anglaise, Chocolate *Crémeux,* Waffle Tuile, and *Gastrique de Cepa Vieja*	85° to 82°C (185° to 179.6°F)	20 minutes	250
GINGER CUSTARD	*Dégustation des Pommes: Génoise aux Pommes,* Candied Apples, Ginger Custard, Milk Jam, Apple Sorbet, and Apple Chips	85° to 82°C (185° to 179.6°F)	20 minutes	230
ICE CREAM BASE, CASHEW	"Ice Cream Sandwich": Vanilla, Chocolate, and Cashew Ice Cream with Banana Anglaise, Chocolate *Crémeux,* Waffle Tuile, and *Gastrique de Cepa Vieja*	85° to 82°C (185° to 179.6°F)	20 minutes	250
ICE CREAM BASE, CHERRY	"Cherry-Vanilla": Madagascar Vanilla Bean Cake, Morello Cherry Ice Cream, Italian Pistachio Coulis, Kirsch Foam, and Cherry Jam	85° to 82°C (185° to 179.6°F)	20 minutes	239
ICE CREAM BASE, CHOCOLATE	"Ice Cream Sandwich": Vanilla, Chocolate, and Cashew Ice Cream with Banana Anglaise, Chocolate *Crémeux,* Waffle Tuile, and *Gastrique de Cepa Vieja*	79°C (174.2°F)	22 minutes	250
ICE CREAM BASE, CINNAMON	Sweet Garden Carrot Cake, Cream Cheese Icing, Candied Walnut Crunch, Black Raisin Coulis, Carrot Buttons, Indonesian Cinnamon Ice Cream, and Gelée de Carotte et Sa Poudre	85° to 82°C (185° to 179.6°F)	20 minutes	218
ICE CREAM BASE, VANILLA	"Ice Cream Sandwich": Vanilla, Chocolate, and Cashew Ice Cream with Banana Anglaise, Chocolate *Crémeux,* Waffle Tuile, and *Gastrique de Cepa Vieja*	85° to 82°C (185° to 179.6°F)	20 minutes	250
SHERBET BASE, JASMINE RICE	White Sesame Nougatine with Sesame Oil Sablé, Plums, Golden Gooseberries, and Jasmine Rice Sherbet	65.5°C (149.9°F)	30 minutes	246

SOURCES

CIRCULATORS AND VACUUM-CHAMBER MACHINES

KOCH EQUIPMENT
866-396-5624
www.kochequipment.com
Vacuum-packing machines

MULTIVAC USA
816-891-0555
www.multivac.com
Vacuum-packing machines

POLYSCIENCE
800-229-7569
www.polyscience.com
Circulators

OTHER EQUIPMENT

BON JOUR PRODUCTS
800-2-BONJOUR
www.bonjourproducts.com
*Small frothers: Caffè Froth Turbo,
Primo Latte Frother*

CONFECTIONERY ARTS
www.confectioneryarts.com
Blue dessicant humidity absorber

JB PRINCE
800-473-0577
www.jbprince.com
*"2 in 1" vegetable slicer D371, chinois à piston
(automatic fondant funnel), dough divider
(5 wheel and lock), #12, #18, and #22 (melon
ballers) Econome Parisienne scooper, Teflon
sheet/silicone paper, Flexipan egg shape
M372A, acetate, whipped cream dispenser*

MY WEIGH
www.myweigh.com
Digital scales

PEARL PAINT
800-451-7327
www.pearlpaint.com
Airbrush

TAP PLASTICS
800-246-5055
www.tapplastics.com
Plastic layering strips

TOTAL APPLIANCE
631-499-3355, ext. 21
PacoJet

VITA-MIX
800-VITAMIX
www.vitamix.com
Vita-Prep

INGREDIENTS

AJINOMOTO
800-456-4666
www.ajinomoto-usa.com
Ajinomoto RM and FP transglutaminase

ANDANTE DAIRY
707-769-1379
www.andantedairy.com
Acapella cheese

ANDREA DORIA (PAUL CAPPIALLI)
917-442-0105
*Trappitu extra virgin olive oil,
Castelvetrano green olives*

ARMANDO MANNI
www.manni.biz
Armando Manni extra virgin olive oil

ASIAN MARKET
212-962-2020
Agar-agar, Indonesian cinnamon powder

BLIS
616-942-7545
Maple syrup

BOIRON FRÈRES S.A.
www.boironfreres.com
*Bing cherry, Morello cherry, banana,
mango, and passion fruit purees*

BUON ITALIA
212-633-9090
www.buonitalia.com
Candele pasta

BUTCHER & PACKER
800-521-3188
www.butcher-packer.com
Polyphosphate (special meat binder)

CHEF'S GARDEN
800-289-4644
www.chefs-garden.com
Sprouts and micro herbs

DAIRYLAND, THE CHEF'S WAREHOUSE
917-442-0105
Guittard cocoa noir, Sevarome pistachio paste

DEVIL'S GULCH RANCH
415-662-1099
www.devilsgulchranch.com
Rabbit

ELYSIAN FIELDS FARM
724-852-1076
Lamb

EUROVANILLE
www.eurovanille.com
Vanilla paste, Madagascar vanilla beans

FOUR STORY HILL FARM
570-224-4137
Poultry, including poulardes, and tripes

FRESH POINT
626-813-5800
Green almonds

GAF SELIG INC.
718-899-5000
Cacao Barry Alto el Sol 65% chocolate

HOBBS' APPLEWOOD SMOKED MEATS
510-232-5577
Hobbs' Curing Salt,
Hobbs' Applewood Smoked Bacon

IMP
510-429-4600
Jidori egg and yolk, Japanese cuttlefish,
Japanese octopus

ISRAELI PRODUCTS
877-289-4742
www.israeliproducts.com
Achva marble halvah

K & N IMPORTS
925-689-7568
Akita komachi rice, kanzuri paste

LE SANCTUAIRE
415-986-4216
www.le-sanctuaire.com
Calcium glutonate, sodium
hydroxymetaphosphate, CP Kelco Keltrol
T630 xanthan gum, Kelcogel F, ascorbic
acid, PX vinegar (Pedro Ximenez), Aleppo
pepper, piment d'Espelette, sweet pimentón

LORANN OILS
800-862-8620
www.lorannoils.com
Apple oil

MANICARETTI
800-799-9830; 707-815-1813
www.manicaretti.com
Cherry-wood-aged balsamic vinegar,
lemon agrumato oil

MILLISSIME
718-777-7808
www.millissime.com
Green apple mustard

MURRAY'S CHEESE
212-243-3289
www.murrayscheese.com
Jasper Hills Winnemere cheese, Coach Farm
goat cheese, Fourme d'Ambert, Chaput St.
Mauré du Manoir goat cheese

PACIFIC GOURMET
415-641-8400
www.pacgourmet.com
Cappezana extra virgin olive oil,
Tipo 00 pasta flour

PARIS GOURMET
800-939-5656; 201-939-5656
www.parisgourmetusa.com
Pastry 1 neutral glaze, atomized glucose,
Feuilletine; Valrhona Manjari 64% and 70%
chocolate, 100% cocoa paste, cocoa powder,
60% praline paste; Pastry Star Le Prestige cocoa
butter; cacao nibs; Cuisine Tech apple pectin,
Cremodan 64 sorbet stabilizer, citric acid

PETROSSIAN
800-828-9241
www.petrossian.com
Caspian Sea ossetra caviar

PIERLESS FISH
718-222-4441
www.pierlessfish.com
Mediterranean octopus

THE ROGERS COLLECTION
207-828-3000
www.therogerscollection.com
Cepa Vieja sherry vinegar,
Castello di Ama extra virgin olive oil

SONOMA COUNTY POULTRY:
LIBERTY DUCK
707-795-3797
www.libertyducks.com
Ducks; duck breast, legs, tongue, fat

SOS CHEF
212-505-5813
www.sos-chefs.com
Whole green Sicilian pistachios, Marivani
banana extract, banana water

SPARROW LANE
707-815-1813
www.sparrowlane.com
Red wine vinegar, champagne vinegar

TMARIM PLUS
www.tmarimplus.co.il
Silan date syrup

TRUE WORLD FOODS
908-351-1400
www.trueworldfoods.com
Japanese octopus

WOLFE RANCH QUAIL
707-678-5651
www.wolfequail.com
Quail

The French Laundry staff

per se staff

ACKNOWLEDGMENTS

A BOOK OF THIS SIZE AND SCOPE, EXPLORING A SET OF TECHNIQUES THAT

are relatively new to all chefs, has required a substantial team. We are very proud of this team, without which we couldn't have completed this book. I'd first like to give special attention to two longtime sous-chefs. Devin Knell has been with us for ten years and has been an integral part of our evolution, including the use of sous vide techniques. Rory Hermann was instrumental in developing and finalizing a HAACP plan for sous vide cooking that was not only accepted by the New York City Department of Health but accepted as their standard.

Corey, Jonathan, Sebastien, and I would also like to thank the people who do all their work behind the scenes at the restaurants. At *The French Laundry*: Timothy Hollingsworth, Michael Swenton, Claire Clark, Jason Berthold, Anthony Secviar, Walter Abrams, Carey Snowden, Jonathan Mizukami, Rodney Wages, Juan Venegas, Mark Bodinet, Naikang Kuang, Charles Bililies, Courtney Schmidig, and Molly Fleming. At *per se*: Eli Kaimeh, Chung Chow, Chico Aguilar, David Breeden, Matthew Orlando, Anthony Rush, Michael Israel, Richard Capizzi, Caitlin Grady, and Sharon Wang. At *Bouchon Las Vegas:* chef de cuisine Mark Hopper.

We are grateful to Peter and Gwen Jacobsen, who are remarkable growers and friends, and to Harold McGee, who not only wrote the introduction to this book but also read the text and recipes to advise us on all matters of safety and science regarding these new techniques.

This is the third publication with our book team. Susie Heller, with Amy Vogler, coordinated the team and recipe development of four chefs from both sides of the country. Michael Ruhlman's words convey not only the chefs' thoughts but also the science behind this extraordinary cooking method.

We would also like to thank Bruno Goussault and Gerard Bertholon of Cuisine Solutions as well as Philip Preston, president of Polyscience.

Deborah Jones, Jeri Jones, and Scott Mansfield of Deborah Jones Studio took on challenging photography and once again showed the beauty of the raw product (even wrapped in plastic) and the finished dish.

David and Joleen Hughes of Level Design complete our team with their ever beautiful book design.

And, finally, thanks are due to the excellent team at Artisan: Ann Bramson, Judith Sutton, Trent Duffy, Jan Derevjanik, Nancy Murray, and Amy Corley.

INDEX